# Gifts of the Spirit

## My Mission as a Healer

By Richard M. Schickel

D1496188

Disclaimer
The purpose of this book is for the author to share personal experiences from his life in hope that others might somehow benefit from such experiences, whether as a general form of support for physical, mental, and spiritual healing, a source of inspiration to conduct further research regarding some of the alternative methods of treatment referenced in this book, or possibly even in some other way.

The author does not intend to make any specific conclusions or recommendations regarding your life. Therefore, the occurrence of any event or the development of any situation that might appear to share some nexus with this book must be purely coincidental.

The author of this book does not provide medical advice, and nothing in this book should be construed to constitute medical advice. Moreover, no one should ever prescribe to the use of any technique or form of treatment of any kind to address health issues – whether physical or mental – without the prior approval of a physician.

RMS Consulting does offer individual readings and healing suggestions and advice. See RichSchickel.com for more information on the process and how to arrange a reading. Also, you are welcome to email any questions or comments to: Richard@ RMS-Consulting.net

## DEDICATION

This book is dedicated to all the people I have ever met, known and worked with in my life. I have learned so much from them and am grateful to share what I have learned here.

Thank you to Jessica and Monica for supporting my mission. Thank you to my friends and family who have helped me to learn so many positive lessons.

Thanks to my fabulous editors - Valerie Porter and Christy White, for their knowledge and suggestions.

Thank you to all my family and friends who read and reviewed this book- they are very patient.

# CONTENTS

| | | |
|---|---|---:|
| Preface | | vii |
| Introduction | | 1 |
| Chapter 1 | Who I Am and Where I Came From | 7 |
| Chapter 2 | Leaving Chicago | 13 |
| Chapter 3 | Coming of Age | 29 |
| Chapter 4 | Growing Up in the IRS | 45 |
| Chapter 5 | My Life-Changing Lesson | 53 |
| Chapter 6 | What Happens in a Reading | 69 |
| Chapter 7 | Finding God, Reincarnation and Karma | 101 |
| Chapter 8 | Being Yourself – Loving Yourself – Changing Yourself | 113 |
| Chapter 9 | Why You Are Sick and How You Can Heal | 137 |
| Chapter 10 | Have a Relationship with Yourself First | 155 |
| Chapter 11 | Romantic and Physical Relationships | 169 |
| Chapter 12 | Disconnecting from Your Past | 193 |
| Chapter 13 | Other Healing Exercises | 201 |
| Chapter 14 | What Happens After Death | 209 |
| Chapter 15 | Abuse and Empowerment | 229 |
| Chapter 16 | Healing Stories | 259 |
| Chapter 17 | Looking Forward | 275 |
| Chapter 18 | How to Allow Change to Happen | 293 |
| Chapter 19 | Final Thoughts | 319 |
| Appendix | | 323 |

# PREFACE

I suppose that I was always different from other people. It was hard for me to figure this out, because everything that I thought, said and did seemed "normal" and correct to me. I thought other people just were a little slow on the uptake.

When I discovered that my life was different from everyone else's life, I was shocked. I was not like most other people; I was not what you might call "normal." I figured out that while I was receiving everything that other people received, I was also receiving so much more information, knowledge and wisdom beyond my years. It was like I was able to hear all the words being said on 400 radio stations all at the same time. I was a little kid when I figured this out and did not know what to do with so much information.

I tried to hide from it - pretend that it was not there. After a while it became a quiet chatter always playing in the background. Being this way and living in the everyday world felt strange and uncomfortable. I lived to retreat back to my home – my sanctuary. I slowly built the walls of my retreat place in my mind - my own, "Secret Garden." This was a place where I could go and feel normal and relaxed.

The theme of this book is using the gifts God gave you in the place where you currently are. Bloom where you are planted. I was with the IRS for 33 years and did the best I could. When I recognized and used my natural gifts and spiritual gifts of empathy, understanding, intuition and compassion, I was able to integrate those into my work life. Then God gave me more and more abilities to service the IRS and the taxpayers. I found that I did not need to be afraid any longer of the IRS, other people, relationships, anger, fear or worry. You can learn this too. This is the story of how allowing myself to use my intuition at work allowed me to grow personally also.

I want to share what I have learned through the many hard lessons of my life. My struggles would have wounded or destroyed some people; but I was able to learn from them and move forward. I am so grateful for my unusual life and its lessons, but it was never easy and never without purpose. It is the same today. I have periods of great learning and great growth, a rest and recovery period and then back to work with new goals. In the end, it is important to have no grudges and no regrets – just peace.

I am finally willing to let go of caring about how other people may think of me or how they judge my life. I will tell you all of my "secrets" to life.

I share thoughts and methods that will help you learn how to *love yourself first, best and always* and support your emotional and spiritual growth. This will lead to a life with more happiness, love and balance.

I dare to talk about God, joy, love, sex and abuse in this book, sometimes all on the same page. My definition of God is a: "Creator Energy with Boundless Unlimited Resources." The terms God, Universal Energy, God Energy and Divine Love are all used to describe this energy of unconditional love and acceptance.

Perhaps you have your own perception and experience with this energy, or maybe even with a stricter religious definition of this God Energy. I respect that and it is useful in your journey through this life. Some of the concepts that I discuss in this book include determining how you define God, looking at karma and reincarnation, and looking at who you were before you were born and who you will be after your body dies.

I am sharing my life experiences with you because I think they may support growth in your life. Perhaps my strange and unusual stories will help you rise to a place of greater understanding of yourself and other people.

I hope my stories will help you to plant your own seeds of unconditional love, acceptance and growth in yourself and others. I hope that you will learn how to dream big and are then ready to receive what you desire, or even more.

I had to plant seeds of growth, wisdom and knowledge in my life so that I could grow to this place that is my current reality. I want to share and teach and listen and learn all at the same time.

Your new life starts when you allow it. The power of the unconditional love energy (some might call it the God Energy) will find you right where you currently are and pick you up and dust you off and support whatever growth you desire. It is not important what you think about yourself; the Love and Light of the Universe already knows that you are an amazing human being full of potential.

In order for me to have grown into the person I am today, there were many good, bad and difficult moments in my life. I had to release old fears, thoughts and ideas in order to become who I am. I am still doing that; I wake up every day wondering what God has planned for me. Despite my current age, I am as excited as a little kid on Christmas Eve.

I hope you will consider the ideas in my book, and pursue those that feel good to you and put others in reserve for when you are ready for them. I think of all knowledge as being like seeds in a bag. When I plant them and nourish them, they will grow in time. But I must also be patient.

My work is about recognizing my clients as they are – exactly in that moment - and then sharing the Love I get from the Holy Spirit with them. I follow up with talking to them about their hopes, dreams and aspirations. My goal is to support their healing and growth.

One of the greatest blessings in my life is that I recognize a spark of God in every person. Everyone has a magical, spiritual energy, a light inside of them that positively glows and I can see it when I look at them. I always expect the best from other people, and even if they fail to do that, I can still learn something from them. I cannot help or support healing in people who are not open to it or ready for it. I receive everyone with unconditional love and acceptance and am slow to see the rough edges around some of them.

When you are ready to review and let go of your old thoughts, feelings and emotions that no longer serve you in your current life, then you are ready to begin. Hopefully the words of this book will help trigger that.

I am a highly sensitive empath who desires to help others reach their full potential in life. I am also a minister, author, prophet, mystic, medical intuitive, spiritual healer, counselor and psychic medium. When people ask me what I do, I ask them "What do you need?" because I have access to whatever they need.

A woman who has witnessed what I do in my work wrote:

God is far greater than a building with pews, but for those who are living stones and know it, should they find that they are not received, shake off the dust and march on to where you will be welcomed. Others are not at the level that you have increased to. God is great! For those who have received blessings from your journey in faith, you will be embraced and those who aren't there may never arrive. We are far more than flesh and blood and were never meant to wake up in a box just as God cannot be. Pray for those who don't know and love them anyway. You are good at this. *You are the church without walls and it's where you belong.* The Holy Spirit says that He will teach us all things, guided by the Word of Life, walking in love. You are a living stone fulfilling your mission and purpose. He will continue to guide you. Where two or more are gathered in His name, HE is in the midst. You carry the Anointed One and His anointing in you and no matter where you go, you cause the atmosphere to change around you, because He abides in you. Some will be sensitive to receive. You have a purpose and a mission. Don't stress about pleasing man. Follow your heart and be blessed in all you do. Forgive them for they know not. Stay amazing! The world needs you! – *Donna Holmes*

Thank you for exploring this book. I surround you with the Love and Light of the Universe as you do so. Reading this book can save you years of therapy and isolation. I am blessing you and sending you love. Now let's get started.

# INTRODUCTION

**I'm a hero.**

The story that follows is not about me trying to find God or my spiritual gifts; it is a story of how God finds me and uses me to serve other people. It is very unusual for a professional person to admit that they have special gifts that might be socially unacceptable to talk about. For me to admit that I am a spiritually gifted healer and psychic-medium is a first. Even the term IRS Psychic is confusing when you say the words together.

IRS work suited me perfectly. It was as if I was my own boss. I was a tax collector - a Revenue Officer looking for people who owed money or were negligent in sending tax returns to the government.

My job required me to be out in the field much of the time driving around making cold calls on delinquent taxpayers. Sometimes I would be looking for people who did not want to be found. IRS Revenue Officers do not announce that they are coming; they simply knock on your door whenever they are in the neighborhood. That way they can observe your actual lifestyle and it is safer, since no harmful situations can be planned in advance.

One freezing day right before Christmas in 1982, I was looking for a taxpayer and was very lost. I found myself lost and alone on an isolated street with only six houses and surrounded by cornfields. There was no one around to ask where I was. But I was about to learn being lost was a minor problem in comparison to what was ahead.

As I was staring at my map book, I looked up and saw a woman drive past me. She went to the house on the far side of the street behind me. I watched her in my rearview mirror. I saw her unload some groceries and then open the front door of the two-story house. When she opened the front door, thick black smoke came pouring out. The smoke was coming from the ceiling, reaching her at waist level. She started screaming.

Strangely, my first instinct when I saw what was happening was, "I should get the hell out of there." Before I could finish processing that thought, I was out of my car running to help.

The woman was hysterical, but was able to tell me that she had gone out to the store and left her eight-year-old daughter Bridgett alone in the house, asleep. Bridgett was trapped in the second floor bedroom. I could see the terrified little girl behind the window and storm window, and saw smoke starting to fill her room. I yelled to her, "Close the bedroom door and stuff clothes at the bottom of the door." She was afraid but did as I told her.

Bridgett was a scared little girl in her pajamas. I could see that she had "bed hair" and had apparently been asleep a short time ago. Mucus was flowing out of her nose from the smoke inhalation, kind of like someone had squeezed a tube of toothpaste from both nostrils. She was trapped behind two windows that were locked up tight for winter. She could not unlock the window or push it open. I had no idea how to get access to her on the second floor. Running into the house was out of the question, so I thought of getting help. This was before we had cell phones. I ran to the six houses on the street and banged on every door screaming, "Fire!" and "Help!" No one was home. It was early winter and no ladders or lawn furniture had been left outdoors - nothing that could help me reach the little girl.

The mother was hysterical and sobbing, and of no help at all. Then two German shepherds came from the back yard and started attacking me, biting my legs, ankles and pants. I yelled at them in what I hoped was a scary, commanding voice that I had never heard myself use before or since. "BACK OFF! I am trying to save the little girl." Miraculously they backed off as if they understood what I was there for, but they looked at me like they would attack again if I messed up.

I ran into the backyard and finally found a metal garden table and chair. I stacked the chair on the table and climbed until only my fingertips could reach the bottom of the windowsill. I am six feet tall but the bottom of the windowsill was still about six feet higher above my head. I was too low to get the window open. I saw some landscape rocks that must have weighed about 10-15 pounds each, located around the house. They were partially frozen into the ground. I broke some from the frost and put them on the table. I told the girl's mother to get more stones, and then I stood on the rickety chair on the rickety table throwing these heavy stones over my head to break the windows.

I was amazed that I could throw these rocks. It was like I was throwing shot putts over my head. Of course, the first few rocks fell short of their mark and bounced off the screen, hit the table and almost knocked me down. Quickly I figured out how to throw harder and kept throwing the small rocks up over my head. I was able to break the screen and then broke the storm window next. When I broke the storm window, shards of glass started to fall on me, cutting me.

Now the little girl was beyond terrified and actually afraid of me. Finally, I broke the inside window. I could smell the smoke from the fire. The girl looked relieved as she gasped for the fresh, freezing air outside the window. I ordered her to jump into my arms. She was beyond processing my directions because she was scared of me and terrified of the fire. She was slowly dying in that room – we both knew that from the look in each other's eyes.

I told her to climb up onto the windowsill so she could jump down into my arms. She said, "No!" wisely pointing out the large pieces of sharp glass sticking out. She was coughing worse now as more smoke was starting to come through her room seeking the outside air to feed the fire. I told her to use one of the rocks and start smashing the broken glass so there were smaller pieces of broken glass sticking up. She did.

Then I told her to get up onto the windowsill and jump into my arms.

She was coughing, bleeding, sobbing. It is surreal to even remember this scene now. I was standing on a lightweight chair on a rickety metal table and I was trying to gain her confidence so she would jump into my waiting arms. When she climbed onto the windowsill her feet and her hands were on the broken glass shards. She started bleeding from more cuts. The smoke inhalation had caused more fluid to pour from her mouth and nose and she was coughing, trying to gasp for more air.

I screamed at her, "Jump now!" I was in an unstable situation and was at first asking, then yelling, at this girl, and finally commanding her to jump. She was too afraid. I told her, "You are going to die in that room if you don't jump!" She and her mother were both hysterical and sobbing. She kept looking behind and beyond me thinking that surely someone would see the thick black smoke and come and help. I told her, "No one is coming. Jump!" She was determined not to jump and then in a move that surprised us both, she jumped safely into my arms. I believe that an angel pushed her out of the window.

When she finally jumped into my arms, the table held. I carried her down from the table and ran with her and her mother to my car. I dropped her in the middle of the front seat onto my tax collector files. I threw a box of the tax papers into the back seat. She had gotten blood on many of them getting into the car. She was going into shock from the combination of freezing weather, the thin pajamas she was wearing, and the considerable bleeding. Secretions were still pouring out of her nose and mouth. I had picked up my dry cleaning that morning and ripped apart one of my dress shirts, and tied it on each hand and foot to stop the bleeding. I also had a grey suit jacket from the cleaners and I wrapped her up in it for warmth.

I started to drive, but the mother was so hysterical, terrified and sobbing, that I could not concentrate enough to be able to drive. I reached over and slapped her face just like in some gangster movie with Jimmy Cagney. She stopped crying and I was able to drive on.

The slap brought her back to reality, but I regretted that I had to do that in the moment.

Although I was lost, my sixth sense directed me to the roads I needed to take to get to the hospital. Bridgett told me that the house was her grandparents' house and they were visiting.

At the hospital I called the Fire Department. The emergency room doctor said that Bridgett had had a close call with death and that another 15 minutes of smoke inhalation would have caused her to die. He said she would be okay. Her mother said nothing the whole time. It was strange, to me, that her daughter was clutching me the whole time when she was on the examining table. I guess her mother was in shock. The father arrived shortly thereafter. That was also a strange interaction, because he addressed me as if I had caused the problem.

I never heard a thank you from Bridgett, her mother or father and I never saw or heard from any of them again. Maybe they did not like the IRS, I don't know. I later learned from the Fire Chief that she had fully recovered and he said that I was a "hero". The story was on the TV news and in the newspapers.

I stopped by the house on the way home and the only things left were smoldering timbers in the flooded basement. The cause of the fire had been a faulty chimney. Ashes from the fireplace fire the night before had smoldered in the wall and ignited the next day.

I received a Silver Medal from the Treasury Department, an Award for Heroic Action and Meritorious Service from the Secretary of the Treasury and a letter from President Reagan. I never really felt like a hero. God had put me in that place at that time for a reason. My destiny that day was to save this eight-year-old girl.

I was pretty shaken up after the rescue. Why was I at that exact place at that exact time when that mother and child needed help? Why me? Was this the Universe at work? Was there a God and a plan? Before that day they had all just been words in a book. Was it destiny, fate, accident or coincidence that brought me there? I now believe that God put me in that exact place to save Bridgett's life.

It was humbling when it first occurred to me that God knew who I was and had used me to help another person.

Little did I know how many more times God would use me to help other people. My life really began on that day. I felt good and happy that I had finally figured out what I was supposed to do in my life. Just show up, be available and God would use me to help people.

# CHAPTER 1

## *Who I Am and Where I Came From*

I was born in the South Shore neighborhood of Chicago, a few blocks from Lake Michigan, and I have good memories of my early years there. We lived in a large apartment building with my grandparents and aunt and uncle just down the hall. So I could roam the halls looking for people to visit with. I loved to talk. Neighbors and friends kept a close eye on the building so I felt safe. As much as I felt that I fit in with the people there, I still felt different.

In my baby book, my parents wrote, "He has a very lively imagination; some of his thoughts are very unusual" and "Some of his stories really throw us" or "Ritchie makes up his own words and languages." There were comments of, "He tells stories about his other families and how they live in different places" and "He has tremendous imagination and tells the wildest stories." They also recorded that, "Ritchie prays for people all day long simply by talking to God. He speaks the prayers aloud and does not want anyone to hear him."

When I was taken to a church, they wrote that I asked why we had to be quiet in church because "God wants us to sing out to Him." I also said that "the church where we were at did not look like God lived there." According to their notes, I told my parents that "God lived somewhere else."

Today, I would have been identified as an Indigo child, an old soul born into a new life in a baby's body. In those days, "having a wild imagination" was a more polite way to describe me, instead of saying that, "this kid tells all kinds of crazy stories."

Growing up, I always felt slightly different from other people. But, I am no different than you, the reader of this book. We are all born with our own gifts of intuition and wisdom. Whether we know it or not, we all seek something greater than what we have in our lives. I think we all have a quiet yearning in our souls that draws on hope, faith, truth, and love. We desire true connection to other people and the earth. We all want and hope for acceptance, nurturing, and love. I believe that we also crave a greater connection to the energy of God.

I have always had the gifts of knowing, seeing, and hearing from Spirit, as well as the gift of precognition (seeing into the future), but these abilities were gradually diminished by my parents, educators, and society as I grew up. Eventually, I lost touch with them completely. Because of that, for a long time I felt a void in my life. It was a great struggle to reclaim these gifts later in life. I had to work hard to remember and relearn my intuition and other spiritual gifts.

When I was in my 40s, I told my mother that I had psychic abilities. She said: "Those psychic gifts are scary and are the work of the devil. That is why I told you to stop listening to them when you were little." That was pretty standard advice in the 1950s and 1960s, many parents gave their children. Remember, in the United States the policy was that we are all supposed to melt together and just be one united America. We certainly were not a nation where everyone was doing what they wanted or listening to ghosts and spirits.

Early in my life both of my parents suffered health issues and it changed my whole life. My mother wrote, "Ritchie seemed to feel abandoned and turned to his Grandma completely." I think that I must have felt abandoned by God when I was first born, also. Then a few years later, my brother was born and he also had health problems which caused me to grow closer to my maternal grandparents.

I remember having great conversations with the spirits I could see around me. It must have sounded like gibberish to my parents, who could not see what I saw. I was never alone, not then and not now. Perhaps sometimes I was lonely, but never alone. But over time, I was forced to keep my connection to the spirits around me carefully hidden from other people. I had to keep it to myself when I felt something or knew something that I would have no other way of knowing about.

Being a spiritual being in a physical body is hard work. Leaving the warm wet world of the womb leads to the cold and unpleasant realities of the world. It can seem like you are just alone when you are born. Sure you have people holding you, carrying for you and feeding you, but you also still have clear and unfettered access to the Heaven that you just left.

The way I remember it was I was like a magnificent rose bush in Heaven and then I was born and while I was still magnificent, I was like a vase of beautiful roses which had been cut off at the stem. I had lost access to the flow of love and energy from God. It took me many years to learn how to allow myself to access that energy again. It was very confusing to figure out how to just be and go with the flow.

When we arrive on Earth at birth, it can be very confusing and distressing. Everything you have known from prior lives and your heavenly rest stop is mostly gone. You are stripped of friends and memories of your time before you came here and now feel so lost and alone. Sometimes you get a warm, loving, compassionate and nourishing connection with your new mother and father, but sometimes not. Some babies, known as old souls or Indigo children, are actually rather belligerent and indignant that they have to come back again and go through all the baby stuff again. They have retained more of their soul selves and wish they could just be placed directly into an adult body.

When we are babies we drool, wet ourselves, see angels and talk to God, and when we are very old we drool, wet ourselves, see angels and talk to God. The problem is that between those two places our mind/ego steps in and tries to tell us there are no angels and no God, except as far as we create a God model at our local house of worship.

This detachment from God and His unending, unconditional love and energy can bring you great pain. The choice is what you allow into your life. When you grow older, even though you may have education, family, love and money, a small still voice in your heart is always reminding you, "There is more! Remember? Do you *remember* why you are here?"

As a toddler I lived in a very happy world of my own creation. I always felt spirits around me, watching me, playing with me, talking to me. I chatted on for hours. Sometimes I still do. I loved to build castles with wooden blocks and play in the sandbox. I was happy to be always building things. As I have gotten older, I have enjoyed connecting people, things, and events to each other. Today, I continue to build bridges connecting people to other people and ideas to ideas.

My earliest memory of being different from other people was when I was three. My mother and I were visiting an elderly neighbor and I was standing on her couch looking into the mirror hanging over the couch. In that mirror, I saw my reflection in the mirror and the room behind me. Suddenly, I saw the figure in the mirror start to move and actually leave the room. The "me" standing before the mirror was still in the same place. Then the "me" on the other side of the mirror came back. He was very playful and very happy. I remember that the image in the mirror was projecting great love and affection towards me. I raised my hand on my side of the mirror to see if he would raise his hand saying, "Hi!" He did. He put his arm down while mine was still up. This completely confused me. We did this for several minutes before my mother came in and asked what I was looking at in the mirror. I told her, but she did not believe me. She said it was just my imagination.

In later years I figured out that my Spirit was having fun with me. I think people take life too seriously. I sure did, and being serious yields little result. Having fun is an important part of why we are here. We often forget that.

I remember even at that age that I would cry or pull away from people who I sensed were sick or getting ready to die. I did not know how to explain it to my mother. I just got a sick feeling in the pit of my stomach and I would start to get sick. Believe me, this did not please my parents when we had company and someone was sick, because I would disrupt everything.

## My First Near-Death Experience

At the age of three and a half, I got double pneumonia and my parents took me to the hospital. I remember burning with fever, coming in and out of consciousness. In Cook County, Illinois at that time, the law said that children with contagious diseases had to be quarantined from society. The most traumatic memory I ever had was when Mother handed me over to the doctor and nurse. They carried me out of the room and handed me over to two large orderlies. I was taken to the Cook County Contagious Disease Hospital. No visitors were allowed. I remember seeing my mother in the background, screaming and trying to get them to bring me back.

Both of my lungs were filling up with stuff that could kill me. I was burning up with fever. When I woke again, I was in a large hospital ward with about 50 other children, some in cribs and some in beds. No adults, just very sick children. It is a wonder I did not pick up an even worse disease just breathing the same air.

I remember the nurses and doctors coming in, wearing masks and giving us medicine, then getting out of there as fast as possible. I remember kids who died being loaded onto gurneys and taken out of the room. What a horrible, lonely way to die, sick and alone.

My first near-death experience, and also my first out-of-body experience happened here. I remember leaving my physical body and being aware of hovering up near the ceiling looking down at myself. I could see the whole hospital ward. I felt so light and wonderful. I had a silver cord connecting me to the body that was Richard. It was very comforting to be up there. There was a Spirit of Light with me there who told me I could choose to stay out of my body or go back.

From where I was, I could see more than just that room. I could see the whole hospital, and then our apartment, and then the whole city of Chicago and all of Lake Michigan; it was like I was rising up, flying into the air.

I thought about just leaving then, but I was worried about my mother and how she would handle it if I did not come back. I decided to go back, but it was really hard because I felt no pain there, just floating around and feeling the vibration of love and joy and freedom.

This was also the first time I was healed by non-medical sources. I started to get better immediately and soon left the hospital. It is such a good memory, being connected to the Light, meaning a higher power. I don't know exactly what that being was, but it felt like pure, unconditional love. I survived but my whole attitude changed about life. I missed being able to float around in the air. My life proceeded according to some plan that I did not yet remember.

# CHAPTER 2

## *Leaving Chicago*

In 1963, when I was seven years old, we moved to a suburb of Chicago called Mayberry. We had a police chief named Nick, a mayor named Delbert, Jim the barber, Eddie and Ray who ran the grocery store, the Brne brothers who ran the pharmacy and the Diekelmans who owned the butcher shop and hardware store. We had a town drunk (in fact many of them) and a large cast of other characters. Oops, sorry, I must watch too much TV. No, really it is called the Village of Thornton; it was settled in 1834. It just seemed a lot like Andy Griffith's television show about the town called Mayberry. In truth, this suburb was more like a tiny, isolated village. It seemed like everyone knew everyone else or at least members of their family.

I want to describe my home place in depth, because I think it is relevant to the story of my life. It was a place where I was in nature all the time - the woods, the water, the tall prairie grass. It was a place that grounded me. This was important because when you are like me, a natural empath and connected more to the clouds than the earth, it is really helpful to still have two feet firmly planted on the ground. Otherwise sometimes, I feel like I could just float away like a balloon.

Thornton was a place where people had lived for thousands of years. Archeologists at the Hoxie Farm dig just east of Thornton have found artifacts from Native Americans on that site that dated to 1400. Later the Potawatomi, Miami and Sauk tribes lived on this land. Traces of their inhabitancy are still found today- where their villages were and other details of their existence. White settlers plowing the rich black dirt of Thornton discovered many of the specimens of pottery, flint, arrowheads, stone chisels and stone bullet molds. Many are on display in the Thornton Historical Society. I remember going to the ancient Indian burial mounds and looking for Indian relics. (Don't judge me; this is just what we did for fun in Thornton). When the interstate was built it went right through the burial mound. The mound of dirt that was excavated was moved to the side of the interstate and we named it Indian Hill and raced our bikes over its many paths. Sometimes we would bring a shovel and dig and often would find treasure.

French explorers had a fort here in 1673 on as they explored the waterways and the abundance of wildlife for trapping and skins. White and Native American skeletons have also been found in the area.

The place now known as Thornton has seen much life and much death for such a small area. That is probably because of old buffalo and Indian trails that joined the area to Indiana and to the places to the west. That is because Lake Michigan was just to the northeast.

When a visitor to Thornton travelled from the north on Chicago Road, they used to go past the Dutch Reformed farmer's fields that grew onions, corn and tomatoes; there was always a sweet smell in the air. Then they would cross a bridge over the I-80/294 interstate expressway. The expressway was about 25 feet below the street level of Chicago Road, the main road into Thornton. Really in my mind it was like crossing a drawbridge over a noisy and busy asphalt moat to enter a castle.

Our house is just south of the interstate on Chicago Road. Just past our house was Mount Forest Cemetery, an abandoned Negro cemetery. It had reverted to land that was owned by the Forest Preserve District. It was a haunting and mysterious place. As children we would play among the gravestones. It was a beautiful, but some say haunted, place. Beautiful Lilies of the Field flowers grew everywhere and had a heavenly smell. As children we always felt that ghosts were watching us as we raced on our bicycles through the cemetery.

A visitor coming from the east would come on Margaret Street / Thornton Lansing Road.

As you continue on Margaret Street heading into town, you go past an old farm on the east side of the Thorn Creek. This farm is remembered as being one of the first places that John and Kate Bender had a farm. They later become infamous for their killing spree in Missouri and Kansas. They also operated a place for travelers coming in from Indiana where they could rest their horses, eat and spend the night. Kate was said to be very attractive and alluring, by some accounts. It was said that she was either the sister of John Bender or his common-law wife - or maybe both. They had a dry goods store. Kate was a self-proclaimed healer and psychic and advertised her ability to heal illnesses. Some travelers came for that and others came to eat. They would seat these people at the head of the table and would feed them. They also offered these strangers a place to sleep.

During dinner, they would find out if the traveler had any relatives and any money, jewelry, gold or silver saved up (and with them) that they were planning to use to start their new life further west. If the Benders thought these people could help them out, the story goes that they had a curtain behind the kitchen table and while the strangers were checking out Kate, John would go behind the curtain and hit them in the back of the head with a hammer (or hatchet), killing them. Then Kate would push them backwards through a trap door into the cellar where their throats were cut. Later they would be buried in farm fields or orchards. Then they would take the strangers' possessions and horse and wagon and sell them. (Chicago is only 24 miles away)

This is rumored to have gone on for several years until the fiancée of one of the strangers hired a Pinkerton detective to find out what happened to her future husband.

After the Pinkerton detective called on the Benders, they disappeared overnight. They became infamous after they were later reported to be doing the same business in Missouri and Kansas, always narrowly escaping the hangman's noose. Then they finally disappeared into Mexico, according to the stories I heard growing up. There are some stories about a vigilante group that caught up to them and lynched them before throwing their bodies in the Verdigris River. They also claimed to have burned Kate Bender alive. I am glad that my spiritual gifts in no way resemble whatever she had. It sounds like her abilities were coming more from the devil, than God.

Growing up, I remember reading an old onion skin copy of this story in a folder in an old WPA desk in the town archives at the public library so I include it here from memory. Some people dispute that it happened, but I present it here for your edification.

Continuing westbound on Margaret Street, a visitor would then cross the old Bielfeldt Bridge over Thorn Creek - the "crick" as it is known to locals. It was a 40-foot-wide waterway in its prime. Now it only gets that big when flooding occurs in spring and summer. I spent dozens of hours of my life building bridges from fallen trees to try to have a shortcut across the "crick". Mostly I would just end up falling in and getting stuck in the muck at the bottom of the creek. Big rainstorms would always wash my bridge creations wash them away - but it was a cool exercise in futility. But we never gave up. I had tried to canoe on the "crick." But it had so many fallen trees that was all but impossible.

On the north side of Margaret Street a visitor would find what remained of the Thornton Brewery - known for making Lithuanian Lager Beer. This was in operation until it was closed by Prohibition in 1932. Then it became a soda pop processing plant. It had vast underground arched cellars and was rumored to have secret tunnels that allowed a person to quickly get out of the brewery if they needed to. Or, they would be able to move goods through the tunnels to other locations.

The infamous gangster Al Capone arrived at the soda pop processing plant one day and offered to go into partnership with its owner.

He wanted to use the soda pop business as a front for a brewery operation. Thornton and surrounding towns were full of Germans and Eastern Europeans and the idea of living without beer or just having near beer was just not going to happen on their watch. The Dutch from South Holland also liked their beer, and I remember growing up and watching them line up after church on Sunday to stock up on beer and liquor, because South Holland was a "dry town."

Sadly, the owner of the brewery declined Mr. Capone's offer. A few days later a fire broke out at the brewery and its owner was never seen again. Capone then took over the brewery for his illegal brewing.

I heard stories that although Prohibition agents regularly raided the soda pop plant, they never found anything and no arrests were made. According to testimony from Joe Sadauskas, who bought the brewery in 1951, government agents discovered the bones of ten men who had been left to die without food or water in one of the vaults under the brewery. Supposedly these men were locked up because they could not pay for their bootlegged beer or may have crossed Al Capone in other ways. Mr. Sadauskas was told to keep his mouth shut about that discovery, but later leaked the story over a beer at a local bar.

According to an interview titled Widow McCleary's Investigation (Google or Bing search on the web), Mr. Sadauskas said he was run out of the beer making operation in 1957 when he refused to pay the crime syndicate for "protection" for his business. He said that the mob dumped 140,000 gallons of beer into the creek. The location is now home to a senior citizen's residence, but the brewery section is said to be haunted.

Coming into town from the south on Williams Street, a visitor would have gone past a huge turkey farm and then past the limestone processing plant and the plant that makes asphalt. The ground up lime is used to make cement and also is used as a fertilizer. I never thought of it before, but it would also speed the decomposition of a dead body, but I guess the Benders would have already known this.

The other street coming from the south was Schwab Street. This led past a former Civilian Conservation Core group of buildings built during President Franklin Roosevelt's administration that brought jobs to the area during the Great Depression. The buildings were later used to house German prisoners of war and it was called Camp Thornton. Some of the German prisoners ran away and assimilated and married local women. Later the buildings were used by the Girl Scouts. The road cut through an old forest where the trees on both sides of the road reached toward each other, making the road dark and almost scary and hauntingly beautiful. It was like a scene out of the Wizard of Oz.

The western entrance to town went past two cemeteries and over a narrow two-lane road that is called Margaret Street/Brown Derby Road/ Ridge Road. This road is surrounded on both sides by the Thornton Quarry, one of the largest limestone quarries in the world. The quarry was enclosed by chain link fences, (no guard rails) the problem with that was that if a car hit the fence, it would just bend open and the car would fly into the quarry and no one would notice for days. Many people have killed themselves in the quarry in just this way. Others have used the heavy train traffic on the old Chicago & Eastern Illinois railroad tracks to end their life. The quarry is half a mile wide and one and a half miles long and in places 400 feet deep. You could put the Statue of Liberty in there and it would be hidden. Four hundred million years ago it was part of an inland tropical sea.

I remember when I was heading into Thornton on Brown Derby Road and suddenly some unseen force stepped on the gas in my car, and I was heading right for the side of the quarry. I reached down and tried to pull the gas up- but nothing worked. I was scared out of my mind and I shifted the car to Park and it stopped. That messed up the car, but at least I survived. Strange things were known to happen in that area.

The quarry blasted with limestone off its walls between at 3:15, 3:30, or 4pm every day except Sunday. This was because the old Wolcott school was built in 1906 and considered to be an unstable building, so the story goes that they waited until most of the kids were out of the building just in case it collapsed. The noise of the explosion, the dust, and the ground shaking caused an effect like a combination of a tornado and an earthquake. When we were allowed to go into the quarry after a blast, ancient limestone fossils were everywhere. Whenever we had company, they got all excited when the blast occurred. I remember my brother-in-law thinking it was an earthquake and hiding under the kitchen table on his first visit to town. The houses shook and stuff flew off the shelves and out of the cabinets. To Thornton residents, it was nothing special, just part of our daily life.

I remember there was an old roadhouse called the Brown Derby Restaurant where high rollers from the nearby Washington Park Race track were said to enjoy the company of dance girls and gambling. Both the race track and the restaurant were said to be affiliated with organized crime.

Thornton was all about work. It was a blue-collar town with 3500 people and about 14 bars. There were also some roadhouses on the way into town, but I can't remember how many. Many people's jobs were associated with the quarry, or with local manufacturing jobs at steel mills and auto production plants. It was the kind of place where almost all the mothers stayed at home raising four to six children while the fathers worked. About five percent of the fathers had attended college and had white collar jobs. My father was one of those few. He was advised when we moved there not to tell anyone because people would treat us differently if they knew. It was a town where everybody knew what was going on with everybody else, and there were few secrets.

But I guess stories like those of the Benders and the Brewery kept their secrets well protected.

In Chicago, I lived a few blocks from Lake Michigan, and parks and museums were close by. There was a lot to do. When I first got to Thornton, I did not know what to do for fun; it took some exploring.

Actually there was a lot to do; it was just different, I had to make up my own adventures. There were 1300 acres of forest preserves and Wampum Lake, a 400 acre nearby lake which held grand adventures waiting to happen every day. It was exciting to just fly a kite over the quarry and the cut the string and watch it sail on the wind currents until it crashed. I did learn to climb both of the water towers, how to sneak into the quarry and go swimming, and how to hop onto moving railroad trains to hitch a ride to the next town. I got used to the busy train lines always blowing their horns, the noise of the blasting in the quarry, and the din of the expressway traffic and trucks that carried all the harvested rock. It was a noisy, dusty town, loud with traffic from dawn to dusk.

I missed being in Chicago. Looking back, I think that I was more than just homesick for my old Chicago neighborhood. I just did not feel connected here on Earth. I missed Heaven. But Thornton provided a good place for me to grow up.

My school was right next to the quarry and hitting a baseball into the quarry was considered a rite of passage growing up. It seemed like there were always chores to do and people worked hard for what they had. I am so grateful for being involved in Cub Scouts, Boy Scouts, and Explorer Scouts because we were always raising funds to pay for road trips and camping. It was the best way to get out of town and see the world. We went to Canada and around the Western states. We went to camp in Michigan and Indiana for at least 2 weeks every summer. Being a part of the Boy Scouts was a great way to feel part of something bigger than myself and I loved it.

We lived in a large old farmhouse built in 1920 by a Dutch woman in the center of her large celery farm that sold to the Chicago markets. It is a large brown brick Chicago style bungalow that from the side looks like the ark. On her death it passed to many owners but was considered a haunted house and owners and renters would be in and out of there, until it was finally abandoned. We built an apartment upstairs when Papa and Grandma retired. I loved living there, but it was not always a peaceful home. Mother and Grandma did not get along on issues like household management and child rearing, so they would get into disagreements with each other.

The house had a history of sadness and disappointment. The Dutch woman that built it was still in residence there, in ghostly form, as was another ghost. Many people have experienced the ghosts. During her life there was a lot of conflict over the land, money and family problems. In fact, when I would sleep in the middle bedroom an opaque, scary, fear-based energy would attack me. It would cause me to have horrible dreams; it would sit on my chest and choke me. The energy would paralyze me completely. It was terrifying. I learned later in life that those were spiritual attacks. (Today, I counsel many people who experience these same situations). At that time, we had a priest come to the house twice and he succeeded in clearing the dark energy of the upstairs area. Only the ghostly old lady who built the house remained afterwards, and she does to this day.

It was very difficult growing up in a place where I felt so different, where there were very few like-minded people who knew about spirituality (outside of religion) or psychic connections. No one else I knew could see dead people or understood the abilities that I was developing or remembering. If they did, they certainly weren't talking about it.

I believe my mother and her mother both had great intuition and spiritual gifts, but they worked hard to hide them, even from themselves. In the 1950s and 1960s, this was not something you bragged about. The only books that I found in the tiny Thornton Library were *The Search for Bridie Murphy* by Morey Bernstein in 1955 (a story of past life memories raised during hypnosis that was earthshaking at the time) and a book about the famous clairvoyant healer and psychic Edgar Cayce called *There is a River* by Thomas Sugrue; it gave information coming from Edgar Cayce readings. Unfortunately, at the time people who claimed they had these abilities were often thought to be crazy or evil. These books seemed almost incomprehensible after all that I had been taught at school and church. I was a teenager, but still had a hard time truly understanding the materials in the books.

I had no access to any other information that would answer the questions I had about the supernatural or my growing abilities to see, hear and feel spirits and things that other people could not.

When you are trying to reawaken, it can be very difficult if your parents, teachers, religious leaders or political leaders have condemned your natural gifts as being evil. Maybe they thought they were protecting you, or wanted to control you. In the long term, it doesn't benefit you. It can take many years for you to remember who you are in soul and bring it back alive in your body and life. There is something to be said about remembering your gifts before you are more mature, about age 40. If people knew that they had the intuitive gifts that they had, they would probably be labeled as crazy or evil. Too much of this knowledge before the age of maturity can destroy your ability to function in the world.

Being intuitive is no walk in the park. When you are receiving so much information from the energy of the Universe, first you are used as a sieve to sort out the information. Then you become like a smelter/refinery for the information. The results can be very productive and produce pure gold, but it is difficult at first.

In my own life, I remember just feeling strange and alone. Growing up I was not like other people. I kept seeing things, knowing things, hearing things and talking about things that I should have had no knowledge of. When I told other people, they would look at me strangely and tell me that I was talking to the devil or it was just plain crazy.

My maternal grandmother and grandfather were the only adults who really seemed to understand me. My grandmother had come from Ireland to the United States and my grandfather had Scottish heritage so they understood things as Celtics would. They listened to me as I chattered on, asking questions and saying whatever was on my mind. They were a great unconditional love experience and they supported me.

Both of them spoke of the "wee little people" that were around us in life. These included:

- Fairies – These delightful creatures inhabit my back yard and are in every garden that I have ever been in. I can see them. They have a very positive energy as long as I respect their space. For instance, changing a garden or spraying weed killer brings negative energy from them. They sometimes hide, remove or steal items in my house.

- Banshees - They signal death is soon to come to a household. (As in "wailing like a banshee")

- Pookas – these spirits could bring beneficial, playful or menacing energy to a household. It could bring wealth and blessings or pain and loss. This spirit can be directed like a voodoo curse. To this day, I can tell when a pooka is in my house, because things go missing or feel strange. My keys, my work materials, the remote for the television are suddenly lost. I used to get so frustrated looking for them. And they just sat back laughing at me, enjoying me getting mad. I then learned that these mischievous spirits just wanted a little attention. In Ireland and in my house that means that I pour a shot glass of whiskey (although they seem to prefer brandy) and leave it out and it will be empty in three days and all such activity from them stops from them - until another time when I have exhausted myself due to my work. They seem to sense my energy imbalances and then take over the house, if I let them.

- Leprechauns are another type of fairy, staying to themselves most of the time; but they are said to have a pot of gold that can be used to pay for their freedom if they are captured. (partial source - Wikipedia)

My life was confusing because I was living a normal human life, but I still had strong connections to my spirit/soul. I still had flashes of déjà vu and I would have strong gut feelings that would warn me to do something or not do something. Not that I would always follow or listen to them, but my antenna was still up. I was still receiving. This really helped me in my career with the IRS. I started picking up clues just talking to my taxpayers and learned so many details that led to audits, collections, seizures, and tax evaders going to jail.

When I first tried to awaken my intuition, I was really left to figure it out on my own. It came through a cloud of negative energy, and that scared me. Many people who are first reconnecting with spirit/soul feel afraid when they have these negative experiences. A lot of garbage comes through when you first start to receive psychic abilities. That is normal. That is where discernment comes in. You have to be able to identify the vibrational energy of the source of the energy and then decide if you understand and believe the message you are receiving.

The gifts that I was born with were not at all acceptable in society or within my Catholic religion in the 1960s. Some people experimented with Ouija boards and attracted negative, scary spirits. Or they found a gypsy psychic who did readings for them that were bathed in fear and profit-motivated.

I also recall having the ability to leave my body in sleep or while I was awake. In a daydream I could look down at the situations I was in, whether I was at school on the playground, at a party, or at some other social event. Sometimes I got new knowledge in those situations when I was separate from my body. I remember thinking how stupid and strange it was to be here on Earth with all these meaningless activities (like cheating, lying, stealing) that people do. I was able to see all of the lies, insincerity, and cruelty that can come from human interaction.

My intuitive messages manifested in many different ways. From a very young age, when I was around a person who was ill or would soon die, I would get a burning, empty feeling in the pit of my stomach. It felt creepy and unsettling. When people would tell the stories that I knew to be false, when people deliberately lied to me, I also felt this burning sickness inside of me. I remember I would get pains in my chest (what I later learned to be my solar plexus area) when thoughts or opportunities presented to me just did not feel right.

I also remember that when I was around people in my family who were ill or dying, I would get this awful feeling because I could see what was going to happen to them. I saw and knew when they were going to die. I was just a kid and having that knowledge was terrifying. When good, wise, or loving people came into my life, I felt warmth, like a tingling of electrical energy. That was so comforting to me.

I was very shy. In fact, when I attended kindergarten, for a three-month period in 1963 I refused to speak to the teacher or the other students the whole time. I had a tremendous speech impediment. I could not say the letters "R" and "S". Believe me, when your name is Ritchie Schickel and it comes out like "Writzy Cickle", it does not make your life any easier! This kept me separated from the other kids. Being humiliated in school because you can't speak properly is not pleasant. I also had ears that did not fit my head so I was bullied in school and called Howdy Doody. I was super shy and sensitive, and as we all know those do not play out well in school. But I survived.

I remember my fifth grade teacher, Mr. Stone, wanted to help me correct my speech impediment. I think he thought I was just I was lazy when I would leave class to visit Mrs. Mason, my very patient speech teacher over many years. I honestly think that I just could not hear how the sounds should be said correctly. While the other kids were doing an assignment, he called me to his desk and tried to do his own version of speech therapy with me. He made me say "rooster" over and over, but I couldn't say it like he wanted to hear it.

I could not hear the difference between how I said it and the proper way. Every time it came out sounding like "Wooster". I do not need to tell you it was rough on the playground after that with the reactions of the other children. He may have been well-meaning, but his method cancelled out his good intentions.

When I was ten, my grandparents moved out. I had an aunt who needed help raising my cousins so they went to live by her. As the oldest child, I took over more and more responsibilities of running the house. In addition to her health problems, my mother suffered from depression. It exhausted her. My mother was a voracious reader and got the equivalent of a college education by reading the whole Encyclopedia Britannica. When she was feeling well, she also did a lot of social work and community projects. But that was not most of the time. I did not feel bad about it since she had been sick most of my life. I just did not understand it. But now she was always asleep when we left for school and sometimes when we got home. I knew that she loved and cared about me; she just did not have much gas in her tank.

The greatest gifts that I have received from my mother are that she trained me in the art of conversation, how to think, wonder, and ask lots of questions. She helped me learn to read. She also directed me to the public library to find answers to my many questions about life and how things worked. I love to read and research and think and write because of her.

The task of running the household primarily fell to me. I got my younger siblings up, got them breakfast, made sure the laundry was done, kept the house clean and presentable, and made dinner too. Once I was old enough to drive, I became the chauffeur and also took over shopping at the supermarket. Funny, I never asked why that was my lot in life; I just accepted it and moved on.

As these changes took over my time, I became very codependent with my family. I define codependence as doing more for others than you do for yourself. It falls in the category of loving others without *Loving Yourself First, Best, and Always.* This type of imbalance always leads to burnout in caregivers and healers, and in relationships. I was good at putting everyone else's needs in front of my own. My father traveled for his work at that time and was often away from home, and my mother just did not have the energy to be a mother. As a result, I worked all the time, between my schoolwork and housework. In fact, I think I have never stopped this pattern of working under some deadline or pressure my whole life. I always felt responsible for myself and everyone else.

Each of us reacts to the circumstances that are going on around us in life. So some of what I was experiencing was typical for a kid raised in the 1960's around too much alcohol, cigarettes and arguments.

I have always loved and cared for people, whether they are good people or bad people. I cannot help it because I see their core energy and it is coming from God. Some people may ignore it or be estranged from it, but I see it and respect it. How could I not? So let's just say I see people differently from most people.

My grandparents' moving ended that phase of my life; it is as though at 11, I became an adult.

There was a magical and mysterious energy in Thornton; it had seen a lot of life and a lot of death and a cast of nefarious characters as long as my arm. But for me it was exactly where I was supposed to grow up. Being so close to the woods and nature allowed me to grow up feeling connected to the earth. It grounded me and made receiving my spiritual gifts that much easier. Thornton was like shelter from the storm of the crazy world of the 1960's and 1970's.

# CHAPTER 3

## *Coming of Age*

I began to develop or recall more of my spiritual gifts at the age of twelve. It is very normal for people to begin to have spiritual re-awakenings around that age. I used to be jealous of Jewish boys, because they had big Bar Mitzvah parties with big cash gifts. I got a Catholic Rite of Confirmation where there is a Mass and the Bishop slaps you really hard on the cheek. My Bishop said "Peace be with you." I responded "and also with you." And then he slapped me really hard on the cheek. I have no idea what this is all about. But I can still feel the sting on my cheek.

Many people begin to seek a more personal relationship with God. They usually turn to organized religion where they study, and seek wisdom and connection to a higher power. Often, they find nothing to help them in their lives, no matter how hard they study or try to follow the doctrine of the church. That is what happened to me with the Roman Catholic Church.

Learning about the beliefs and customs of this religion was a lot for a 12-year-old kid to know. It was way too much for me to process, except for the times when I read about the mystics and saints who had the same type of strange things (gifts of the Spirit) happen that I experienced. Otherwise, I was not able to connect to the teachings of the Catholic Church. The whole religion seemed so far removed from Biblical teachings.

My paternal grandfather (Papa Frank) had experienced a lot in his life. He had been very successful as a candy store owner in the 1920s and 1930s. He sold candy in the front of the store and then as you walked behind curtains to the back of the store, he had One-Armed-Bandits (slot machines), and in the room beyond the next curtain was the "hooch" (illegal whiskey and beer) for sale. This all ended when Prohibition ended in 1933.

He did not complain or look back at what he had; he was able to enjoy it in the moment and that was a great lesson to me.

He also taught me that I should enjoy what I had at the current moment, before I could ask for more. So I learned that if I wanted more money, I needed to be grateful and thankful for the money that I already had.

He worked many jobs, but his passion in life was playing golf and teaching people how to play golf. He said that I had a natural talent for golf and could easily make a million dollars just playing a game. Sadly, despite his best efforts I was not interested in golf, despite the hundreds of hours we spent practicing. To me, golf was a game played out in your mind, before you even picked up a golf club. Papa Frank said that I "had to watch the club head hit the ball." This took me a long time to figure out. Finally, I got it. If I was worried or obsessing about putting that little white ball in the tiny cup, I was focused on that, not the actual mechanics of hitting the ball. By that "wanting and needing" to place the ball in the hole, I was sending out a vibration to the Universe that was actually blocking the ball from going into the hole.

The lesson I learned from him with this was about faith: I made clear my intention to the Universe that I wanted the ball to go into the hole or at least close to it. I next needed to have faith that it would happen, simply because I was at the golf course that day and picked up a club. No thinking, no planning, just relaxing. He was the most relaxed and natural golfer I have ever seen. His swing was so fluid and just by his faith the ball usually went into the hole. He enjoyed the game and that inspired me to enjoy life, whether I had a lot of money or not.

## Me and the Roman Catholic Church

A good example of faith was when I went to Mass one day at our local church. A group of parishioners seemed obsessed with amassing a huge building fund to pay for a new church. One Sunday there were six collections during the Mass: collections for the Pope, for the building fund, for the mortgage, for the starving children in Biafra, and so on. The church was packed that day, and by the end of the third collection, one lady actually stood up and said, "I came to pray, not pay." The priest told her to sit down, but she refused. Two ushers came and escorted her out of the church. No one got up and went with her, but I wish I had been brave enough to follow her out. I never saw her in church again. This experience made me really question what kind of church I was in. It was more about dollars collected, than souls saved.

It was common in those days for our Catholic priest to issue warnings against hanging out with non-Catholics. He would talk about the "Jews that crucified Jesus" and the "God-forsaken Lutherans". He warned us that if we ever went into a Protestant church, even for a wedding or funeral, we would be struck dead by a bolt of lightning. I later wondered how many people were actually struck by a bolt of lightning. Children believe that kind of stuff when they are growing up. Some people still believe it as adults! Although they may be away from religion now, they never release the fears that were ingrained in them at such an impressionable age.

When I went to Catholic catechism school, I asked questions about spirituality, and knowing, seeing, and hearing things from spirits. The teachers looked at me strangely and told me that that was not coming from God. They said that I needed to pray the rosary more, or go to Mass more frequently, to make that go away. Later in life, I wondered if someone had told the mystics of the Catholic Church the same thing, mystics such as Saint Theresa of Avila, Meister Eckhart, Saint John of the Cross, Saint Faustina, and Saint Padre Pio. I share similar spiritual gifts with them. Now I fit the description of a mystic. I have self-surrendered to the power of the Universe. I can see and experience spiritual truths beyond my intellect. I am open to and continue learn from inner experience.

I recall going to confession and confessing my sins: I had been smoking cigarettes and sneaking looks at my father's Playboy magazines. The priest told me that of course I did those things because I was an evil sinner. I had been born an evil sinner. Nothing I could do or say or think would make that change. It was only Jesus who could save me from Hell. But even that was not a sure thing. I understood that God would decide at the time of my death where I would go.

Later that year when I saw that priest smoking a cigarette, I was shocked. I guess he had grown comfortable with being a sinner. I wondered if he had Playboy magazines too.

Since then I have found churches, temples and synagogues that attract spiritually connected people and places where Divine Energy is flowing. But these are few and far between. Most religious gathering places have a cold, formal energy that does not welcome the Living God energy which we all have inside of us. Most church congregations think that the rules of how you should worship God are more important than the connection itself.

The problem for me, being raised as a Roman Catholic and also as a Christian, is that so many things I was told just didn't add up and balance out in my accountant/tax collector's mind. The people who were there to answer my questions at the time couldn't keep up with what I was asking. Believe me, this did not get better with age. My natural intuition says somebody tinkered with the story here and I do believe that is what has happened. I seek to clear up some of these matters by sharing what I have received from direct spirit communication and offer it for your consideration. Whether you agree with me or not, I think it is important that people can entertain new and different ideas. In other words, they do not have to embrace these new ideas in order to be enriched by them.

## My Trip to Heaven

When I was 15, my beloved Grandpa Milne (Papa) died. I was with him in the long weeks leading up to it, and also at his deathbed. I was so close to him and my grandmother that this was a horrible experience for me. My grandfather believed in what you could see, hear and feel. He believed that God was in everything and you didn't need a church to see or know God. He was a churchgoer by necessity, mostly just when it came to baptisms and funerals.

He married my grandmother, an Irish Catholic immigrant, but they were not allowed to be married in the Catholic Church because he was not a Catholic. He was allowed to be married to her at the priest's house instead. Still, he paid for all four of his children to attend Catholic schools, along with making required donations to the church.

When he died, my uncle, Grandma and I went to the Catholic cemetery to purchase two gravesites - for him and for my grandmother. At first our request was denied because the salesman said my grandfather did not qualify to be buried on consecrated, holy ground. That was when my grandmother jumped over the desk and gave him a black eye. We later got the two gravesites without further trouble. This spiritual snobbism I grew up with, that only Catholics would be going to Heaven, confused me.

I was worried about my grandpa going to Hell because of all the Catholic stories I heard over the years. I prayed and prayed, falling further into despair at the idea that he would be in the "fiery pits of Hell" simply because he was not a Catholic. And yet, even at that age, something did not feel right to me about that story.

One night, shortly after he died, Papa came to me in a dream and said he was taking me for a trip to see where he lived now. I can still see it so clearly. When he touched my hand, we flew off far away and over a city that had bright yellow- colored brick buildings. It looked like pictures I have seen of Chicago in the 1930s. The city was glowing and bright - almost like a city of gold. The sky around it was sparkling clear. There were a lot of steam locomotives. Papa had been a fireman on a locomotive in his life, so I guess he liked seeing them in his Heaven.

The next thing I knew, we were in a building that looked like a government building and we had to wait our turn. There was a lot of activity there. People were constantly coming in and out. There was furniture like you might find in a courthouse in the 1930s. It was a waiting room. There was a clerk who was wearing old fashioned clothing, with a green shade over his head and sleeve protectors that people used to wear to protect from getting ink stains on their clothes. He came to the counter, seeming friendly but very busy. Papa told him my name and that I was there for a visit. The man, who was very old with round spectacles, said, "Let me check." He went past several file cabinets and then pulled a card out of one. It had my name and my picture on it. He came back to the counter, looked at me and then looked at the card, and said, "Yes, you are in the right place. Go on and look around. Don't stay too long; you have work to do!" We turned to go and he said, "We like having your grandpa here except when he beats us at cards."

Papa was so excited. He took me flying through this city. He just thought of where he wanted us to go, and we would sort of fly through the air and arrive at that place.

We went past a room where there were people who had just died. It was like a place where they were resting and letting go of their bodies - where they let go of the illness, and aspects of death. I was told they could stay there from a month to three years. When they have died from diseases like cancer that drained them not only physically but also mentally, emotionally and spiritually, it takes longer. People with Alzheimer's move thru here very quickly, because they have already been out of their bodies in spirit - usually for a long time.

There was another room where they went to review movies of their lives to see what they did or failed to do for themselves and others. No judgment - just self-evaluation without all the excuses they might have offered while alive. They either did thumbs up or thumbs down in response to their actions in life.

There was another room where Life Planners worked with people on future life plans. They decided if they wanted to go back to Earth and if so, when, and what lessons to work on.

There was a records room with thousands of file cabinets and large bound books and those recorded every action and lesson that a person had done in life. They also showed me the intricate web of connections that each of us has to other people. These were the "serious rooms" - I was just supposed to see them and know that they were there.

But mostly I was with Papa to have fun. Heaven is all about fun and joy and love and compassion. Each of us creates our own Heaven. There is the central Heaven, which is portrayed as a 1000-story building where we all get in.

The strongest memory of the city was that it was so very clean. The whole place was very organized, and the people were all happy, smiling and laughing, enjoying whatever they were doing. It gave me such a great feeling in my chest to be around so many people who had so much love flowing out of them. We went to the park and rode on the backs of huge swans who gave us a tour of the lake. We never had to talk to communicate. Whatever thought Papa had, I knew instantly, and whatever I wanted to say, he knew instantly, too. It was so wonderful and magical. We went to a place where he said that he lived in a building made of stone. It looked like a manor house from where his family had come in Canada. The whole building practically glowed. It had such charm and resonance in my soul. I was so happy to be there with Papa that I never wanted to leave. This Heaven that I met my Papa in was his idea of a perfect place. For each of us, Heaven is what we make it. It is all based on love, so there are no negative thoughts or emotions.

After meeting his friends, old (from his life) and new (from this Heaven place), I started to feel guilty. First, Papa had left me and Grandma, and now I had left Grandma as well. I wished we could all be together in one place as we had in the past. My whole time there, I felt a warmth in my heart that I can now describe as a higher vibration. It felt like pure love. I was happy. He was happy. Being together made us both happier and our vibrations increased because of it. I knew that I would never need to worry about him again. He was okay and we were going to be okay as well. I think that was the point of the visit. He showed me that he was always around me; I just couldn't see or touch him anymore. Otherwise, everything was the same as before. I discovered that I could talk to him and feel him around me, and continued to experience a connection with him many times in the years that followed.

This vision happened in 1972. I think that it is interesting that as a 14-year-old I would learn so much that other people would later write books about over the next forty years.

Heaven was so very different from life on Earth. You did not need to talk to other people/spirits that were there - you could do it, but it was so slow. They just talked mind to mind, spirit to spirit. Whole thoughts came from one person into the other person. There were no misunderstandings or poor word choices, just instant love and under-standing. There was no place for negative words or feelings. You just did not need them. It was unconditional love all the time, like being locked in the best hug you ever experienced.

My Papa was a carpenter and at one point Jesus was there working on building a table with him. There was such a quiet, positive energy around him - very loving and comfortable. While there I felt a kind of buzzing - like a high vibrational energy that ran a current through my body and made me feel wonderful. Papa had also been a fireman on a locomotive engine but could never make engineer of the train because his vision was not quite good enough. Now he was able to once again enjoy the thrill of being around the steam trains of his youth.

I remember we had this amazing meal and then went to an ice cream shop that looked like it was owned by Willie Wonka. Everything was so perfect - so delicious, so amazing. I have found in life that sometimes it is not the actual physical act that gives me the greatest feeling- it is the memory of the event that provides the pleasure. This can be in remembering food, love or sex. I can remember it perfectly over and over forever. This makes for a low-calorie way of living.

In Heaven I found absolute faith, absolute trust, absolute caring and unconditional love from the Creator God and all the spirits around Him. There was such a high vibration; it makes me so happy and high just remembering it.

I saw that there were other areas of Heaven that had a slower vibration and the spirits seemed more sluggish. It was harder to communicate with them using our telepathy.

In other sections, we found people at a much lower vibration and they were moving around weakly and sluggishly. Some were still connected to their bodies and were dragging their bodies around, thinking that they would need them later. (As is suggested in the Bible – that your body will be resurrected.)

We knew from the vibration and the bright colors around each angel and spirit we met that everyone who had a good intention toward others was right along our path. People who were further away from our path did not bother or attract us.

Since that day, I have never had another moment of fear or worry about illness, pain or death. Seeing my Papa one last time is still such a sweet memory.

Papa said he had more to show me that I needed to know for my future work before I went back. Then an angel joined us and we flew over what was described as Purgatory. This place was grey, foggy, dank and dismal. It was very cold. Lost souls roamed here, caught up in their own misery.

I saw thousands of them walking back and forth, cursing people and events that happened in their lives. One man said, "My wife ruined my life! If I had not married her, everything would have been okay. She is to blame for all my troubles!" They were all blaming others, "my boss, my parents, my kids, my business partners." The souls there wanted to blame everyone else for their current situation. They were caught up in confusion, anger, blame, and denial. They were completely absorbed in their own misery. Each soul had an arm up in the air, trying to pull us down into their pile of self-created shit. They were trying to pull us down into their miserable situations. I remember them grabbing at my ankle. It was not as much fun to be so miserable if they could not share it and pull me down as well. They were all looking down, moaning about how other people were the cause for them being there. There were angels around, but not down in the purgatory space.

Every few seconds, I could see a bright flash of light. I was told that those people had finally figured out that they were 50 percent responsible for every situation in their lives. When they understood this, then they had finally forgiven themselves. Before then, they did not feel worthy of God forgiving them because they were self-described sinners. They didn't know that God had already forgiven them, and what's more, that there was no actual need for forgiveness at all.

Since they had come to Earth to learn lessons, there was no such thing as Divine Judgment or blame. It was an affront to think that they could decide for Spirit what the Divine forgives or does not forgive. When they finally forgave themselves, the flashes of light that I saw were their souls being transported to Heaven by the angels. The angel who was with us told me, "It all happens on your time, not God's time. God never stops loving you and providing for you. You just get so involved in your body on Earth that you forget."

The Angel told us that the flashes of light were when people actually looked up, saw the face of God and felt the unconditional love of God. Then they were finally ready to pass over to their version of Heaven.

Next, we flew over Hell. It was cold, down in a vine-covered hole. It was a snake pit with darkness and vague shadows that threatened to suck us into the misery of the place. Some of the souls there had both arms up and narrowly missed grabbing my ankle to pull me down and suffocate me with their guilt, hate, anger, abuse, unworthiness and misery. Some were so numb they looked like the face of death, so shocked at what they had done on Earth that they were horrified now to be able to view it from a distance.

But even in Hell, God had his love for them, no matter what they did or tried to do. There was one soul there that was the soul of one of the doctors at the Auschwitz death camp. He had experimented on, tortured, and killed thousands of people in the name of so-called scientific research. He felt pretty good about it at the time, like it was his mission and duty to the Nazi Empire to do this work.

The angel showed me what had happened when he had killed himself. The doctor came before God and there was no judgment, only unconditional love. But God asked him to judge himself and made him see not only the death of all the people he had killed or allowed to die, but also all the connections that this meant for each person. They showed me that we are on a giant web and all of us are interconnected. So, in the death of one person, dozens or hundreds or even thousands of other people's lives may be affected. There are babies that would never be born, husbands without a wife, a mother without her daughter, an employer without an employee. There is no one to do all of the things that a person would have done in their life if they had lived. Kind of like George Bailey in that movie, "It's a Wonderful Life."

Then, they showed me this doctor crying and crying, feeling every emotion of those who were killed or denied the presence of the person he had killed. He had already filled seven large lakes with his tears. The angel said that this was his judgment of his own actions. It was his penance, not God's. The angel said when he was through punishing himself and had settled all his karma with those people, he would be free to go to Heaven.

My Papa kissed me on my forehead and said, "I love you Ritchie. You are a good boy!" Then I realized that I was still attached to my body by a silver cord, but this time it functioned like a stretched out rubber band. I was propelled through space and slammed back into my body in my bed. I felt nourished in soul, body, and spirit - but I was also exhausted. It seemed like I was in a dream for days after that. I will never forget a single moment of my visit to Heaven or my time with Papa. I am so grateful for it. Little did I know what a major role this trip would play in my future life.

## Second Near-Death Experience

My second near-death/angel experience happened the next summer. I was on an Explorer Scout trip on a river that had Class IV rapids. The outfitter advertised that a class IV area contained difficult, long and violent rapids with significant hazard to life in case of mishap. As a group of testosterone-filled young men, we were enchanted with danger. But we had also been told that, since we had a guide, it would be safe. I remember wondering how a guide actually made it safer and wondered even more when I saw their cargo (many cases of beer). It was a five-day trip. It was super exciting and scary when we went through rapids.

When we got to the rapids in what I think of as "Hells Canyon," the story was different. It was anything but relaxing! As we were going through really rough waters, I was thrown out of the raft. I had a life jacket on, but no helmet. I was immediately sucked into the space in front of a large boulder on the downside of the rapid. It was a protected place with some air, but it was also impossible to get out of due to the tremendous power of the current. I could not stand or push myself off of the rock to get out. I think for me, a healer and minister later in life, it makes sense that this happened in "Hells Canyon."

I watched my whole life flash before my eyes on a huge movie screen, like IMAX movies are today, but this was years before they had thought of that. The movie showed me all the good and bad things that I had done in my young life. At the age of 15, there was more good than bad. Actually, there still is. I remember seeing a large glowing presence which I believe was an angel. I could not distinguish any features, but I felt the love coming from this presence. Then, after my movie was over, they said, "It's time for you to go!" I felt huge hands under my bottom that thrust me up into the air. I shot up like a rocket, and then I floated downstream with the other scouts. I was exhausted. I told everyone I could about the movie and the angel. The raft guide said that I had probably struck my head and that is why I was making up all those stories. They made me lie down for a while and then asked me questions - my name and where I was from - and then said that I was fine.

## An Angel Prevents Accidents

I have avoided many traffic accidents because of angels. One time, I was with my wife in my little Nissan Sentra on a two-lane road that was under construction. It had concrete barriers on each side of the road. There was nowhere else to go when we saw a large Ford Explorer coming straight at us in our lane. The driver was weaving between the two lanes. It seemed sure that she was set to hit us head-on. Then, when her car was about six feet away from us, the wheel suddenly turned and she just barely missed us. We saw she had a wild, confused, drunken look on her face and a can of Budweiser in her hand. She looked as surprised as we were that some force had taken control of her car.

Another time we were on an expressway and it was blizzard conditions and a Chevy van fishtailed and was broadside blocking the left two lanes of the busy interstate expressway. I tried to brake, but went into a spin and then completely flipped around and stopped about two feet in front of the van. Inside the van we saw the anxious faces of a large family with 4 kids. Again, I was saved from injury or death. Thanks be to God.

I was beginning to realize that these incidents were not just lucky; there was a trend here. Some higher power had a plan for me.

At age 18, I became a student at Thornton Community College. The college had an even larger library and I loved having access to so much information. Their library had many books about religion, philosophy, meditation, Eastern religions, metaphysics, and mysticism, I loved being there. I was finally able to learn that I was not a crazy freak and that other people had experienced visions and voices like me. That was such a relief.

One day, a transcendental meditation (TM) class was offered in the open library. But it was $25 and I did not have that much money at the time. I know that does not sound like much now, but the minimum wage was only $2.10 an hour then, so it makes sense why I did not have that much money. I went to the library at the same time the class was going to start and sat behind a partition so I could hear everything being said. I followed every instruction and was able to achieve full meditation in my first attempt. Later, I figured out that I had already learned how to meditate during all of my trips to a dentist who did not offer any pain medicine before he started drilling. I used an innate kind of meditation to relieve myself of the pain shooting through my body at every dental visit.

At age 20, I moved on to attend Northern Illinois University. A new life started for me at that point. Everyone I met when I arrived there looked just as confused, lost, poor, and thirsty as I was. I fit right in. I connected with many people who were also seeking answers to the question, "Why am I here in this life?" I had posted a saying on my dorm room door that said "People should build bridges, not walls." Little did I know how that would also be played out over and over in my future life. I attracted many friends who felt the same way. Things were forever changed after that. I saw that I was no different than some people, although I was very different from most people. I was comparing myself to the wrong people and it is why I felt alone for so long.

It seems like some unseen Spirit kept me moving, always learning and experiencing new things. Like how a seed knows just when to sprout in the spring, there is some inherent force in each of us that allows us to be exposed to many things in life and then, having learned some lesson, move past them.

We all have so much imagination and love and lust for life when we are children and it is driven out of us by our educational and religious systems, our parents, and our culture. Along with that, our intuition is often suppressed and lost completely by adulthood. Albert Einstein said:

> Imagination is more important than knowledge.
> Knowledge is limited.
> Imagination encircles the world.
> Logic will get you from A to Z,
> Imagination will get you everywhere

# CHAPTER 4

## *Growing Up in the IRS*

My life progressed. I fell in love, got married, started work at the IRS at the age of 24, and became a father at the age of 38. I experienced many aspects of family and life. Everything was going pretty well. I had work, my garden, and various interests that I enjoyed reading about. I enjoyed studying people and liked to draw floor plans for houses and gardens. I was pretty settled, and even happy. I was able to help people who requested my help with the skills that I had.

This chapter shares how I survived the hectic pace of the IRS using my spiritual gifts and this allowed me to further develop my intuition.

What I learned was that I could survive and function no matter what circumstances I found myself in, or with the limited tools that I had on hand. I learned firsthand how to *do what I could with the tools and gifts that I had right where I was.*

I was alone most of the time while working for the IRS. I was almost my own boss, but it was not a 9-to-5 job. This was very helpful, I learned later in life, because I am also an empath and very sensitive to the energy of others around me.

The stories my taxpayers shared about their lives and circumstances, and the sometimes horrible living conditions they endured, were enough to wake me up in the middle of the night. Other times, trying to do the right thing for the taxpayer and the government was difficult because the IRS is often so hostile to settling cases in a simple and reasonable manner.

But my job was also to hurt people - to make examples of them - in an effort to prevent other taxpayers from thinking about not paying taxes on time - or at all.

I remember my first day with the Internal Revenue Service; it was like walking on to the set of the old police sitcom, *Barney Miller.* We sat two to a table and shared a telephone. I knew everything about everyone else in the office and about their cases as well. Some of my fellow employees were kind and friendly and helpful to me. The mood in the office every day ranged from nice to mean to extremely aggressive at each table. It was not a nice place to come to work every day. The energy of an IRS office is often so low that fear, anger and resentment are the daily result. It is a miracle that I survived the first week, let alone all those years.

While writing this book, one of my editors said "What are some of your happy IRS stories?" So I thought – and I'm sorry if this doesn't sound typically happy - about seizing people's homes and their hidden bank accounts. I thought about how happy I was when I outsmarted some tax cheat. I relayed stories to the editor about the camaraderie I felt when all these lone wolf tax collectors got together and did enforced collection. The editor said that was not what she was looking for.

She said, "I mean positive things!"

I told the editor exciting stories about how I had almost been killed by a pipe bomb that blew up the entry way to the IRS building that I was supposed to open that morning. It started a fire and shattered windows. Thank God I was running 15 minutes late that day.

I told her that I was thankful to be alive, because taxpayers could be verbally abusive and it can get physical quickly. I was assaulted physically five times in 33 years. I am talking about being hit, choked, and thrown against the wall. Throw in the threat from a mobster to blow me and my family up and you begin to get the idea.

There was a thoughtless disregard for the law and for other people. But at the same time, I saw so many acts of kindness, where IRS employees went out of their way to help taxpayers who had messed up their lives. IRS enforcement employees are trained to be mean but to smile at the same time.

After a while I was indoctrinated into the mindset of the IRS. I started to lose my feelings of concern and compassion for my fellow man. I remember some of my fellow tax collectors calling the taxpayers dirt bags and scum. I never let it go that far, but I often was reminded of the saying, "Absolute Power Corrupts Absolutely." The IRS is much insulated from the real world and pretty much does whatever it wants with little resistance and no explanations.

As a Senior Revenue Officer for the Internal Revenue Service I was also a bill collector, psychologist, credit counselor, loan officer, auctioneer, marketing specialist, marriage counselor, financial planner, social worker, paralegal, mediator, asset evaluator, negotiator, judge, jury and enforcer. It helped that I have a natural ability to instantly connect with people. We start talking and I would jump into their lives, learning everything they wanted to tell me. My gut feelings (intuition) would tell me everything else I needed to know to investigate their case.

My job required me to make cold calls on individuals and businesses that had not filed tax returns or paid employment, income or other taxes. I would knock on their door and ask the most personal questions about their finances, lifestyle, relationships and living arrangements, questions about their style of living, their marital status and their children, and would want to see inside their house and business, to look for other assets, like artwork or antique furniture.

Most of the reasons why people owe taxes came down to my unofficial "D" list that I compiled over the years. Many people experienced death, depression, divorce, drugs, drinking, deception, dumb choices, or dumb behavior. Add to this some non-D words such as illness, adultery, bad luck, stupidity, incompetence and a gambling addiction.

Some people say they are too busy, or too afraid to open the IRS letters. They are so overwhelmed with their daily lives and the whole tax filing system that they try to hide. Sprinkle greed and deliberate tax evasion in, and it makes for an interesting cast of characters.

Most taxpayers figured out how to get me the information that I needed and start paying taxes again, after those collection actions. Most taxpayers could barely survive on the money that I (IRS) allowed them for their expenses. Some people did not survive, and suicide was a common way to finish things up on the taxpayer's end. Seven of my taxpayers killed themselves; dozens more suffered mental break-downs, attempted suicide or experienced health issues like strokes and heart attacks, and some just died. I always liked the cases where the person died, because then I could quickly close my case. I was not the only one that caused their problems. I was just the last one - the last one to take away their money, their home, their business and their pride. I rewarded them with fear, worry, despair and anger. The weak ones did not survive. But I truly didn't care, because the IRS had hardened me. I could be swift and merciless if they lied to me or did not do what I told them to do.

It's not that I had no conscience. I helped taxpayers who helped me close my cases. I was just merciless on those that I judged to be tax cheats and criminals.

In my life as a tax collector, I dealt with people who lost hope after their dreams died. They may have survived a death in the family, disease, divorce or losing everything they had, but the awful fear of having to deal with the IRS caused some people to go into shutdown mode. I often asked myself, "Why do bad things happen to these otherwise good, hard-working people? Why have they invested every-thing they had into this business and lost all their money plus a lot of the government's as well?"

I instinctively knew when people were lying. In my early years, I thought it was because I had been so well trained by the IRS in inter-viewing taxpayers. Better yet, I knew specifically what they were lying about and what they were trying to hide. I could not talk about this until after I retired, but during all those years in the IRS I was using my secret gifts, my intuition. I was able to "read" my taxpayers and discover assets and secrets that they did not want me to know.

Co-workers used to say that I had a sixth sense about the tax work. I didn't know at that time what it meant. I just knew that I was really good at what I did. My skills and ability to pay attention to my gut feelings led to 22 criminal tax fraud referrals. I just knew stuff about my taxpayers that went way beyond anything that I was trained in. I thought it was because I was trained in reading taxpayers' body language and verbal clues to determine when they were lying, but this was so enhanced by the spiritual gifts I have.

Early in my career when people were lying to me, I would get a bad feeling just under my stomach in an area that I now know to be my solar plexus, a chakra energy point on my body. It felt like a sharp pain. I knew when people were going to die or when they were really sick.

At the age of 40, I had a 2-year-old, a wife with health issues, and my own significant health challenges. In my sick bed, I had time to think about why I was here on Earth. These life-changing events reawakened me to the fact that I was more than an IRS revenue officer. I was also a human being.

I came in touch with how I felt, how others felt, and the cause-and-effect of everything, so through a combination of circumstances the "mission" of my life was revealed to me.

I had an incredible amount of power in my job at the IRS. I had used it to hurt and even destroy some people – just to close cases. I decided to change my ways and try to help my taxpayers. I could still be aggressive if tax collection was in danger, but that was the exception.

Looking back, I had few friends outside of the IRS, because no one else really understood me and my work. Not even my family. Looking back now, I see that was not very healthy. But mixed in with this were many dramas and traumas in my life that led me to greater and greater lessons. Always with the lessons! I remember thinking sarcastically, "Wow! God must really love me to give me this life."

At the age of 40, I wrote a book on my own time that I gave to the IRS called the *Asset Recovery Guide*. It explained how to collect taxes in various situations, and about financial analysis and finding money and assets. It was well received and the Financial Analysis section of the Internal Revenue Manual (IRM 5.15.1) is patterned after my book. I was never sure if I had written the book or simply been chosen by Spirit because I would allow it to be channeled through me to the paper. It came so easily, as if each paragraph was delivered to my mind right before I wrote it. It was all based on my knowledge and experience, but repackaged by Spirit and delivered back to me.

As the book was being written, every morning at 4 a.m. a voice would wake me up and tell me, "Time to get up and pray!" So I learned to get up and say some prayers. I have never been a morning person, so this was a big deal! Then, after I finished my prayers, my fingers hit the keyboard of a borrowed computer and it was like automatic writing; it just came though me. The book really was a pleasure to write, and so much was recorded for future generations of IRS tax collectors.

Even after I finished the book I continued to be awakened by the voice telling me to get up and pray. When writing the book, I had prayed, gotten my tea, and then the words flowed through me. I wondered what this was all about. So I went to a Catholic priest and told him about it. He said, "This is clearly the work of the devil!" I said, "But Father, the voice is telling me to pray to God, not the devil!" He looked very seriously at me and said, "Young man, I have been a priest for 43 years. Don't you think if God had wanted to talk to someone, He would have talked to me?!" I agreed with him. He gave me a laundry list of prayers and a bottle of Holy Water and sent me away, making me think that I was not only crazy but being pursued by the devil.

Later, I spoke to someone who told me that I could negotiate the wake up time with the Spirit. I chose 6 a.m. and that worked out fine. I woke up and prayed and kept my prayer stream open throughout the day, at least on a spirit/soul level. Spirit and I were both happy for a while and I got more rest. Eventually, I was able to direct my spirit to pray unceasingly while I went about my day.

Every day I wake up a new person, slightly different from the person I was yesterday, always learning – always growing. Sometimes I am in joy, sometimes in pain, sometimes in stillness, but always growing. .

I love the 23rd Psalm. It says:

> *The Lord is my shepherd; I shall not want.*
> *He maketh me to lie down in green pastures:*
> *He leadeth me beside the still waters.*
> *He restoreth my soul:*
> *He leadeth me in the paths*
> *of righteousness for His name's sake.*

I feel like my soul is restored and rearranged almost every day. When I was in sixth grade I received a message from Spirit that said:

> *If you are not progressing,*
> *then you are regressing,*
> *but you are never standing still*
> *Avoid regressing whenever possible.*

I think that an angel had whispered it in my right ear. I think this was about the same time that I started to lose most of my spiritual connections. From then on it was gut feelings and rarely direct messages from Spirit.

# CHAPTER 5

## *My Life-Changing Lesson*

In the fall of my fortieth year, I suddenly got very sick. Three discs in my neck and three in my lower back herniated and swelled to levels that caused me pain, loss of sensation, mental confusion, and numbness down my entire left side. I did the normal thing a person with great health insurance does; I went to the doctor. I ended up seeing many doctors and physical therapists. I had many x-rays and MRIs, and all of the news was bad. I would need surgery, as my muscles were already starting to atrophy in my left arm and left leg. I was getting mentally confused and even having trouble forming sentences and keeping my thoughts straight.

Finally, one doctor, a brain surgeon in fact, discovered that I had a tumor on my pituitary gland (brain tumor) and he said that he would have to go up through my nose to remove it. The pituitary gland is right up there next to the brain. He told me most tumors are benign and not to worry. Easy for him to say, I thought. He was very casual about it.

I went home and fell to my knees in front of a kitchen chair I used as a prayer kneeler. I was so sad, worried, and afraid. I was crying and I said aloud, "God! You are scaring the Hell out of me!" Then I heard a voice I had never heard before, and I have since identified as the voice of God, say, "And when the Hell is all gone, I will still be here." Now, this really scared me! I was sobbing at this point, thinking that this tumor was making me crazier than I already was.

My sister-in-law, a Catholic nun, told me about a priest who did healings. I laughed it off. "Right!" I thought, "Like he can heal anyone! And even if he could, why would he heal me?!" But the pain and loss of feeling did make me feel very distant from my old self, and so I went to the healing Mass. There, I met an 80-year-old Roman Catholic priest, Father Peter Rookey, who was doing healings before an audience of about 1000 people. There were cancer patients being wheeled in and a lot of people who looked very sick. I looked fine on the outside compared to most of them; I was just breaking down on the inside. He put holy oil on my forehead and palm of my hand. He did it to each person there. He didn't use any words, just gave his silent blessing. When he put the oil on me, I felt nothing. He moved to the next person and put the oil on them and they fell backwards into a group of people who are called "catchers" and they would guide the person to lay flat on their back on the ground. The person who was blessed in that way was said to be overcome with the spiritual ecstasy. Then the priest stepped back to me and said, "It didn't take. Now, relax and don't fight it this time." He put the holy oil on my forehead and palms again. I did not know anything about chakras (energy centers) at the time, but he anointed me on my third eye chakra which governs spiritual connection and intuition and on the chakras in the middle of each hand.

I later found out this was called being "Baptized in the Holy Spirit." The second time worked for me. I felt a jolt of electrical energy go through me. I felt dizzy and confused, and I went and sat back down. "Okay," I thought, "at least now I can tell my wife and sister-in-law I have done what they wanted."

I did not feel any different that night. The next morning, I woke up, and still could not feel three of the fingers on my left hand, three of the toes on my left foot, or anything down that side of my body. Nothing had changed. But as I got up out of bed I felt different. Then I realized

I felt no pain. All the pain that was going down my back and shooting from my neck to my breastbone was gone - completely gone! Within a week, all of the feeling in my hand, arm, leg, and foot had returned. A doctor later told me that since my nerves and muscles had started to atrophy, it was normal for it to take seven to ten days for feeling to return.

That is when I learned that the absence of pain is a healing in itself. Even if people still have the disease a great prize is when their pain is removed and they are somewhat restored because of it.

I was amazed, but still the tax collector part of me was skeptical. How could I be healed when that church was full of really sick people who surely needed healing more than I did? How did it happen, and why me? I wanted to know more and did not know where to begin.

I went back to the two doctors that were treating me and one starting poking into me with a sharp needle. I jerked away from him, and he said, "Looking at your MRI, you should not be able to feel this at all." But I did. Then he did the same in other places on my body, and it hurt like hell. The doctor ordered a new round of x-rays and MRIs. When the results came back, everything had returned to normal. Everything! The doctor, being a true scientist, ordered another set of tests, which also came back negative. Even the tumor on my pituitary gland was gone. He kept thinking than the MRI operator had messed up the tests. He referred me back to the brain surgeon, who compared all sets of the test results. He said, "No doubt about it. You are completely healed." I asked how, and he said, "I have no idea." Then I told him about the healing Mass. He said, "Then there you have it. God has healed you. Accept it! Go home and figure out what you are supposed to do with your life, and then you can discover why God healed you."

Since that first healing, it seems I only get sick suddenly and profoundly, so that God can show how quickly I can be healed when I allow it. When I allow God into my life, then I become a living witness to this work. One of the most amazing things that I have learned is that when you do not have pain, you can feel so much better. You may still be sick, but without pain you can still live an active life.

I became friends with Father Rookey, the old healing priest. He told me that he had been blinded as a young boy from an accident and then he was healed in much the same way that the healing happened to me. After my healing, I had the gift and ability to do hands-on healing. The priest was always careful to say that the power to heal was not his, but was God's, administered through the Holy Spirit. I also grew into the abilities and gifts that I have to be an emotional and spiritual healer. The priest counseled me and said that I was now a "Charismatic Catholic Healer." I was very skeptical of all this at first. He said he had not given me anything that was not already in me. He compared it to God just turning on my light switch and the power coming through.

Father Rookey used to call me his Tucson Branch Office. I learned about his story of having the gift of healing and then having it suppressed most of his life by the Catholic hierarchy. The lesson of spirituality and religion being related but not necessarily connected together was shown to me over and over in my life; the two do not seem to mix well.

After my healing, I was allowed two months of rest. Then, the next phase of my life began, in earnest. Why had God chosen to heal me? Why? Surely I was the least of his flock, which is what I had been taught throughout my life anyway.

Then, my spiritual gifts started to come back, slowly at first. They built upon what I had already learned. I had only to read the Bible to figure out that what I was getting was normal, and even expected, for a Christian. My gifts of prophecy, discernment, wisdom, visions, healing, and praying in, and interpreting, tongues, were reawakened. When I read *1st Corinthians* I found that these abilities were called the "Gifts of the Spirit." I saw statues cry and witnessed prayer cards that were tear-stained. I knew that I was supposed to do something more than being an IRS Tax Collector, son, husband, and father, but what?

God never seems to make it easy for me in any lesson or reawakening, or maybe I am too stubborn to be easily directed. In fact, I have been told that the exams are tougher for those at a higher level - the old souls. The first question I had was, "What is my mission on Earth?" I was guided to the fact that all I had described were obligations: having a career or being a son, a parent or spouse. The obligations are not missions. That is why people who put too much emphasis on only taking care of those obligations are in such spiritual and emotional trouble. When their parents or spouse die, or the kids move out, when someone retires, or when a friend or family member dies, or they lose a job or a business, they lose their reason for living. The people that you have relationships with were supposed to be part of your life, but they were not the *reason* for your life.

Because of my healing, I met many like-minded souls who did healings and had visions. I met with other Charismatic Catholics. They explained that everything I was experiencing was very normal and not to be afraid, to embrace all that came, but also to question and use my discernment to determine its source.

I had been tormented by attacks from devils for years because I forgot that I was from God. This body I was in was not the be-all, end-all of my spirit and soul. Coming into this new life was tough. My mind/ego fought it every step of the way. Everything was tough, but I came out okay in the end.

I felt much empowered by my ability to pray, and learned that every word and every emotion is a prayer. Words can be a powerful sword. I found that I needed to be careful when I sent out any message to the Universe because I could get a swift and immediate response.

I started with intercessory prayer and prayer lists. This means praying for people who are mostly strangers, usually regarding their health, jobs, or relationships. Suddenly people started coming to me asking me to pray for them or for someone they knew or loved. Often, these requests came from people who I didn't even know. Each time I wrote down the name and the petition they asked for. I prayed and healings happened, by the Grace of God, I am sure, because I do not believe that I had any influence in the matter. This became quietly successful. I discovered that it was my mission to pray for people. I was happy to share my love for people that way. I do not think it had anything to do with me. I was just an instrument of God allowing the healing power of God to come through me.

I would get up in the morning, brush my teeth, and shave, and then say my prayers in a small bathroom in my house. I had all of the names written on a piece of paper on the wall there. I said my prayers. But my intention was that my spirit/soul would continue praying for the rest of the day as I went about my job at the IRS. I call this "praying unceasingly." I gave up part of myself and allowed my spirit to be connected to the God energy all day. Prayer is so easy and it begins with good intentions. It can be done any time in the day or night, aloud or silently. I learned that good things happened to me and others when I prayed. Good things happened.

I think that it is amusing how so many people can define God. This energy that is God is impossible to perceive, comprehend, know or understand on any mental level. You may witness manifestations of the God energy in things that occur, but never more than that, until you rise up to the spirit level again.

When you learn to recognize God-energy in every single person that you meet every day, you are on a good path to feeling God more. There is a Hindi expression "Namaste." This literally means "I recognize the God/Goddess energy in you." When you say this to another person who is also enlightened, they will usually respond by saying "Namaste" back to you.

Some people pray a lot and get no peace from it. In fact, they have trouble praying and not asking, demanding, and telling God what to do. God already knows what to do. You need to catch up. The best thing is that you owe nothing to God, at all, ever. There is no judgment, criticism, condemnation or punishment. The only person who can do that to you is you.

When you pray and make petitions, you must also be ready to receive a response. Many people only want what they want on their own terms.

Sometimes God gives you what you have asked for. Sometimes God gives you even more. Sometimes God says "maybe later or we will see." Sometimes God just says, "It's not time right now." Sometimes God just says "no."

It does not matter the answer; it matters that you were sharing yourself with God, maybe to help others or maybe to help yourself. It does not matter; the lesson is about being in community not only with your fellow man, but also higher spiritual powers. Praying always raises your energy and the energy of hundreds or thousands of other people who do not pray.

One day, I saw an apparition of Mary, Mother of Jesus. She told me that she was proud of how my healings were going and that she had a new job for me. She said I needed to get out and touch someone - to do hands-on healing. I argued back that I was not comfortable with it. I was just fine with praying in my bathroom. Mary indicated that this phase of my development was ending. Her greatest message to me, and that I have applied to hundreds of other people in their lives, was, *"Just do it - Just start!"* I could ask all the questions that I wanted, but just like a firm and loving mother, she wanted me to follow her instruction and just do it.

I wanted to know what to do and then Mary was silent. But I knew that I was being guided in this process. I would know what I needed to know, when I needed to know it.

How many times have we as children or parents faced this difficult task of accepting the will of another that we did not ask for or maybe don't even agree with? This was one of the first tests of overriding my mind/ego. It was also one of the first ways that I learned to submit to the will of God. What I know now is that submission to the will of God will lead to me walking along with God. And walking along with God will lead me to feeling the Spirit of God inside of me. It is quite amazing! Submission leads to supplication which leads to recognition of the partnership that we all have with the God energy. Eventually this partnership becomes oneness with all of Creation.

Since then, I have done hundreds of hands-on healings with great results. I am mostly a spiritual and emotional healer. The body is more temporary, so while physical healing does occur, it is not the primary place healed. My only true gifts are unconditional love, acceptance and compassion for my fellow man. The real healing energy comes from God.

When I work with a client I seek the issue that caused the physical problems. It could be abuse, the inability to forgive, or emotional lack. Usually, illness comes from lack of love, lack of worthiness, and other feelings of lack. If the client will only practice acceptance of, and forgiveness for, whomever or whatever has hurt them, then they will soon find themselves on the road to health, happiness, and peace. It is a process, but also a good place to "just start!"

I am not saying that clients I have worked with do not still die on my watch — they do. But all die with a new awareness of the Living God, however they define it in their lives. They are not going to take anyone's crap anymore, and they are doing this because they *love themselves first, best, and always.* They have been healed mentally, emotionally, and spiritually through various ways.

In my readings, sometimes I am gentle and sympathetic, and sometimes I can be brash, pushy and forward. It seems that if I simply follow the messages and directions I receive from Spirit, each client hears exactly what they need to hear at the time that they need to hear it. Many people are so happy because they say that I have confirmed for them everything they already knew inside but were afraid to accept.

Some clients are angry with me because I lay everything out on the table. Even when this is done with love, some clients are in deep denial because their own ego is so in charge of them. They want to do everything their own way and it has to be perfect. I tell them that they are not God; they are not perfect. I try to help them let it all go. You would be amazed at how much better everything will be when you turn your ego down to a minimal level. When I work with clients, I also have to remind them that they are not the Savior. I remind them that trying to change others will never work. They can only change themselves first, and then others may follow them if they choose. You can support healing that a person chooses for themselves, but you cannot force anyone to change or heal.

Over the years, I learned that most clients heal in stages. They have many layers that must be healed, step by step, as they allow it.

After many readings with individual clients, I was directed by Spirit to go out and rent a shop to do public readings. I met many people and learned a lot. I tried to reach people where they were, not where I wanted them to be. It was a great educational process. All I was doing was sitting there offering people hope and love. I think that was when I recognized the true spiritual nature in all people.

I confirmed for them that they did have intuition and spiritual gifts, and that was a great blessing to both of us. Many people who are intuitive or healers carry it as a secret that they do not want others to know. This also applies if they have a higher calling and march to the beat of a different drummer. So it was a relief to them when I recognized them and directed them on how to reconnect to the power of the Universe, the Creator God energy.

I learned that even using that word "God" is traumatic for many people. This is usually due to people's experience with, and interpretation of, religion. They have been harmed and pulled away from the God depicted by religion. I do not discuss who this God is because it wastes too much time. I share with clients my view that God is a creative, loving energy at a higher spiritual level than you or I. The Bible, among many other religious books, has already covered that.

I prefer to direct people back to the Creator God. I ask them to define the energy that created the Earth and all our ancestors. That is the energy I want to reconnect them with. I am told by Spirit that there really is only one God and all the petty divisions over concepts such as "My God is better than your God" are amusing to them. I often refer to God as "The Great He-She-They-It Energy." This pretty much covers it. It is more like God is a blend of every energy, every feeling, and every emotion we feel here on Earth. Since many can agree on the many attributes of God being all-knowing, all-seeing, and more, this clears things up for most of my clients.

Regarding organized religion, philosophies, and spiritual beliefs, I do not believe that we should throw the baby out with the bath water. If religion works for you and leads you to ideals of the Living God, then embrace it. I hope that you are bold enough to go to your church and ask for more. Ask where God is within the four walls of the church. Ask for more spiritual connection and self-realization in the surroundings of your existing church or religion.

I think many people feel a longing for something that they cannot even describe -perhaps for God, once their lower chakra needs are met (the need for food, shelter, clothing, basic comforts, sex, and children to take care of you in old age). They feel the need for community and connection. They do not feel the need for control, correction and deception.

Since birth, I desired to know why exactly I was here in this life. I discovered that the web of interactions that I had with thousands of people directly also affected tens of thousands of others indirectly. I discovered this in the days before we knew anything about the power of connections on the internet. But that is the purpose of my life, to be a part of all the creative connections that result just by being here. It is a tricky area when you get divine inspiration. When it first comes, most people are afraid and reject it fearfully. People can actually be afraid of you if you are spiritually gifted, and that attitude pleases the dark energies very much.

When you live for others, the purpose of your life becomes clear. When you love what you are doing, this passion will allow you to make the most of your life. When you make connections to the Universal

Energy, it's like filling up your gas tank. It gives you an unlimited supply of energy.

I have learned through my own experiences that one of the biggest mistakes I ever made was to try to do healing on people using my own energy. I only have a limited amount of energy. When I gave it away to others, no matter how well-meaning I was, then it was not available to help fuel me in my own life.

Education, society, and parents love to over-schedule, over-control and over-demand their children's lives. Many people spend most of their time building boxes in the lives of their children. They set goals and time requirements on their children. There is the box that says that if you are a white, male, Protestant, you must go to a certain college if you are to be happy and successful. Or if you are a girl you must wear a dress and make babies to be happy. So many rules, so little quality of life. Anything outside of the box is deemed wrong or dirty. After so many years, the children can no longer see outside the walls of the box. The box around them is comforting, but also limiting.

Thinking of the world in such a small and limited way crushes intuition, joy, happiness, and the ability to grow with the gifts that are given to you. The gifts of intuition, knowledge, wisdom, healing, and compassion for yourself and every other living thing on Earth are very valuable. If you are lucky, someday a person like me will come into your life with a box cutter and make a small hole in the box of your life so you can look out and begin to wonder about the world beyond. Perhaps you will get the urge and strength to find your own box cutter to come out of your box. One day you will look up and begin to see what's outside of your box.

Often, through a reading, I create a spark that allows my clients to be reignited, reconnected to the Universal Energy of Love and Light. Often this happens at age 38 for women and 40 for men. We all yearn for that "something more" in life. This is how we have everything we could possibly want, but still feel unhappy and disconnected. This is so often the case, and it is sad and unnecessary.

When we begin to remember who we were before we came here to this earth, and when we thirst for connection to Spirit/God, our soul rejoices. When we are happy, we attract people who are happy to be with us. When we are sad and miserable, we attract the same and later wonder why these people have tried to destroy us and our creations. But we must not blame others, because no one is present in your life if you do not invite them in and tolerate them. You cannot be abused or mistreated if you do not allow the abuser into your life. You are always in control.

It is not an easy journey to go from where you are to the place you are meant to be in this life. In fact, it can be very difficult. The Chinese symbol for chaos is the same as the symbol for opportunities. But it is a blessing when the pain, anger, fear, and loss push us to new places of soul growth.

Spiritual/Soul growth can take place over many years or it can be very rapid, depending on how quickly you lower your walls of defense. You must first learn to quiet your mind/ego. When you truly allow spiritual growth and reconnection, it will happen very quickly.

When I began to rediscover and reconnect with my God/Source/ Universal Energy, I began a journey that forever changed my life. It is a long reawakening process, with joyous results in the end. The road is not easy. If you live life to the fullest, it never is. But, it can still be amazing and fulfilling. Sometimes you do not even recognize how strong you are until you have either nearly died, or actually died and can view your life from the other side.

Perhaps because my own life was more chaotic than other peoples' (and more exciting), I searched for connections every day. I still do. Every time I was open for spiritual growth, the fear came in very strongly. I was seeing things, knowing things, and getting huge déjà vu moments every day. I started to remember things that I should have had no knowledge or even access to knowledge of. It was really strange how precise my visions and memories were.

I have great respect for all people I have met because I see the highest good in each person. I think we all want the same things. We all want to find a mate, friends, someone to love and care for us, and we may want to have children, to have safe and affordable housing, to be able to pay our bills, eat, be warm or cool and properly clothed, not go to bed hungry — we are all the same. Yet the darkness in the world wants us all to believe we are different because of our race, religion, nationality, social status or economic class.

While this is what we want, we often settle for far less. The love turns out to just be about the sex, or the other benefits your partner gets from you. The security turns out to be sporadic and temporary. Every day the glow that may have previously surrounded your relationship continues to be extinguished.

As I began my 20s, I started to deny these inner truths, that knowing, that intuition. I was beginning to lose faith in the future and my gut feelings, and starting to trust only in what I was told to do or say or think. As I grew away from the God Energy, I start to get slower and unable to resist pain and mental attitudes that attracted physical illness into my life. I started to trust in what I could see, hear, count, and touch, not what I could sense or feel. I started to lose the sparkle and excitement of my youth.

The question must have come up in your own life many times: If you have done everything right, then why have you still suffered pain, loss, and regret? Why have you suffered? Why have those who you love suffered? What is causing you so much unhappiness may just be the way you perceive your life as this single chance, this one shot deal where you have to get everything right. That is impossible, to know all the things a person must learn about love in a single life. Stop torturing yourself!

When bad things happen to good people, it is simply because that is part of the plan for your growth. If you look at your life in the context of reincarnation, when the pain and loss is spread over dozens or even hundreds of lives, you will find the momentary pain no larger than a pin prick on your finger. This can help you through your worst moments. Knowing that you will be okay in the end, no matter what happens, will help you to heal.

In reincarnation as it has been shown to me, we are all like actors in a play. We usually have 150 other souls in bodies playing key roles in our current life. Then we have another 1,500 souls in bodies that may be in our lives but just for a moment, distant family, friends, work associates or partners. Everyone plays a role in your future. Some are cast as good and some as bad or even evil. It is all required- just like an actor reads his lines in a play. But when he walks off stage, (returns to spirit/soul form) then they are equal and loving with us again.

If you had asked me 40 years ago if I was happy in my life as it was then, I would have said yes. Helping people helped me feel good. My life at that point was full, and my ego was satisfied. But a strange emptiness was always within me. I was yearning for connection to something more than what I could see. The closest I could see or feel this energy was when I was working in the dirt while I was gardening. I felt completeness when tending my garden. My backyard garden was turning into my Secret Garden.

Now, I am more developed and I am able to help more people using God's energy, not my own energy. I am able to love myself more because I am not afraid to love you, my fellow human being.

When we are on Earth, mind/ego is often in control. I ask clients, "Who do you think is the 'Prince of the Earth'?" Usually they answer that they think it is Jesus. But, really, does that make sense? Would Jesus make a mess like this and then allow it to continue?

According to the Bible, the Prince of the Earth is Satan (*John 12:31, John 14:30*) and that should make some sense to you at this point in your life. But Jesus and all the energies of the light around Him are always available to lift you up to the next level and pull you out of karmic situations which are no longer productive.

I think that many people have felt empty and alone, even in great houses and with wealth, at various points in their lives. Socrates said:

I am not saying that it's not important
to make beautiful statues and to have
fine battleships and city walls.
But none of this matters
unless the people inside
those city walls are happy.

I do not think many Americans are happy today. That is not just my opinion. It is an observation. Look at our poverty rate, our mental health cases, depression, suicides, education levels, teen pregnancies, employment prospects, our declining standard of education, and our declining standard of living. Look at our spiritual poverty and it is no wonder that many people are disconnected, feeling sad and depressed. When people seek their perception of God, and do not find it in organized religion, that hurts us all.

At age 40, when the layers of my past life had been peeled away from me, my ego was forced into retreat. Then I saw I had been living with many negative emotions for a long time: unworthiness, fear, anger, low self-esteem, low self-confidence, lack of love, non-forgiveness of myself, sadness, and loneliness. Much of this I had picked up from the people who were around me, within the IRS and even my own family and friends. When I was able to distinguish that these things were not coming from God, I was able to better sort them out and reject them.

What is important to my mind/ego is not always important to my spirit/soul. It is my ego's job to protect my psyche, to make me think that everything is all right, even as I create artificial reality. Mind/ego goes to great lengths to make you think that you are right, and others are wrong, to make you think everything is going well when it is not, to make you think that you are superior to your brothers and sisters in life. Mind/ego does not want you to improve your spiritual lot in life, but loves if you can get more power, control, sex or money.

# CHAPTER 6

## *What Happens in a Reading*

If I had a sign outside of my house promoting my healing business, it would say:

> It doesn't matter who you are
> Or where you came from.
> You are here now and I have a secret to share with you.
> God and I accept and love you unconditionally and forever.

All of my readings and healing sessions start out the same. I shake your hand and start receiving your energy on many different levels. I am able to access your energy and read your heart, mind, spirit and soul. I ask if it is okay to share with you whatever may come to me. This can include information from deceased love ones, plus information about relationships, jobs, career, and what the future might bring. It can also bring information about abuse, bad memories, and other thoughts or behaviors you may not want other people to know. I am privileged to be able to drop behind the façade that you show to everyone. I am completely open and honest with you about what I find inside you.

I always visualize it this way: we are all like giant, secure castles. We have thick walls, and many layers of walls around us. Perhaps we have moats and alligators (you can have all of these things built up to protect you), but during a reading, I am gifted to be able to go beyond that wall. I simply parachute into your castle courtyard and walk right up to the treasure room where all of you is on display.

In those rooms, you store the lies you told, the hurts you received and caused, shame, regrets, and the secrets that you do not normally allow people to see. It is almost like I am allowed the experience of being you. But here I am, and as I look around and assess the "you" inside the you that people know about, I project Love, Light, and Unconditional Acceptance of whatever it is that you are made of. Whatever you have experienced that has hurt you is ready to be exposed to the Light I bring, so that it can be healed and removed from you.

It can be slightly uncomfortable for you at first. You have to trust that I will not hurt you, and that I will protect and guide you to where it is you need to go to release the pain of those things that no longer serve you. The readings are always private and confidential. This will allow you to forgive yourself as you forgive others.

It is very intimate and can be either disturbing or comforting to the person I am reading. That is why it is important at every step along the way to verify that I have permission to go in depth.

While every reading I do is different, they all start out the same. First, I write these two phrases on the top of a piece of paper: The first is *Love Yourself First, Best, and Always!* The second is *Pray, Meditate, and Shut Up and Listen!*

Many clients, when examining their lives, see that they have not put themselves first. Often, they have loved others more than they have loved themselves.

This hurts them. This attracts energy vampires who have sucked up their time, love and energy. They have experienced codependent and harmful relationships.

When I say to *Love Yourself First, Best and Always*, I do not mean to love yourself in a selfish, narcissistic, or damaging way. I mean to not be an emotional or physical doormat for another person because you love them, are afraid to be alone, or want to change them. Many people I have spoken to want to help others. They want to do the right thing for other people, but often forget about doing the right thing for themselves. So, they bend over backwards to help other people, often people that could help themselves if they chose to. And then they end up hurt, lost, alone, and exhausted.

I remember a homeless man who I gave a $10 roll of quarters to; he thanked me and opened the roll and took out $2 in quarters, then handed the rest back to me. He said, "I could get mugged with that much money in the shelter." I did not understand it at first. I was trying to help him, but he was wiser than me; he was loving himself. He accepted all the help that he could at that moment and we both benefited.

This is why so many self-help books have been written on this subject. My favorites are *Women Who Love Too Much* by Robin Norwood, and *Codependent No More* by Melody Beattie. In the United States, we all are encouraged to be independent. That is why we may have nice houses, televisions and stuff but are all alone, unloved, and lonely. We are all interdependent, though American society does not promote this. We are not all rugged, self-sustaining individualists. We are all connected to each other and to God.

To learn to love yourself, I use the example of a parent traveling on an airplane with a child. You are advised that if the oxygen mask comes down, you should put the oxygen mask on yourself first, so that you are still breathing. Then you can put the mask on your child. This seems counterintuitive to a parent who always puts their child first. But your child cannot put the mask on you.

When you attempt to heal, love, save, support, and change other people directly from your own limited pool of energy, it wears you out. You drain your emotional and physical energy, and eventually this leads you to getting sick. Accessing the universal love energy of God is like putting your oxygen mask on first. What I will show you is how to access the universal love energy of God.

Many clients are doing healing, counseling, and using their own energy to help other people. This hurts them, first emotionally and then physically. Your health is a mirror reflection of all the stress in your emotional life. We can pray for and support others in the life changes they have chosen, but we cannot make those choices for them.

Before you try to help others, you must first try to help and heal yourself. This is where you learn to *Love Yourself First, Best and Always* in every situation. This will allow you to build a strong conduit through which the healing energy can flow. But no amount of self-improvement can make up for a lack of self-acceptance and self-love.

Regarding the *Pray, Meditate, and Shut Up and Listen!* phrase that I received directly from Spirit, it might be hard to hear, but I am just delivering the message. Some clients do not like it, but who am I to judge Spirit?

I offer clients prayers and a guided imagery meditation, and the "shut up and listen" part is up to them. Meditation is simply quieting the mind enough to allow you to connect with the God energy. It is so important to have access to, and trust of, direct revelation. We cannot know the world until we know God's world, but discernment is also important to everyone in the world seeking to learn the wisdom of holy books such as the Bible, the Koran, the Torah, and the Bhagavad-Gita. Seeking the counsel of like-minded people, or enlightened religious people is helpful, but I prefer to run everything through my own list first. The Bible is very clear that we must exercise discernment in every area of our life.

*First Thessalonians 5:21-22 states,*
"But examine everything carefully; hold fast to that which is good; abstain from every form of evil, but test the Spirits to see whether they are from God; because many false prophets have gone out into the world."

I find that many current leaders in organized religions have really dropped the ball on this. Jesus said that a good tree can only produce good fruit, and a bad tree can only produce bad fruit. (*1 John 4:1*) In each message or vision we receive, we need to determine if the message promotes love and spiritual growth for ourselves and others around us, or if it will injure or destroy ourselves and others.

During the reading, the next phrase I write on the paper is: *Remember: Forgive Yourself and the Person Who Hurt You, and Release It All to God with Love.*

After you learn to love yourself, you must forgive yourself and those people, religions, organizations, and circumstances that have caused you pain in your life and left you feeling unworthy, exhausted and damaged.

When we heal ourselves and turn everything over to God, it is a major step forward. Your new life can begin. Once you rid yourself of the emotional baggage and painful memories of your life, you will feel free and youthful. Like-minded people and love will be attracted to you on many levels.

It is important to know that all of the joy and pain, and in fact, all of the events that made you who you are in your life, has been stored in your soul. The soul is connected to God and is like a reference library. You need to forgive and forget, not just others involved in your life, but yourself as well. Your past simply is not important in the present day. Not that your past is not worthwhile; the past has many lessons, but none of them need to be in your active folder of life. It works the same as computer memory - you know it is there or stored in a cloud somewhere, but you do not need to keep dragging it along with you to every new situation.

You will have many painful and also joyful lessons that happen in your life. That is life. You will experience many things that you must go through to learn how it feels to experience that action. For instance, when a loved one dies, you need to accept it and mourn their passing. That is normal and expected. But sometimes, you may be unable to get over it.

This is where I tell my clients about the energy of the Violet Flame and a mystic named Saint Germaine. Do a Google search for more information about him. This energy helps a person going through a difficult lesson. It allows them to still experience the mourning, for example, but to burn off residual feelings and emotions that are slowing healing. This supports them in getting themselves "sorted out" and empowers them to move forward in a shorter time. I call it "paying off karma with little or no drama."

You will learn in this book how identifying the vibrational energy of another person or situation will help you match that energy and make you better able to deal with it.

The most miraculous healings take place when the pain is taken away from the client. It might be physical, emotional or mental pain. But instantly it goes away. You can endure so much in your life if you do not have pain and suffering, just like you can enjoy your life more if you do not have fear, worry, anger or anxiety.

Healing can take place during the readings themselves, or in the weeks, months, and years that follow. Healing always occurs on one or more levels: physically, emotionally, mentally, or spiritually. The degree of healing is up to you. How much will you accept, and how much will you allow?

When you leave the reading or healing, you may be in a better place to not only help yourself but also to help others.

As I progressed, I learned which people I could tell more to in one sitting, and which people needed several consultations. Some people did not understand the answers I was giving them that could help support change and growth in their lives. Again this is because my client may have built up layers of fear, over many years, so it is normal for it to take some time before we can remove all the levels of pain and heal what is left. During the readings, I learned many things. But I especially learned about active energy vampires that are in the lives of my clients – these are people who want to drain your energy, debate you, and tear you down.

During my readings, I've learned information that changed how I felt about myself and how others viewed me. An example of this is how one farmer/healer saved his sister's life, but it had to be kept secret.

A surgeon came to me with his wife. He was being pressured by her to have a reading. Instead, I just talked to him about my observations, just like a doctor would do after examining me. I told him that he was so successful as a surgeon and as a professor of medicine because he had great intuition. He bristled when I said that. He said, "No! I do not have any intuition." He only believed that what you learn and experience are all that you can ever know. I later learned that the word intuition was a trigger word for him, like a voodoo curse. I rephrased it and said that he was widely respected and admired for his medical abilities because he followed and trusted his gut instincts. This he very much approved of. Then I told him I could see that his great-uncle was a doctor as well. He said, "He was no such thing! He was a farmer." I said I could see him in my visions operating on farm animals. He agreed that this had occurred. I said, "I can see him operating on your great aunt, who had congestion in her lung. He is doing an open lung surgery and sucking this matter out with a tube and then dusting the area with a white powder, cauterizing the area while he stitched her back up."

The surgeon admitted that this story was true. He told me no one outside of his family knew that, and suddenly he wondered where I was getting my information. He said that his uncle had healed his sister from profound tuberculosis and she was fully restored, but they did not tell people because many people thought the uncle was crazy already. The surgeon thought that my reading was very accurate and told me he was ashamed that he judged his uncle through the eyes of other people. While many people experience great spiritual gifts, it can be unwise professionally to proclaim the source of their gifts.

We all have the choice every day to decide if we will be happy or not. Every moment brings us that choice. It does not matter what your job, health conditions, or financial circumstances are; you can be happy being a homeless person dying from cancer if that is what you allow in your life. Each of us must choose what we want and then allow the Universe to provide it for us.

When you try to take control of the direction of your life, there are many memories and situations that will suddenly come back to you. Events that happened years before will instantly be fresh. You might first see images in your dreams or begin to have actual visions or memories that you would have no reason to have otherwise.

You can envision how we do this process of forgiveness and healing. You are filling a beautiful gift box and getting ready to put all your hurts and disappointments into it, along with anything that is still causing you pain today. We present that "box" to God to dispose of for you because you have learned everything you could from each situation. This will allow you to return to a new reality that makes it so much easier for you to reconnect to the God energy.

I have two things that I do when I am doing a reading. First, I see myself as a conduit for the energy to come through me; then I imagine a drain in the floor of the room and all the stuff that comes up from my client goes down the drain and leaves me and the client, never to harm another person. Then after the session, I say "I Let Go of Whatever is Not Mine."

Unpleasantness, pain, and fear can often cause great positive change to occur in our lives. Sometimes these will force people to climb out of the ruts they have lived in. There is a book that I really enjoy called *If You Want to Walk on Water – You Have to Get Out of the Boat* by John Rothberg. It shows how, when you release the fear, anger and worry, you come into your own power.

Another example of this is when you think of your life like a river - always moving, always changing. If you stand on the bank trying to protect yourself or hide in your castle, you miss out on life. If you jump into the river and constantly swim against the current, you get exhausted and miss out on life. If you jump into the water and go with the flow, you will have an amazing adventure. You will learn so much more if you do not fight the lessons in life that you are meant to accomplish. In the Bible, *1st Corinthians 10:4*, St. Paul refers to Jesus as that rock in the river that you come up against but also are polished by just from passing.

Another area that almost immediately comes up in a reading is recognizing what in your life is benefiting you and what is harming you. We look at behaviors and classify what they are and whether they are coming from the God Energy or coming from the opposite of the God energy. During my time with my clients, I write on a piece of paper a list to help them see where they are, in the initial stages of reconnecting with the God energy

I make two columns – one labeled Coming from Good Energy and the other labeled Coming from Bad Energy. You will notice that the Coming from Bad Energy list is much longer than the Coming from Good Energy list. This is based on my experience of asking clients to write down 20 of their most positive aspects, traits or behaviors and 20 of their worst. Few people are able to come up with 20 positive, without asking for help from friends. All of my clients can easily list 20 of their negative aspects, traits and behaviors. So this appears to be how clients view themselves.

## The List

| Coming from Good Energy | Coming from Bad Energy |
|---|---|
| Love yourself | Anger |
| Love others | Worry |
| Faith | Fear |
| Faith in a force greater than you | Unworthiness |
| Trust | Guilt |
| Confidence | Shame |
| Ecstasy | Anxiety |
| Joy | Self-hatred |

| | |
|---|---|
| Sexual union | Depression |
| Peace | Powerlessness |
| Acceptance | Low self-esteem |
| Wellness | Low self-confidence |
| Forgiveness | Poor self-image |
| Mercy | Jealousy |
| Relationship | Rage |
| Intimacy | Dis-ease (illness) |
| Community | Dis-harmony |
| Understanding | Betrayal |
| Compassion | Chaos |
| Empathy | Need |
| Acceptance | Lack/Want |
| Desire | Self-doubt |
| Learning | Shame |
| Wisdom | Abuse |
| | Regret |

All of these emotions are created and allowed by God. We could also use the terms Good & Bad or Positive & Negative. It makes no difference. There is good in the bad energy and bad in the good energy. Everything in the Universe is perfectly balanced. They are to be used as tools to help you with your life lessons and your spiritual growth. But when they are blown out of proportion and used at inappropriate levels they can act as your own personal demons, and veer more into the realm of emotions that belong to the dark side. We must be careful in accepting those emotions that are exaggerated in us because they do not let us love ourselves first and best.

You need to be aware that if you are mentally, emotionally or physically exhausted, items that you may have already resolved in your current life may come back to bother you. When you restore your body to a better condition, you can close up those old chapters, also.

It only takes one spark to reignite communication with Spirit. Like striking a match in a dark room, in the instant you strike the match the entire room is exposed to light. After that, you cannot abide in the darkness any longer. It will simply no longer feel good.

When you let go of self-doubt and allow faith in something greater than yourself in your life you begin to make progress. (Don't be in the how – be in the now.)

I arrived at this conclusion from personal experience. As I released control over what I thought I had some control over in my life, I gained more control over my mind. I kept it busy with prayers, affirmations, rosary beads and I made my direct connection with the Holy Spirit, the source of my intuition. I gained more connection with source energy and more control over my own life, feelings and emotions. Gaining control of my mind let me direct it to ideas that produced growth and abundance for me.

Knowing that these emotions can control you and overtake you is the first step to battling them and releasing the power they have over you. You must first identify the source of the emotion or behavior as coming from Good or Bad Energy. Now, each of us needs to be able to express these emotions, such as fear or anger, but some can be in limited ways and not make up the substance of our whole day or life. If you are perpetually angry, anxious, sad, or worried, you can be assured that this is coming more from Bad/Mind/Ego/Negative Energy than from the Good/God/Positive Energy.

Fear makes people afraid that if they trust another person, one day they will wake up and that other person will find out that they are really a fake or a fraud or a failure. Fear causes people to suffer from more fear. I had this fear when I first started doing public readings, because it is not like I have a degree in being intuitive; I don't have a training certificate hanging on the wall, signed by the Holy Spirit.

In cases where these emotions become too great, I advise clients to put them into a bubble that will shrink them back to more normal levels. If your life is particularly difficult, I suggest that you envision yourself in an egg, instead. You identify the behavior that does not serve you, and make it get out of your life. You say, "Anger or illness, I am pulling all my energy away from you. I am shrinking you to fit in this small bubble." When you take charge of your life and your responsibility for the anger, that will help erase the victim mentality so many people seem to enjoy. Knowing that the Universe recognizes whatever you want, and gives it to you, will allow great change to begin in your life.

Allowing change can be so very hard. Your mind/ego wants to be in control ALL the time. But desiring change and achieving it are two different things. Mind/Ego is afraid of what it cannot understand or control, such as love, prayer, faith, spiritual connection, or unconditional love.

Allowing change in your self is hard; being patient and allowing for it in the people around you is so much harder. It is important to be respectful of the growth process of other people. They will grow or change when and if they are ready and that may not be with you, or in this life.

When you insulate yourself from the drama of the trauma (those things coming from the bad energy), you also build your walls of protection higher and higher. When you do that, the darkness that seeks to make you feel small, weak, and unworthy cannot come in. When darkness can no longer hurt you anymore, it may go after your family and friends. So you expand your circle of unconditional love to include more and more people.

Having faith, hope and trust are three things that the darkness cannot take away from you once you have chosen them.

Many people focus on what they don't have, what they want, need and lack. So the Universe gives you more of what you are missing. More lack of love, lack of understanding, lack of relationship, lack of good health, security and prosperity.

We have to love ourselves, care for ourselves, be honest with ourselves, respect ourselves, and allow ourselves to be healed. We have to do this before we seek a relationship or business or situation we want. Before we try to help or heal others, we must help and heal ourselves first.

Learning how to respect and honor yourself is very hard work. Many clients want change to come into their lives, but with little effort on their part. Many are coming for the reading because they are afraid or have been wounded or destroyed by another person or circumstance. Fear is a powerful motivator to seek and allow change.

When I meet anyone, no matter how they look, I feel their energy. Usually, I can look into their eyes and see the beautiful and amazing person that is inside their bodies. I advise clients to look at themselves in the mirror and make love to their eyes, but for many, that is confusing advice. They see the wrinkles, the hairs that need to be plucked, the bloodshot eyes, and the sadness. They have forgotten who they are and why they came into their body. They have had teachers and religions tell them they are not good enough or smart enough or worthy or slim, or whatever, and they believe it. This is not coming from God.

The next area that we address in a reading is why clients are allowing people and events in their lives to hurt them, and sometimes destroy them. We discuss the idea that we are all co-creators of our own destiny. It is important to remember that each person is at least 50 percent responsible for being in a relationship and situation, so to find fault with the other person is to find fault with yourself. You always have a choice. You can stay or leave. You always have a choice.

Of course, there are usually costs involved with any choices you make. You might be without the lifestyle you enjoyed or the money, or you may have a million other excuses and reasons for staying. Sometimes staying in an uncomfortable or abusive situation is easier than leaving. Sometimes you have not yet resolved the karmic lessons that brought you into that relationship in the first place.

Whatever you choose is the right answer for you. The problem is that people often complain about their relationships, job, family and more, and that complaining needs to end. When you decide to stop paying attention to, and feeding the energy of, people who seek to control you or destroy you, you will feel stronger and live happier.

## Trying to Change Other People

We should never waste our efforts trying to change other people, but we do well to support the changes people want to make for themselves. Often, we impose our ideas for how we think they should be. It is not wise to tell people, "If you love me, you will stop…" smoking, drinking, drugs, sexual addiction, robbing banks," or whatever it is you want them to stop. It never works when the behavior changes you seek are forced on them; they will always resent you for your efforts. It works better if you talk to them about how much you love and care for them, and wish the best for them, but the current behavior is not only harming them, it is also harming you and those around you. It is causing you to pull away from them on one or more levels.

## You Are Not Crazy! – But You Are Special

One of the most important ideas that I'm glad to share with my clients is when I tell them that they are not crazy and they are not alone. They have never been alone. They are in a group of people that I referred to as being in the "5 percent." These are emotionally intuitive, empathic, sensitive people, who, throughout their whole lives, have been treated differently and felt differently than the people around them. They have been comparing themselves to the "95 percent."

I tell them they are not crazy, even though they may have been previously diagnosed with ADD/ADHD, manic depression, bipolar disorder, or any number of other personality disorders. I explain to them that they are a part of something much greater than themselves. They may not be understood by others who are not like them. I joke that there is a fine line between being psychic and being labeled psychotic. The whole thing is something much greater than anyone could ever conceive of. I don't need to teach anyone anything; I just remind them of what they already know. It is amazing to me how this all works. It is important because their whole lives, they have felt like outsiders, never thinking they were seeing or hearing as they should, as the majority of the population does. Yet, these special individuals are so lucky to be wise souls.

## Change Can Be Easy or Hard - You Decide

Usually the biggest impediment to change and growth in your life is **YOU!** Your mind/ego is a collection of all thoughts, feelings, and emotions you have had up to this point in your life; the pain and disappointments have led you to the place where you are today. You are in a box of your own creation. Often, you are your own policeman, prosecutor, judge, jury, and jailer. You are usually guilty according to that group of people within your mind/ego. No one knows your life situations better than you. No one can judge you and hurt you better than you.

Life is what you decide to make it.

Your ego wants to protect you. It is in control of your mind and is a huge block to any change that you wish to make. Allowing mind/ego to control your whole life also diminishes or delays your connection to spirit/soul. Too much control robs you from feeling the nuances of life.

It is very difficult to release the thoughts and beliefs we have attracted and accumulated throughout our life. Usually growth happens only after experiencing moments of great pain and distress. It is important that you seek to go back and examine your life to determine why you are the person you are today. Then forgive yourself and others. Know that when you turn it over to God, it will be resolved.

But can people really change? What does it take to allow that to happen? Does the pain have to be so bad before they release the past and embrace the future? One friend of mine, Stacey Louise, said that, "My changes have been fueled mostly by loss, long suffering, etc....

my soul's agony and sorrow. The extent of the suffering has been the utmost blessing…because it is what inspired me to allow my core essence to rise to the surface…and bring to the surface truth, true compassion, unconditional love, and sincerity, and the changes make this trueness grow even more."

Sadly, mere desire for change will not make anything happen. It must be a determined effort that you approve of at an ego level. Receiving outside support is also a huge plus. Usually, we are able to spell out what someone's higher purpose is. When they realize they were put here as instruments of God for service to their fellow man, it brings great relief to everyone.

We are all sent here for service and learning, if we allow it. I share what has worked so well for me over the years: to *radiate love without concern for results*. You could also radiate healing or joy. "I come to serve, not be served," said Jesus. So the more you give of yourself to others, the more you can expect to receive.

Be in the place that God wants you to be, to act as His healer in that moment for the person you are with. Do your best work every time, then turn that person over to the Universe, the Energy of the Creator God, and let it go. Have faith and trust that you did exactly what you could to heal and support the growth of that person.

The next part of the reading is when I thank the client for whatever spiritual work that they are doing and tell them that they *"were not selected to be the Chairman of the Universe!"* It usually comes as a big relief. Then I tell them, *"You were not selected as the Savior either. We already have a Savior."* But they can work for the Savior. Many people's egos are so self-involved they cannot see beyond what is directly in front of their faces. Many people want to cure and heal other people, especially in cases where they themselves are in a situation or relation-ship. But, they must first heal themselves and make themselves whole, part of the delivery chain of the God energy.

A person who is newly receiving healing energy may wish to heal friends and family and loved ones. This is normal but at first the healing energy is coming mostly from their own bodies, not from spirit. That energy cannot be sustained for long, because it exhausts the new healer. I think all healers have limited success in healing family and loved ones; that has been my experience also. I have mentioned this before and it is very important to reiterate it here; I tell my clients that to be fully successful, they must:

## PRAY, MEDITATE, AND SHUT UP AND LISTEN!

I have some prayers I offer my clients. I like them to start with formal prayers to cover all the basics dealing with their past. I also use two prayers that I wrote called the *Miracle Prayer* and *Family Healing Prayer* to support their healing. These prayers offer spiritual protection and facilitate family healing *(see Appendix)*.

Meditation can be however you like it. I offer the 20-minute free download from Winter Robinson called *Talley's Lullaby*. This guided imagery journey takes no physical effort except to push the play button and lay down on your bed to listen to it. This can be found at http://vimeo.com/37491591 and at http://www.winterrobinson.com/medical.html.

I also recommend the Meditation Regression Series offered by Dr. Brian L. Weiss, the best-selling author of *Many Lives, Many Masters*. There are books and CD's with hypnosis on them that are very effective in educating newbies to reincarnation and past life hypnosis. (See Appendix)

I bless people with Holy Oil (a preparation of Frankincense and Myrrh) and Holy Water (water that has been prayed over for a period of time) preparing them for their own reconnection to God. I offer them prayers for spiritual protection and offer a prayer that deals with "*Sins of the Fathers*" because it offers generational healing. I also have a prayer that allows "forgiveness healing." All are non-specific to any religion; they are just what I say when I talk to God.

No matter what walk of life, religious, or cultural background people come from, when I discuss this reconnection with the God energy they all know in their hearts what I am talking about. It is amazing. They all describe knowing for years what they were put on Earth for. When souls and kindred spirits come to them, they know they will finally get on to what they came here for.

The next words that I write down are: *What is Your Mission?*

This could also be written "What is your passion? "Or "What is your life purpose?" What are you passionate about in life? What makes you happy when you are doing it? What makes you feel good? What really turns you on? At this point, we must differentiate between obligations and mission. Obligations are your relationships with loved ones, your partner, spouse, and children. This also includes your work. It is all something you are obligated to do. Your mission is something you are called to do and it pleases you.

A mission is usually something to do with greatly moving forward in your personal/spiritual growth, and is about attracting like-minded people to be around while doing your work. It usually involves helping people or situations where you will get little or no monetary, emotional or physical reward. It is simply doing the right thing for people who are unable, unwilling, or unknowing because they are not at your same spiritual level. Your mission challenges you, engages you and makes you feel good, deep inside yourself.

Teaching people they can do something about their lives simply by releasing anger, fear, worry and resentment, forgiving others as they forgive themselves, is the key to emotional freedom. As a friend or teacher you can only support those people who are willing to release what is blocking them. You cannot do it for them. When you learn this, you release the need to control the circumstances of the healing. Otherwise, you are just wasting your time. *(Radiate Healing Without Concern for Results)*

When you can imagine what your mission is, then you are one step closer to making it happen. We all have specific agreements, contracts, missions and goals we've already agreed to work on in our current lives.

It is exciting and interesting once we remember what our mission is. We rediscover the opportunities of our mission, the opportunities the mission will bring, and it opens up a whole new world.

The most wonderful part of life is when your job or work actually intersects with your mission. This allows you to be functioning at a very high level most of the time. I advocate that you "Make Your Passion Your Profession."

When you are on your mission, it will lead you to your own self-actualization. Your mission will bring you joy and happiness. Serving others, in whatever form or capacity, is loving yourself, serving yourself, and serving God. You will likely team up with many like-minded people over the years as you raise your frequency. You will attract those whose frequency is as high as, or higher than, your own. It is a process of continual growth. Do not be afraid to grow forward in this new higher energy. No one else has your same exact mission, obligations, or responsibilities.

My whole life has been spent building a bridge between my spiritual gifts and the real world of family, business, and the IRS. One of the aspects of my mission is to be a bridge builder between people and ideas. I also work to plant seeds of hope, love, faith, compassion and universal connection.

Sometimes, Spirit will share some aspects of the mission of my client. Clients are always surprised when they hear from me exactly what they already know about their reason for being here in life. Sometimes, I am able to define my clients' spiritual gifts, such as physical touch healing, emotional healing, and other aspects of healing. Missions usually involve helping more people than yourself, your friends, or your family. They involve people who you don't owe anything to and people who may be very different from you.

Sadly, many clients when asked this question have no idea what I am talking about. They have conditioned themselves to hide in their castles for so long that they don't even remember what makes them happy. They just try to get though each day. It takes longer to get them to the point where they can begin to even wonder what their mission is. It is a question that smolders in their mind and will always result in an answer. When they first start to live in the moment and feel everything that is going on in real time, this is a start.

The next big topic that most clients want to discuss is – relationships. We will discuss this later in the book. It is important to realize right now that your new direct connection to God will not only give you direct revelation, but you will also be able to freely draw unlimited amounts of energy from it.

Continue to *Pray, Meditate, and Shut Up and Listen!*

When you have reconnected with source energy, with God, you are able to more clearly receive the true messages of God. You do not need to rely on a minister, a priest, a pope, or a book.

The first step is to acknowledge the God energy. Then, we can submit to that energy and after vetting it out, surrender to it - not simply because it is a higher energy than yours (even Satan has a higher energy than yours), but because you feel the goodness of the Light of God and are attracted to it. This is where your discernment comes in. At this point many people seek to supplicate to the energy. This means asking, begging, and praying for specific things to come from God. When we have submitted to the reality that God exists, however you so define God, then you are ready to enter supplication with God.

Next comes recognizing God as a powerful, creative energy. God is like a friend you would enjoy walking and talking with on your path of life. This is merely walking down the same path with the Light within you, the Light of God.

When you do not pray for stuff, you get more gifts of the Spirit. When you pray with faith, this confidence allows you to experience whatever happens as the lesson for growth that it is. Bad can always be found in good and good can always be found in bad. When we examine the intentions and motivations of people, we see the real truth behind their actions.

To truly find God, we must come to God as God comes to us. We must recognize that part of God that is within us. When we treat ourselves like God and treat others like God, then the world will be healed.

As you walk through life on your path, many people will cross your path and many more are ready to walk along with you on the path. Not in front of you or behind you, but walking along with you. Then there are also those who are racing down your path, using you, wasting your energy, and ready to knock you off into the mud.

## Just Start

In counseling, Mary, the Mother of Jesus, often appears over the left shoulder of the person I'm speaking to and advises me to counsel them to *"Just Start"* and *"Just Do It."* What is important is to simply begin whatever it is you need to start in your life, or to finish whatever it is you need to finish and then you can start once again. It is after you have started with trust and faith that the resources of the Universe will come to you. Christ taught us that it is important not just to feed people, but to teach them how to fish.

When you are *Going with the Flow,* you will be amazed at how much spiritual, mental, emotional, and physical growth happens in a short period of time. Many people have said that being engaged with the flow allows them to accomplish in a matter of months what would have normally taken them years.

Some people question this advice. They ask me how they are supposed to" *Just be and allow joy into their lives."* They ask how they are to *"Just Be"* and *"Just Start"* and *"Just Do It"* …all at the same time. There is no contradiction here. These all involve action. *"Just Being"* is hard at first, because we are used to toiling away on projects. We are always "working on ourselves." The only work you need to do is to daydream your life into what you will allow it to be. Make your order at the deli - choose what you want. Pay for your order and then have faith that it will be delivered. Then you just wait. There is nothing more to do. Make the order. Then go sit down at a table and wait for delivery.

When you decide to *"Just Be"* you are quietly filled with confidence and faith and hope, and you are ready for the creations that you desire to manifest in your life. Manifesting means to make real. You allow things to be created. If they are not, you would do well to have a reading with someone like me who can read you down to the deepest level. "Allowing" is just as hard as "Just Being"- at least it was for me - because when you have full faith and confidence you begin to see endless possibilities; you allow the dream to be presented to you. Or maybe your order will be modified. It may be greater than anything you could have ever dreamed of.

Sadly, most people never put in the order for their future; they are like a cork in the ocean, always being pushed about by the waves around them, never knowing if they will be in water or on the beach. Never knowing, never choosing can kill you.

When you seek reconnection with the Universal Love Energy of God and *go with the flow*, you are able to get free uplifting, powerful, loving energy into your crown chakra first, which is located at the top of the head. Then you are able to be very focused and intellectual, plan things and be organized, but you cannot hold that energy in your head or you would have a stroke. Then you move the energy to your throat chakra, opening that area so you can say what you need to say. Then, you allow the energy to move down to your heart chakra and experience compassion, understanding, wisdom and sensuality. You truly feel like you are part of the whole system of life on Earth. However, if this energy is held in the heart, a heart attack could result. So the energy moves down to the 1st and 2nd chakra levels which provide for your security - home, clothing, heat/cold, food, and your reproductive and sexual function. You get everything you need there and then you can move this energy to the place where you usually store what you need, your intestines. As this energy flows through you, you are once again completely satiated and find this energy is still as strong as ever. It is overwhelmingly positive.

Next, the energy passes up to the solar plexus chakra, which is a place about the size of an orange just below your breast bone. It is from this place that you can give away all the energy, love, healing, and compassion you are receiving. The supply never stops and it never diminishes, but it can grow to huge levels. The benefit you receive from this is that you will have increased health, happiness and joy in your life.

Now it is easier to understand the phrase, *Going with the Flow*. This is where people usually get gut feelings. This is early intuition. It is that feeling you get when you just know someone or something is not good for you. Sometimes you follow it and sometimes you do not, but there is great risk to yourself if you do not.

It can be overwhelming to see for the first time that we are all connected to each other. From good to bad, and from brilliant to barely functional, we are all one – from the same Creator God energy. When you see how you fit with the rest of the world through your actions and your mission, the world becomes smaller and smaller, and you see how we each are part of a whole. We don't get any credit, wealth or satisfaction if we do our mission for prestige, ego, sex, or money, but if we selflessly share all God has gifted us, then we will abundantly receive more than we can imagine. We will learn that helping others is helping ourselves.

Often when we try to help others, we do so with a willing heart motivated by love and compassion. This can turn into a damaging, co-dependent type of relationship that attracts people who are energy vampires if you do not remember to *love yourself first*. For every positive action you take, an equally negative action can occur. Light is attracted to dark and dark is attracted to light.

## Sleep Problems

When clients are first being reconnected and begin to reawaken to the God Connection, many experience being disturbed by dark energies in the early morning, often about 3 a.m. This can include, but is not limited to, the feelings that someone is watching you, feeling pressure on your chest or that someone is trying to sit on your chest, someone is trying to choke you, someone is trying to violate you, sleep paralysis or someone is trying to suck all the air from your lungs. These feelings are real and usually occur in what is called "The Devils Hour." (3 to 4 a.m.)

You can stop the sleep paralysis and other attacks by willing them to go away in your mind. You can also think about good, love, God, Jesus, the cross, or other religious symbols that you identify with. This is darkness trying to scare you away from the connection. Beginning psychic awareness is all garbage, scary negative stuff combined with the fear of death. Reject it. Fear takes over. Identify the fear and determine what you can do about the fear. Don't let the images terrify you. Know yourself and resolve those thoughts, beliefs or habits in you that seek to harm you. Go where angels fear to tread and turn all this negative stuff over to God, so He can handle it for you.

## Energy Centers

Energy centers are called Chakras in Sanskrit. A study of all the points on your body that send and receive energy can be quite exhausting. So I will try to describe them simply. See the Appendix for more suggested reading.

I can see energy moving, just as if I were watching a river where water is flowing. I can see places where the water may be caught or rerouted due to obstructions. The human body works the same way, when energy gets "stuck"; it attracts fatigue, exhaustion and then illness.

The **first chakra** is at the base of the spine. This center is about survival-housing, clothing, and food.

The **second chakra** is below your belly button. This is the center for sex, procreation, work and community.

The **third chakra** is behind your solar plexus (gut feelings). This center is about your ego and personality.

The **fourth chakra** is next to your heart in the center of your chest. This center contains love, compassion, and community,

The **fifth chakra** is behind your throat. It allows you to speak and say what needs to be said.

The **sixth chakra** is in the center of your forehead (also called your third eye); this center enables you think clearly, to be wise, insightful and to send and receive intuition.

The **seventh chakra** is at the top of your head and allows you to receive all the energy of the Universe.

Disease is usually associated with the organs closest to the chakra. For example, imbalance of energy in the second chakra can in a man lead to urinary problems, prostate cancer, and lower back problems. In a woman, infertility, vaginal disorders, cervical cancer etc. can result. See the Appendix for these excellent books – *Anatomy of the Spirit* by Caroline Myss, and *Feelings Buried Alive Never Die* by Karol K. Truman. They explain how emotions can attract illness and how chakras interact.

## Body Scan

Next, I do a body scan.

I have learned that most people have some intuition and use it to determine if they can trust another person. In my work, the nature of which can be very intrusive and intuitive, most of my clients will be scanning me to determine if I have some other intention than to do the reading and healing. I have known healers who exploited clients for money, sex and power. So I try to be pure of heart and have a positive intention. It is so very important for the client to be able to trust me and count on me delivering my best work every time. (*Radiate healing without concern for results*)

I place the palm of my hand over my clients' third eye (mid-forehead) and I allow our energies to connect and synchronize. I start at the top of the head and, using one or both hands, simply scan their body. The chakra in my palm is like a human MRI. My hand will tremble when I get to places where they have physical illness, or physical, emotional, energy imbalances and mental trauma from this life or even past lives. I may see things inside their body or know of past, present or future illnesses.

After I scan at this level, I find areas containing anger, illness, worry, fear, or a broken heart. Then, I stop scanning and direct energy through my hands into those areas that need to be cleaned up and re-energized. I imagine that I have a huge vacuum that is collecting all the negative energy.

Next, I scan again to see that the energy is now flowing. Sometimes I will sense other spirits in the body of the person. These could be positive spirits that may have entered to help the person through a specific trauma in their lives, or they could be negative energies. Sometimes there are demons, but not often. Full demonic energy in a person is rare. Usually, the dark side will use the energies you already have, such as anger, fear, and worry, and increase them to levels that are dangerous to you. The goal of the dark energies is to make you unhappy, sad, unbalanced, chaotic, worried, and fearful. Anything you would describe as bad is good for them and their team.

I have been shown that all illness – physical, mental and emotional, is the result of generational karma (sins of the fathers), situational karma (being part of a nation that commits atrocities, for example), karmic repayment, environment, DNA, or is caused by personal demons such as anger, worry, and fear. Some illnesses have elements of all of these. What you think and allow in your life can make you sick or allow existing seeds of illness to grow.

After completing the body scan and I share my findings, it is time to discuss the Disconnecting Cords Procedure with the client. This is where we identify people, emotions, and past situations that may still be linked to the client. Many times we find that people still dream, fantasize, or think about people and situations that occurred many years before. Often clients have gotten divorced and moved, sometimes halfway across the world, and will still have these etheric cord connections to people who have used and abused them in the past. We do the cord disconnection in an attempt to settle past karmic or active situational karmic relationships the client may have with other people and circumstances in their lives. I discuss this method in many places in this book; I am also including it in the Appendix at the end of the book.

## Disconnecting Cords Procedure

One of the greatest gifts and blessings you can do for yourself and for another person is to disconnect spiritual, emotion, mental, physical and ethereal cords with them. This allows you to see them as they really are in the present life. It resolves old karmic connections and debt, and has been known to change people's lives and relationships for the better. Disconnecting means forgiving them, praying for them and turning them over to God with love. You can also disconnect with your old self, your old emotions (self-defeating habits, anger, worry, fear, depression and anxiety) and people who have used or abused you.

Over the next three days you will see the person you are blessing in the Disconnection with new vision that will allow you to see who they truly are in this life. You will release old feelings, allowing for a fresh start in the relationship, if you choose.

Begin by asking God to bless and protect all involved in this process.

Then say: "Please come here in Spirit, _____" and read your list of names. You can call them out in spirit since spirit is not attached to their body.

The person or persons you are blessing will gather in spirit on your right side. On your left side is the Golden Doorway to Heaven.

Then say: "I'm doing this with the Love and Light of God.

As I set you free, you must set me free.

No two spirits should hold each other as we have.

Now it's time to let go.

I undo all that I have created in you.

I owe you nothing and you owe me nothing. All is forgiven."

Then tell the person you love them and bless them, and anything else you want to tell them.

Then say: "I dissolve all cords, contracts, commitments, agreements, vows, spells, curses and all other karmic connections with love. All connections between me and _____ (read your list) are null and void.

Remove any resistance and help us to let go.

You are no longer allowed in my energy on any level of my being unless you come with the Love and Light of God."

"Anything you do in any way to harm me or those around me will reflect back to you, and you and that which stands behind you will absorb all karma.

Whether it be by your actions or the actions of others created by you, you and that which stands behind you will absorb all karma."

Then say: "I let you go, and now undo all that I have created in you. I set you free."

Then say: "God - I give you _____ (read the list) — He/She/They are no longer my responsibility.

Take them where they need to go, to heal and grow.

I will not hold you anymore.

I set you free.

Go into the Light!"

When you feel this has happened, say: "Amen" or "So Be It" three times.

Then envision a giant bubble around you that protects you from any reconnection. Stay in the bubble for seven days. Do not discuss past or emotional issues with the person you are dissolving from. This will let you decide if you want them in your future.

The cord cutting gives you an opportunity to speak to the person safely and truthfully, without fear, while they are in Spirit form. You can say what you need to say, release what you need to release, express your love for them, and then turn them over to God. It is important to forgive the other person for whatever they have done against you. I used to tell people that they needed to forgive, not necessarily forget. However, that was short-sighted advice because while the forgiving part usually comes along, it creates another cord. We want to get rid of *all* those cords. This is important because once you release, it is not something that will come up in your memory and is simply part of your past.

The result is what I call baggage, such as old pains and abuse that you continue to carry around into every new situation in your life. When I talk about disconnecting from those old events and leaving all your baggage for God to store and deal with, you would be amazed how quickly you forget and grow.

When a client comes to me seeking advice and counsel, and sometimes healing and prophecy, it can be amazing. I see the Light of God in each of us. But how do you make the desired change actually happen? Sometimes all I can do is plant seeds of hope, ideas, wisdom and knowledge and advise them to dream of the future they desire so that it can become their reality. It is easy for me to tell them about the wonderful things that can happen when they *"Let go and let God work in their lives."* But, as a practical matter, mind/ego and self-defeating attitudes all seek to keep you in bondage to your past.

We all have the power to change the future based on the feelings, thoughts and emotions we are putting out right now.

How and when you will be able to leap forward to the future you desire is scary, but it can happen instantly and be supported by the Spiritual Universe. We all need to pack our bags with the old lessons, the old hurts, defeats, feelings, and experiences and turn them over to God. We already learned what we needed from those times. Now, they are a hindrance to our future. Old, self-defeating, and negative ideas will only hold you back and cancel out your future desires. This also applies to what you say. When you learn to listen to the negative things that come out of your mind and mouth, you will be shocked at how negative they may be. When you think or say things that are self-limiting or negative just say "I cancel that".

The strange part is that fear, tragic circumstances, and loss can often trigger the desire for change. We actually do change from some primal desire to be one again with some power or energy greater than ourselves. We all experience the desire for reconnection.

Change can also come because society, culture and religion dictate that change, or karmic circumstances can bring you to a crossroads, or perhaps God presents you with an opportunity to be lifted to the next, higher level. Free will, though, is always present and will guide the circumstances of the change. When we are able to surrender, submit, and walk along with the new change and behaviors, then we are finally able to grow.

Many people have asked their ministers, rabbis and priests questions like:

"Why do bad things happen to good people?"

"Why did my friend, or lover, or family member have to die so young and so tragically?"

"Does God hear my prayers?"

"If God loves me so much, how could He let this happen to me?"

They are usually being told that "It is just the will of God" or "It is God's plan." This makes people angry that such limited, control-based thinking is applied to their lives.

My work allows them to see the big picture and to determine the reasons things happen, and why. My work brings healing, peace, compassion and understanding to them. It allows them to go on with the rest of their life.

The reading and healing is only the beginning. It is merely a presentation of the future as it might be, not what it will be. With this knowledge, you can make changes in your life. You will make your future. You are always in charge. It is important to know you are always in control. In fact, looking at the life you have already lived, you can see the positive and negative aspects that being in control brought you. There is always good and always bad. Imprudent decisions can be painful, but they are also learning tools for your growth.

Importantly, decide to "chill" for even a moment and allow the future to unfold as fully as it wants to. It is best to never make projections limiting the future. That is trying to define God, and you simply have no comprehension of the great things waiting to come into your life. So, when you can just be still in the moment, you allow for spiritual reconnection and that *always* brings great rewards.

My goal is simply to accept each client as they are and offer unconditional love, just like God does for each of us. Knowing everything that I know, see, and feel, I am able to empathize and walk a mile in their shoes. I feel nothing but love for them and their circumstances, and knowing their heart helps me to become them for a brief moment. This forever changes my life as well.

No matter what your secret was when we started the reading, releasing fear is very important. When you know you are still loved unconditionally by me and God, it is a breakthrough. Then you can go and love, and attract more love. The healing happens in the doing.

When you understand, you will be understood. When you love, you will be loved. When you cry with another person, they will cry with you and healing will result for all. When you comfort another person, you will be comforted too. The hardest transition that most people have to make is to go from merely contemplating change to actually implementing it. What I do is guide them on the path to their future and offer support. Support is important because our efforts often fail if we think no one cares.

When the reading is over, often it is all a person needs to move to a new and higher spiritual level in their life. It might take more than one reading to help support the changes that my clients wish to make. Often their lives are so complex that one reading may only resolve part of their issues. Some people need support, and that is called life coaching. I can continue to monitor their progress directly in their life situations for a period of time. I am firm in trying to understand them and guide them forward. Change is hard. Major change can be terrifying for some people, but the results are always gratifying. At the end of the reading, I ask them if they have any more questions, and I answer them as best I can. Then I ask if I can hug them. This connects our heart chakras so I can continue to channel support to them while they are in the process of allowing their own direct connection with the God energy.

When I first started doing readings, my mind/ego kept sending me the message: "Who the Hell do you think you are to be giving people what you give them?"

This is normal for mind/ego to question or attack what it cannot control. Then I was shown in a vision that I was actually more like the Wizard of Oz. I don't give anyone anything they don't already have; I just recognize their gifts and support them in their growth.

# CHAPTER 7

## *Finding God, Reincarnation and Karma*

Before we are born, we are in consultation with the Creator God energy. We plan every single event, every circumstance, every relationship, every lesson we need to learn in our upcoming life.

**The Idea of God**

Early in a reading, I ask my client what they think about God and if they have a religious upbringing. This can help me to define what I tell them, or how to put information into words that they can better understand. This is because we cannot undo learnings from the past until we know what they were. Usually the client picks up their perception of God from the teachings of their parents.

Some clients are more advanced and say that they believe in a God Energy, but not in religion. Many clients have said that they think that God is God. Other clients have used the following words to describe "their" God - Jesus, Jehovah, Quan Yin, Gautama the Buddha, Lord Ganesh, The Divine Father, The Divine Mother, Father God, Lord Krishna, Taos Worthy Lao-Tzu or to the God of Abraham, Moses and Mohammed. Native Americans simply call God "the Great Spirit." Some think God is love or found in nature. I accept whatever they say and acknowledge it. I offer them my unconditional love and acceptance.

My idea of God is the Creator Energy of the Universe. The God Energy is like a council of energies, the Great He/She/They/It. It's beyond comprehension or definition, and beyond whatever our wildest imaginings are. I believe God is not only in every living thing, but also in each of us. We each hold a spark of God. For some people, God is Jesus. You get to decide what God is for you, and then let's all move on. You only need to accept that this energy of God is a higher vibrational energy than what you operate at in order for healing to occur.

When discussing religion, we usually find the more intuitively inclined have started to reawaken to God and have gone the religion route, only to find it empty and unfulfilling. Everyone I talk to has a yearning for reconnection with something greater than themselves. Maybe you call it God. This one day must be addressed in each of us, just as a woman is genetically programmed to have babies, or a man to have offspring, the desire to connect with God is in you already. You must recognize it and deal with it, make peace with it. Pursue it, or not. We could have a great discussion about religion and spirituality, but why bother? I am here to deliver the messages I have received so that you can move forward more quickly and easily in your spiritual growth. You choose your own path.

I do offer this warning to those who are consumed with allegiance to organized religion: If your religion advocates limiting who is or can become a member – then you need to ask - is that what Jesus would have done? Or if your religion claims that only certain people are saved or loved by God, then that is bad. If it actively advocates hate and division among other people, then it is a source of evil itself.

Did Jesus ever take hope away from another person? Did he curse or condemn anyone? If not, then who are you or your religion to close the Gates of Heaven to some of your brothers and sisters? Jesus is all about love, mercy, grace and acceptance – perhaps your God is like that also.

My mission is to teach others that when you recognize God in others then you will also find Him in yourself.

Each person I speak with has parts of them that are like God. Many attributes are described as being with God. At some point everyone comes to the realization that no matter how much they have in terms of education, social status, wealth, or possessions, there is a certain emptiness associated with it all. When people know there is more to life than what they are living, then their quest for the truth truly begins.

Sometimes the quest causes them to go to church or temple, or seek out someone like me. Some crisis has happened in their life that has awakened them to the fact that everything they have learned, been taught or accepted from their church, society, or education is missing one key element — the energy of the Universe, the energy of God.

Baba Meher from India had this message for me about that one key element: *"Many people that you serve are in their spiritual infancy, yet they are spirit beings in human form, not the other way around. Many have gone to temple, church, priests, and religious leaders seeking God and have found nothing but pews and prayer mats. They sought spiritual connection and were offered candles and incense. You will free those in organized religion to know God from their own souls."*

In describing my mission, he said,

*"The time for teaching and learning is over. The teachers have diluted and corrupted the messages and now all you have time to do is to awaken people to who they really are — to tell them that it is time to just love God! You must collect souls who are ready for this. Wash and kiss their feet. You are not special; you are an instrument of God."*

He continued, *"Of all the world's religions, Muslim, Catholic, Jewish, Buddhist, the message of God has been diluted down to 10 percent of what is true."*

The fact that we were already with God and are now here inhabiting bodies can be a bittersweet memory. You left the warm glow of eternal, unconditional love and you thought it was a good idea at the time. You and God planned your life, but now it does not seem like such a good idea as the cares of the world fall upon you every day.

During the reading, we will briefly discuss the ideas of religious works and how incongruous it all seems that the Creator God would banish anyone or condemn them to eternal suffering. It is bizarre and obscene to even discuss it.

One of my clients was an elderly Jewish man who had been held prisoner at Auschwitz. He was preparing for his eventual death. He was terrified of dying, because he was not a practicing Jew and allowed some ideas from Christianity to infiltrate his mind. He said, "I am going to Hell, because I do not know Jesus Christ as God." Spirit told him through me, "You have already lived in Hell; Jesus Christ was another Jew who also lived part of His life in Hell. You enjoy the company of others. Allow yourself to picture, after your death, you and Jesus walking down a path together. That path will lead you to Heaven - not what church or synagogue you did or didn't attend."

The message that I have consistently received from Spirit is that God loves us all, all of the time – unconditionally - and accepts us just as we are right where we are at that stage in life. It does not matter what we do or what we don't do. It is all about abundant and eternal unforgettable love and acceptance. God is always guiding us to higher energy and self-love. God is always there trying to provide answers when you ask questions and are ready to listen.

In my work, I meet people where they are in life - honoring where they come from. I seek to recognize and support the interests and gifts each person presents. The goal is always reconnection with the positive spiritual energy that is greater than them. This is the God energy.

Sometimes we will talk about déjà vu because many people have it in varying degrees and frequency. Déjà vu is simply remembering at the appropriate moments in your life that you have already witnessed the life you're living. You have already planned everything happening in your life, as if your whole life was a movie on a theater screen. The less frequent your déjà vu and dreams, the more you have likely strayed from the creation of your life you planned with God. We have free will to do whatever we want when we come to Earth, and often wander off in directions that are painful to us. When you receive chills or goosebumps or the hair on the back of your neck stands up, these are also signs to verify that you are receiving the God energy.

## Reincarnation

When I am speaking about a person having more than one life, it can be confusing to someone who does not understand or agree with this concept. This leads to a discussion about reincarnation and karma. There's never been a person I have been reading for who does not have at least some basic understanding of reincarnation. But the reincarnation concept that I described is not in the terms readily understood by a Hindu or Buddhist. Reincarnation is simply your soul deciding to come back into various bodies, male or female, to experience life, compassion, understanding, conflict, and every aspect of human interaction. That is why we speak of the common sense approach offered to me by the Holy Spirit, which is reincarnation. Some readers will protest, but I ask them to read the Bible, especially everywhere there is the word "resurrection". Substitute the word "reincarnation" and it all makes more sense. The Bible has actual instances of reincarnation. Although it has been heavily edited, some still remain. (See Appendix) Also, you can see where karma is spoken of throughout the Bible. The Bible speaks often about "everlasting life" and that is what I am explaining also.

The message I received from Spirit over the years is actually that there is no reincarnation - just many incarnations. We are all born once and all die once. We already have eternal life, but our spirit is not tied to one body. You have one soul, one spirit, and many bodies and many lives.

We simply cannot learn everything there is to know about the lives, feelings, and emotions of other people and their circumstances in one single life. We need the actual experience of being born without legs, or being born blind, or losing a child, or losing our own life. This serves to create patterns of understanding much like a giant spider web connecting us to every other person on Earth. We will build empathy, compassion, caring, tolerance, acceptance, and the ability to recognize that every living soul is connected to our soul. We will begin to recognize that our soul is connected to God, and so is the soul of everyone else.

I give my clients this visual of how incarnation/reincarnation works: First, I have them envision a huge diamond with 1000 rough facets. I ask them to see that, in order to completely polish the diamond, every facet of the diamond must be polished. This is done by experiencing and learning lessons we come to Earth to learn. In every life, some of those facets of the diamond will be polished and finished through the karmic lessons chosen in that life. In a normal life, a person may choose four to six of these lessons, but many people choose more, many more. Lessons will involve physical, mental, emotional, and spiritual lessons.

## Karma

The next big topic is the word karma. This is a Hindu/Buddhist term that says whatever you do in this or prior lives, good or bad, will come back to you. The Bible talks about karma when it talks about the concept of what goes around, comes around (an eye for an eye, a tooth for a tooth).

The Universe is not random and in chaos; it is perfectly balanced and orderly. Karma results when we have had lives in the past and used our free will to make choices that either harmed us, like killing another person, or helped us, like helping others. Karma can be an award of knowledge and gifts you received in past lives, such is the case with child prodigies or people who are viewed as saintly, or it can be found at the opposite end.

*"Do not be deceived.*
*God is not mocked, for whatever one sows that*
*will he also reap." - Galatians 6:7*

In every life, you are surrounded by hundreds or thousands of people that you have positive past life connections with. You are an actor in their play and they are an actor in your play. This mutual support is important and provides you with a base to learn and grow from.

God also always arranges for you to be reunited over and over with people and situations you left under negative circumstances in past lives. I call these "negative past life connections." The reconnection is often glorious and wonderful and magical for the first four to six months, and then old issues will come up, and the pain of a new negative karmic connection will be felt. Other people can also be in your life to support and care for you. Karma presents both positive and negative.

Examples of positive karma are helping others, donating money, making change in the world and planting seeds that will allow people to bloom in their lives. This is like that old quote that says that "A society grows great when old men plant trees whose shade they know they will never sit in."

If people do not resolve karma from past lives, and proceed to accumulate new karma that is negative as well, it simply is played forward to be dealt with at another time. The structure of all of our lives is so carefully woven that it will always allow for us to meet people we have hurt or benefited from in the past. The best goal of every relationship is to be at peace with one another.

Circumstances in life can lead people to start asking questions such as why they are here and what life is for. The death of a loved one or serious illness of someone close to them usually will trigger them to seek my prayers for health or healing. They may want to contact someone who has died. Religion works for some, but most of my clients have gone this route and found that what organized religion offered was lacking in some way.

When a person is ready to be reconnected to the truth of who they are and why they are in their bodies in this life, they begin to recognize and honor the yearning for more, for something greater than what they have. This yearning to bask in the presence, or in the glow, of the God energy is enough for them to seek that connection. In later stages they will likely seek the spiritual glow of other people also.

Your mind/ego is only at rest when you meditate or sleep; otherwise it must be directed to some goal to keep it busy, and even subdued if only for a few moments - enough time for that spiritual reconnection to happen. I describe this as the *Soulgasm (Spiritual Ecstasy)*. This is when your body, mind, and spirit reconnect with your soul. Your soul is always connected to God.

This is where true spirituality triumphs over religious practice. Because soul reconnection/connection is so powerful, so satisfying, and so mind blowing that even if a person is exposed to it only for a few moments in their life, it is an experience they will never forget.

When we discover we are more than our body and mind, we discover we are connected to this collective consciousness (of every other living thing on the planet) as every single person is. Then we see we are connected to the people we know, to people who we do not know, and to all of the people who think and see and hear as we do and all those who do not. We are connected to every person who ever was or ever will be through our blood and DNA. It is like looking at a gigantic spider web - and it is amazing to see how we are all connected. We can call this giant web the collective consciousness which really totals up to the energy that powers every living soul on Earth. It is like a giant pot full of all of the energy of the Universe. Then we might begin to understand our connection to God, individually or collectively.

## Prayer Power

The collective consciousness reflects the lowest and highest energies of the population of the world. We learn that every single thought, word or action causes a ripple to be sent out into the air that affects other people. This energy also affects all the plant and animal life, the climate, and the Earth itself. Each of us is like a power generating station. We are always producing either positive or negative energy, and are rewarded with the same energy back from the Universe. The idea that one person praying can raise the vibration of thousands of people is not new, merely unacknowledged on a wider basis.

Just as the energy of the body is very dense and heavy, the energy of the person who reflects spirituality and mental facility contains a higher vibration. This is why someone who is operating at a much higher frequency can raise the energy of so many thousands of people more than someone who operates at a very low frequency. We need both high and low energy to keep balanced mentally, emotionally and physically.

When we make reconnection with the God energy, we are at last fulfilled. We can work toward achieving the goal set out in the Lord's Prayer (Our Father) of creating a "Heaven on Earth." We feel complete. We feel the quiet knowing, the yearning we have always had, that we had something inside of us that was special and different, and is actually true.

When we are able to remember we are more than this body or spirit, then we can remember we are souls connected to God, and we are in bodies temporarily. Then our lives can begin to change. We only need this miracle for minutes or even seconds to change our entire lives. That bond, that cord or connection, is so strong and it has never *not* been there, but it has been forgotten or not recognized by us after we were born.

In fact, in time the "new normal" in your life will be rapid growth and change. It will be about learning to embrace change - how to step quickly forward and keep focused on your hopes and dreams. But it is also important to rest as needed to assimilate these new ideas and to recharge your physical body.

Our parents, teachers and religious leaders may have steered us away from our spiritual gifts, thinking they were protecting us. In truth, they were disabling us and making us feel like we were different or maybe even crazy. We could not remove our receptors, but we could tone them down and try not to listen to the messages, but the messages never left us. The yearning never left us. We just conditioned ourselves to ignore the obvious gifts from God. We all want unconditional love, acceptance, security, to have hope, to have dreams, to be on our work/mission, to be cool, to be beautiful, to feel important, to be wanted. It is what God brings to me that I bring to other people.

A *Soulgasm (Spiritual Ecstasy)* is actually very difficult to describe. It can be like a huge electrical vibration that peacefully runs through your entire body. It calms you, consoles you, nurtures you, challenges you, and makes you feel at peace with yourself and the entire world. To bring it down to a physical level, it reminds me of the feeling you get at the peak of sexual orgasm. It is a one-to-three-second peak that every person has at the climax of their sexual orgasm, but it is even more powerful. It covers your entire body and can last for an hour or more. There really are no words to describe these feelings and the benefits you receive. Some in religious life would call this being "slain in the spirit." It is how it feels when you reconnect to the Source, in other words, the Energy you came from.

It is definitely an experience that will change the rest of your life. This same connection can also be found in dedicated meditation, dream states and out-of-body experiences. I like to think of it as how it would feel if God was hugging me. I just receive the love, and then have so much love and energy that I can give it away in support of my brothers and sisters.

Whenever I have been in the flow of energy, which some people will refer to as God, it is like a continual spiritual orgasm. It is unmeasured bliss. It is a vibration inside of me that brings joy, bliss, being, and nothingness, all at the same time. When you are in this flow, there are no expectations, no rewards, no punishments, nothing to do except to *Just Be and Allow Joy into your Life*. When my spirit rejoins my soul, which is already connected to the primary source energy - *The God Energy* - I am happy. When we are in that source energy, miraculous things happen. Spiritual, mental, emotional, and physical healing all happen at an unbelievable rate. Your life begins to change.

# CHAPTER 8

## *Being Yourself – Loving Yourself – Changing Yourself*

Welcome to my world! When I received the outline of this book from Spirit, I was told that it was now safe to welcome you into my Secret Garden. I could open the heavy door which had been closed so long to the outside world and show you the world I have lived in for 59 years.

When I trusted myself, I learned to be more open and trusting of people and ideas that resonated with my soul. I have found many people who understand me and have joined me in the Garden. I used to be afraid to show people all of the parts of me. I was afraid they would not like, respect or love me, or would think I was crazy. I gave them this power over me and it nearly destroyed me because my life was all about them and not me. This was not *Loving Myself First, Best and Always.*

Even when I wrote my two earlier books about taxes and the IRS (*IRS Whistleblower* and *What to Do When the IRS is After You*), I was afraid that if people knew that I was intuitive and had all of these spiritual gifts, then they would think that I was crazy. So I continued my readings on the down low. Now the books are done and this book is my public announcement that I can "be all that I am—again."

Deciding who you are and what you want in life is the first step to the rest of your life. Are you tired of always being under someone else's control? Your boss? Your spouse? Your parents? Do you sometimes feel like a cork floating in and out on the tide at the beach? Every life must have a plan, a goal and a mission. If you are ready to dream, and dream big, then God can accept your order and put it in motion. Sadly, many people have forgotten their dreams and lost hope.

We all want so much to be accepted for who we are so we give in to the ways of others becoming who they say we are and who they want us to be. We try so hard to love and to be loved. It is never enough. Intuitive/Empathic/Sensitive people know they are different, but we also know we are not crazy. We want to love and serve and care for others - right or wrong. Although we can choose to do this, we also hope for love and acceptance in return. This rarely works. *Conditional* love and caring do not work in the long run.

First, we have to learn to accept and love ourselves, not as some image we create of who we hope to be in the future, but just as we are right now. It is hard to look in the mirror and see the real you - to love the person you see with your eyes.

True unconditional love is you loving others without expectation of reward, and not in a way that degrades, depreciates, depletes, drains and destroys you. You just send out love to everyone all the time. Then God gives you more love and your life improves. *Going with the Flow* brings great rewards.

When you remember that unconditional love relationship you had with God and allow it in your current life, you will never feel scared or lonely again.

Any memories or feelings you have from before you were born can be very confusing to you because it is hard to live in a three-dimensional world when your soul remembers you being greater than that. On the other side you don't need to talk. Your thoughts, with all the emotions and knowledge attached, are instantly transmitted to another person and they respond back instantly.

When you realize, or remember, you are a spirit in a body, not a body with a spirit, and you are always connected to the God/Universe/ Love energy, your life begins to change. The amazing part of this energy is that it is free, everlasting, and always accessible. When you allow for it, it will come. Some call this the Christ energy, others call it Universal energy. You have your body, heart and mind, and directly above you is your spirit. Your spirit is connected to your soul. Your soul is always connected directly to God and the energy around God.

(Universal consciousness)

You are a beautifully-crafted work of art created by God. You are like a Tiffany lamp, able to radiate so much light into the world; but you may not be fully plugged into the power yet. I help my clients reconnect.

Every day your needs change and every day you access the energy differently, depending on what you wish to accomplish for yourself and for others on that day. It is important to realize this is not your own energy. You can do physical, emotional, mental, and spiritual healing with people simply by using your own energy. However, this takes a great toll on your body, mind and spirit. The energy to make everything happen in your life is free and freely available to all who allow it. (*Go with the flow!*)

This healing energy, and my attitude of acceptance, has allowed me to heal herniated discs in my neck and back, and a spot on my pituitary gland, and saved me from gallbladder and thyroid removal, bilateral carpal tunnel and ulnar nerve impairment, and fungal pneumonia.

I admit, I had no belief in healing work at all. I had no faith that I was even "worthy" of healing. I thought it was all crazy talk. But when I showed up to a Catholic priest doing a Healing Mass and I was instantly healed, I quickly changed my mind.

Great healing is always available if we seek the source of all energy - God. There is an abundance of clean, positive energy if we only allow it in.

Spirit has shown me that the body is designed to protect and sustain itself, to filter out and destroy those things that cause disease. The body is also equipped to regenerate itself. All of the body's cells are kept fresh and healthy by our ability to make new cells. The problem is that our bodies were not designed to be under 100 percent stress, 100 percent of the time.

Stress is a factor in all of our lives every day. We may have less physical stress because we are not doing farming or physical labor, but the stress has moved to higher levels. We worry about work, money, food, housing, health, sex and love. We worry about our families and our futures, and then we get angry because we are so worried about everything. So we self-medicate and try to forget about it all.

Emotional and mental stresses are the greatest enemies you have to your health and the human condition in general. You are most likely not receiving adequate and restorative sleep, nutrition from your food and water, and you are not having much fun. We are here in life to learn, and also to have fun. This comes up over and over in my readings. People today have so much "stuff" and so much money, but so little pleasure and so little fun. Life was much quieter and simpler even 100 years ago. It was not easier; it just had less constant mental and emotional stress.

Today we are constantly being attacked by water with chlorine, medicines, metals and dozens of other contaminants that our government deems to be at acceptable levels for our safety. Even if we try to eat organic food, it is still raised on land that has been reduced to "acceptable levels" of contamination. Farm fields are not allowed the time to naturally recharge themselves. As a result, we are nutritionally deficient. We do not eat or receive those vitamins and minerals that are needed by our bodies and we never have enough vitamin C, a stress-fighting vitamin.

As the old world receded and a more modern, progressive and darker energy became our new world, we began to live in stress. This is when the darkness of the Earth sought to overtake the light of our spirit. Now we must all awaken the sleeping prophets within us. We need to unleash the healing power in ourselves.

We are under some form of stress all the time. We have schedules and clocks constantly upsetting our natural rhythms. We are living in disharmony with the world around us. I was so busy trying to live in this world of my own creation that I forgot I lived in the Creator's world.

When is the last time you sat on the grass, walked in the woods or had your bare feet in dark, rich soil? You are bombarded with electric waves, radio waves, artificial light, artificial food, unsafe water, and microwaves. Your body can process some of this as there are energies like this in nature, but you should not have to process this all the time.

Your emotional and mental health suffers first. Then it makes its way into your energy field, your ethereal body, or aura, around you. Then it enters your physical state. This causes disruptions of energy in your body's systems and then the dis-ease starts. Dis-ease means dis-comfort, caused by anything that interrupts your energy flow or makes you sad or unhappy. It is also related to dis-ability and dis-content.

Let's examine the word dis-ease a bit more. When we find we are sick, we must look behind the obvious symptoms to the spiritual, mental, emotional and physical causes. We no longer need to suffer because the medical profession is treating only the symptoms. This is essential information for you to know. You do not need to be sick unless it serves some purpose, i.e. learning about that disease or about suffering or settling karma.

Dis-ease is also a partner to dis-stress, dis-agreement, and dis-harmony. Spirit tells me that we are supposed to not only have fun in life, but also have no stress, no discomfort, no disagreement, no disharmony. Spirit tells me that you must experience the pain of your lessons or disease and then grow from it. Accept it, bless it, go through it, get rid of it and then move past it. Yet, you have been told you still have to die, and you actually think that is the natural order of things. It may actually be a good thing for some who act as if they really don't want to be here at all.

I love to watch birds flying around. I love how they know what to eat, where to find water and shelter and mostly avoid predators. They make babies and then one day die. But they are different from man, I think, because they do not exhibit signs of stress and anxiety. If they want food they are directed by some internal radar where to find it. If they want sex, they find it. They do not feel worry or guilt. Birds may appear simpler than man, but also happier.

I had one client who, in meditation, saw herself as a giant hawk. She was flying and described her range of vision as being so much greater than a human being's vision. She described how she felt flapping her wings and then getting to heights where the wind currents let her glide for hours. She described this feeling – like radar - that the hawk had that prevented it from flying into buildings. Also when it was capturing food how it "just knew" exactly how low to the ground to fly. She described feeling hungry and then flying to a river and catching a fish and ripping it apart. She said that there was great power in that vision. The hawk had absolute authority over itself and just trusted its instincts and did not want for anything. She ended by describing the blood on the hawk's beak and the feeling of the full belly and then it closing its eyes until it was hungry again. It had a peaceful knowing and faith that all was right with the world.

You have a schedule that does not give you enough time to live. Actually, the clock is watching you all night as well, telling you that you only have so many more hours before you have to get up and do it all over again. Many people spend so much time working and earning a living and buying homes and "stuff", that they are exhausted. They forget that though their soul lives for eternity, their bodies do not. So they have forgotten how to relax and enjoy life. This goes on and on. Some days you are too busy and stressed to even have a bathroom break. Do you have a daily bowel movement? Or are you too busy rushing off to work or school? Do you get bloated, tired, groggy and mentally confused? When you ignore the natural systems of your body, waste starts to accumulate in the body. You get fat and then you worry about that. Your waste backs up and putrefies, inviting all kinds of problems. It backs up your liver and gall bladder and you start to store fat which attracts more fat. Your pancreas is always confused as to how much insulin it will need so it produces too much or too little and that makes you sick also. You don't know what to do with all the fat so you line your arteries with it as well as storing it in other organs, and then you start taking medicines to treat your high cholesterol levels. The human body is designed to work together, not in separate sections. You cannot have a chemical-laden breakfast and expect good results.

The craziest part of this illness thing is that it appears that your government and the medical industrial complex are in partnership to allow you to get sick, and then bill you as they heal you, or as you die. We know cigarettes and tobacco products cause sickness, but we do not ban them. We know growth hormones and GMOs make their way into our food chain along with hundreds of other chemical compounds, but we do not ban them.

The fact is that we are exposed to many substances and events that could kill us every day. But we do not all get sick equally. Why? First, let's look at the causes of physical illness.

Spirit tells me that illness is a lesson we come to learn on Earth. We may have a karmic need to learn how it feels to die slowly of a terrible disease. Or you may have to pay back karma for illness or injury you caused to others in the past. There is generational karma (paying back the Sins of the Fathers) and there is situational karma (group karma), where the thinking is, "I am in this group or land and this is what we do to others so this is what we get back because of it."

Illness can be the result of emotions. The emotional part of you will either attract or reject illness. It is truly a case of mind over matter. In many cases your emotional attitude will determine if you will get sick or not. Spirit tells me that in future generations we will develop bodies which are naturally immune to disease. We will be able to match the energy of the illness and defeat it naturally.

In many cases, before healing can occur, we do the body scan and have a long talk about the memories or talk about things that the client has long suppressed, but that I am able to sense or view. We do not need to review every negative circumstance, but we look for patterns and trends. If they even allow for the idea that they were abused, it makes a difference in their healing.

The Disconnecting Cord Process can not only rid you of people or memories that have hurt you, but also feelings, emotions and personal behaviors that no longer serve you. Many clients have reported that they started to forget about the pain in the abuse and the misery in their lives because it was no longer important. Or that it had been replaced with a new abuser. When they identified that, they were ready to let the person or situation go and turn it over to God.

Your life can be all that you see in your mind. You should decide what you want, imagine it like it has already occurred and been created for you. Start working to try to find it. It is this quiet knowing that makes all the difference. Having faith in your dreams and visions gives energy to them being created.

Spirit is forever telling me, "Why get sick if you don't have to?" I'm told you can learn the lessons without the physical pain of illness and early death. Spirit talks about preventing illness, healing yourself and being strong enough to *Love Yourself First, Best, and Always.* When you are in good condition on all levels, you are able to maintain emotional, mental and physical balance in your life.

We are all exposed to germs and illness from birth. We survive and thrive, we get sick and recover, which builds our immune system, or we die. For most people those are only seeds that may have been planted but need never grow and blossom. Doctors have told me that we all have active cancer cells in our bodies at various times in our lives. They may have been there for years, but our healthy immune system and healthy body prevent cancer and many other diseases from killing us.

I have seen so many healings not only in myself but in many others that I know your attitude makes an important difference in allowing healing.

Everyone wants to talk about cancer and cancer treatment. Spirit talks to me about preventing cancer and never needing treatments. I have read that one in six men will get prostate cancer, and one in seven women will get breast cancer. The healthy cells in your body must be weak for this to happen. Cancer treatments are not very effective. No one needs to get sick and live in pain. In the past I would have said at this point, "But we all have to die." Spirit tells me that we do not. In fact, the Bible tells us that we all should be living to 120 years old. To even quote this sounds crazy, but in the time since the last century, life expectancy has gone up 75 percent, while the quality of life and connection to other people appears to have declined.

Our systems get so overwhelmed that usually one part of us fails and we die, perhaps from heart problems, stroke or cancer. But most of our body still wants to live. When we get emotional blockages and damage in one organ it affects our whole system.

Where are the fun and joy and happiness in your life and in your relationships?

We have too long equated a good life with a long life. That is clearly not what you find in the elderly in the United States today. Their lives are the result of years of breathing cigarette smoke, polluted air, ingesting insecticides, medicines, chemicals and hormones that have entered our water supply. In addition, they have been eating chemical-laden foods and suffering exposure to radio waves, microwaves, and nuclear energy. The burning of fossil fuels alone causes many people with sensitive health to be so out of breath they cannot cross the street without needing to stop and take a rest.

Even treatments of food like pasteurization, the boiling of milk, eggs, cheese and butter, heating beer and wine, alters or kills what beneficial bacteria and enzymes we expect to get from that food or drink. But the government does not ban smoking or companies that build cars or machines that pollute the air or harness dozens of other life-threatening events.

When people find they are deficient in vitamins and minerals despite a seemingly healthy diet, they turn to artificial chemical compounds for vitamins and minerals. It is not the same. You do not get the same benefit from drinking processed milk as compared to raw milk. For thousands of years our predecessors drank raw milk and lived healthy lives with strong bones and muscles.

Today some doctors claim that many people are deficient in vitamins B-12, B-6 and B-1, Magnesium, Vitamin D, Sulfur, Zinc, Chromium and Iodine, not in any particular order. We look around and see people carrying so much weight. We see them eat huge portions simply because their bodies are craving the vitamins and minerals. They instinctively know they should be able to get certain vitamins and minerals from certain foods. In the past, you could eat one apple and get many positive benefits. Today you need to eat two apples to get the same benefits. This is discussed and debated, but the low quality of our food is causing us to eat larger quantities of food which are making us fat and unhealthy.

The United States Government fails to protect us from the junk food and bio-engineered food on the market. I think we need protection from the government. We need to make self-appreciation and self-healing *our* priority.

Everything has its time and its purpose. Your body is simply a manifestation of some desire you had in Heaven - to come to Earth and learn or experience lessons that will make you closer to your fellow man and, eventually, closer to God.

We are in a time where the more we let the Love and Light of God back into us, the more it will increase. Our energy, our ability to receive love and light and direct it to others, benefits us. Our bodies are reawakening. We are learning to feel, to trust, to discern again. This doesn't come from our own knowledge or abilities but instead from what we feel and know to be true in our hearts. Spiritual reawakening will bring so many new situations into your life. You will feel wellness and energy, you will receive healing at whatever level you are allowing it to occur, you will have more energy, and you will be able to attract the things that you want: the things that allow you to *Love Yourself First, Best and Always!* You will look back at your old life and wonder why it took you so long to get to this place. It does not matter. What matters is that you are here now, with all the rest of the souls that are on a similar migration to Love and Light.

This is easy to follow if you think about the *Going with the Flow* example previously mentioned. As we move higher up our chakra system, life becomes less about "stuff" and more about feelings. We have the ability to transmute (modify or cancel out the effects from) whatever it is that bothered us before. Illness, mental stress, emotional attacks - all can be modified so they no longer harm you or have any power over you.

We will go into this more in the future. For now, think about the best quality of life that you can dream of, where you take care of yourself and are provided what you need from the great abundance that is all around us. Think of turning off your phone, your TV and your computer and being outside in nature. Enjoy the moments in the day. You just need to increase your energy to get to that place.

The human body is an amazing instrument. I am told that all poisons in our food, air and water can be transmuted and cleaned up by our endocrine system and our liver and kidneys. There is nothing we cannot filter out. But when our intestines are so clogged up because we are unable to eat and release, as is natural, due to the use of drugs and chemicals in our food, in medical treatments and in the air, food and water, and you allow fear into the equation forgetting that God put you in your body for a specific purpose, then you begin to experience a breakdown of your natural systems.

If you allow fear in particular to manifest, it will make you sick. The disease will flourish in your mind - this is your ego allowing it, giving it standing and permission to go on. Then you fall into the medical trap - tests, accompanied by worry, fear, surgery, bad news, bad news, and bad news. Then you go to a doctor and turn over your power and authority to a perfect stranger, asking him about your health. He will judge you as sick and pave the path to physical illness for you. He will claim to know more about you than you know about you. He will take direction and control over your life. He may be well meaning and have good intentions. But he is not you.

Many people identify with and own their illnesses. They may tell their friends endless stories about "my heart condition," or "my cancer." This further weakens them and gives more energy to the illness.

It is when fear and lack of trust in the healing energy of God are introduced to you by some technician or medical professional that you allow a disease to grow. Often these things happen when a major trauma has occurred in your life. Divorce, unemployment, death of a family member or loved one, financial insecurity or loss, job loss - all of these can trigger huge emotional responses. When you are unhappy, the Universe notices and sends you matching energy! When you feel unloved or incapable of love, when your dreams have been destroyed, when you have been cheated on or betrayed, then you are ready to begin nurturing the seeds of dis-ease you planted.

Dis-ease is watered with your fear and anger. Then it grows. You wonder why *you*? Why did I get this dis-ease? You turn to God for explanations and find silence. God did not make you sick, but He allowed it for the lessons it would bring you. Why do babies and children contract dis-ease and suffer and die? If you seek counsel from a priest or minister, they might tell you that it is God's will. They do not know what else to say to you in that moment.

You should see a medical doctor if you are sick to get a diagnosis and treatment plan. But you can also allow in the healing that I will teach you to access. I have done this many times in my own life. I have been diagnosed with various health issues and have been healed from them completely. This is the cool part because you have your x-rays and MRIs proving you are sick. Then you get naturally healed and you have the clean x-rays and MRIs proving that you are healed. You have experienced your own healing from God. Miracles happen in great and small ways every minute of every day once fear is released.

I have allowed the image that "I am well and I am healthy" to overtake and subdue any image of illness or death. I have submersed the illness in love and empowered healing in that area of my body. I am my thoughts and I want to be well. I will be well. I am well. All is well.

The point of this is that you have control over your emotional state. You have cancer cells present in you, and you also have hundreds of other cells and bacteria that can make you very sick and cause your death. But they do not. There is a natural system in the Universe of positive and negative energy that keeps you safe and supported. You also have control over the illness. When you identify the illness as not being welcome in your energy, you release the illness. By rejecting illness, you build good cells that overpower it. When you actually think, "I am healthy and well and ok!" you will become just that. Even if you are dying, it is all about you having a positive attitude about where you are in that moment. Healing will occur in more than just your physical state. Emotional, mental and spiritual healing also takes place.

Fear of death is another problem that makes you more susceptible to illness and results in death. When you accept the possibility of you dying one day, then that takes away the fear of it. You are going to die someday but probably not right now as you are reading this book.

So many clients have said that they want to negotiate when and how they die. They want to be in control of their body's functions. They diet and exercise, they deprive themselves to preserve and protect their health. Yet they still die. They might trip while out jogging and break their neck or a cherry tomato gets stuck in their throat and they stop breathing. You still might die if that is some lesson you need to learn, but you are in control over the circumstances of your death also. Before you even came into your body- this was all scripted out. You and God formulated the plan and it was approved at the highest levels. Accept knowledge of your eventual death as a blessing.

Spirit always tells me that we have control of when we will die; we simply will it and then allow it. I am not talking about suicide, but there are departure points built into every life, I am told, where you may choose to leave. When you are blocked energetically in your ethereal/energy body it will eventually also block some places in your physical body. Then illness will result. We can will ourselves into a happier, healthier state once we reconnect with the energy of the Light. What we put out is what we attract back. The question is how are we to remain vibrant and alive until we decide it is time to die?

Determining your quality of life is very important. The medical community can keep you alive for a very long time even though your brain and heart may be technically dead. However, some people have no quality of life due to their medicines or treatments. The end of their lives can be painful and horrible.

When you set your intention for your health then you can manifest healing, wellness, joy and bliss. You will also then come into your highest power. When you take authority over your life, you will begin to connect with higher energy from God and from other people. You will no longer be subject to attacks from germs, illness and attitudes that allowed you to get sick in the first place.

The power of the collective conscious is unlimited. When tens of millions of people direct their energies, prayers and good intentions to a problem or situation like a war or natural disaster recovery, the pain of the problem is less. That is what the power of your intention can do. Prayer and positive intentions can make miracles happen in your life as well.

Every day we connect and collect other people's stuff, whether it's facts, gossip, fears, worries, information, or misinformation. It is constantly coming at us. TV and radio news assault you. Now is the time when we can still be in the world but not of the world, not harmed by those people, events or illnesses that would kill other people. We will survive as we move closer to the Light.

When you wake up in the morning, decide to release all that you no longer need. You can say, ***"I release everything that is not mine."*** This will cover spiritual, mental, emotional and physical cares that hurt you or may fester and grow to hurt you. Let them go! Just let them go! You can heal from your own words. Your intention is your prayer. God honors all prayers, but sometimes we cancel out our prayer with poor intention. You might say "I wish I would win the lottery, but then I bet I would have so many problems and so many relatives chasing after me." See? You want to win but then you say it would hurt you so you cancel the intention of winning.

It is when we connect back to those positive energies that are greater than we are that we begin to experience the lessons we need, and also grow to move on to new lessons in a more positive manner, and lots faster.

Once you see how this happens, you will see others in a new light. You will see that your old attitudes were killing you. We do not need bombs to destroy us; good people ignoring the way their fellow man is being treated is what is hurting us. When people identify and stamp out racism, greed, and disconnection from each other, we can begin. The term "I am my brother" will begin to make sense to you. You will soon learn we are all connected. It is the connection with others that keeps you young and feeds your soul.

When you decide to no longer feed the negative energy of other people or of government, political, educational and banking systems, you get a fresh start. No longer will the processes that have used you, abused you, and tried to destroy you be feeding off your energy. When you re-gather your energy, you are pulling back your power from the old, negative systems. Those systems will eventually notice that you have pulled back your power and that you have survived. Then you will be transmitting your own higher vibration of pure unconditional love and compassion which will flood these old institutions and either reform them or destroy them.

When you see the movie "The Secret", it looks very easy to change your life. But you need to apply considerable effort toward making your dreams come true. You cannot do it alone. I am told you must dream, then apply yourself and allow your vibration to rise up to the level of the circumstances in your future life that you desire. Otherwise, you get yourself all excited and then you come down hard when the Universe does not give you that new Mercedes. When you become part of this new vibration, it will feel different, even uncomfortable at first. Then it will feel better and better until you have trouble remembering the way you were before. You can't cherry-pick only those things you want in life. Good and bad things are all part of your life.

I have found that people hardly ever change, at least not essentially of their own accord. But there are forces that believe in the redemption of each individual. These are the forces of good in the Universe. Wise people try to not even define this energy. They just seek the compassion and understanding that it brings forth. There is no mercy or forgiveness because none is needed. Each act a person does in their life is essential, not just to them but to the rest of us. Every good or bad thing that you go through blesses the rest of us. This knowledge gives us what we need to carry on. All is well - there is no Hell - except as you create it yourself. When you are prepared to shed your old self and all you have known and suffered in your life, then you are planting the seeds for your future life.

When we talk about vibrational energy, we talk about the feeling that you get about a person or situation when you talk to them or meet them. Being aware of how that feels is important. When you recognize that some people have an energy that feels bad to be around, you can avoid them. If a person has a good energy you will want to see them more.

Your spiritual path is like you are climbing steps towards your goal and when you reach a higher step you stop, look around and see where you are. More importantly you notice how you *feel* being there. Then you imagine how you will feel at the next step and the next step. It is only when you stop and look back that you can appreciate how far you have come.

This allows you to be in harmony with yourself and be in harmony with the new vibrational energy that surrounds your dream/goal/

situation. If you want to live big, you need to dream big. When you *go with the flow*, even when illness drops into your system like a giant boulder in the stream of your life, you have the ability and power to go around the boulder. I often think that God is the boulder in the stream of life and as we pass a boulder a little bit of the fear, anger, worry and our mind/ego gets sanded down. Our true beauty is revealed.

A Chinese proverb says:
*"The gem cannot be polished without friction,*
*nor man perfected without trials."*

Some people get angry with the boulder in their stream. So they get sledge hammers and machines to attack the boulder and try to turn it into dust. They are completely missing the point.

We experience various situations and illnesses in life because of karma. We are given in body what we need to learn in soul. When you are sick you can see yourself becoming well. Then you have learned the lesson. We all learn many lessons in life, but some people are afraid to let the lesson go. I always received help from the Violet Light and the mystic St. Germaine to burn off whatever after effects remain from karmic lessons.

You need to go through the good and bad events in your life. It is essential to living. You need to learn these lessons and the new emotions that come with them. You do not need to carry around these old lessons like old baggage for the rest of your life. You simply turn them over to your soul level. You do not lose the knowledge of what you have learned, only the pain. Knowledge learned is knowledge retained. You do not need to carry all the books you have read in school to be thought of as intelligent.

When we look at the big picture of life, and reincarnation and karma, we see that all illness does fit right in God's world. When you do get sick it may seem like friends and family all tacitly support it, and they may think, "Well he was old! Of course he would get sick." That attitude does not help. It sends an energy wave out that makes us think it is normal for people to get sick, suffer and die. We should cherish life, and the ability that people have to continue to contribute and care for others long past the age of 65.

Disease is planted by anger, fear and worry. It flourishes in your mind and is born in your body. However, this is not coming from God.

The self-defeat or hopelessness you feel is from the world and the energies here. When we look at Jesus we see that chaos, poverty and sickness, or behavior forbidden by society like corrupt tax collectors, prostitutes or adultery did not bother Him at all. He knew that the Christ energy was in each of those people. He did not judge them, He just unconditionally loved them. In the instant that they felt this, tested it and then embraced it, Jesus healed them, in body, mind, soul and spirit. So simple.

Your new life can begin when you ask yourself, "What would my day be like if I had no fear, no worry, and no anger? What could I accomplish?" What if death and fear no longer had any power over you? What if you had the power to decide when and where you will die? What circumstances would you choose? What age would you be? What would you want to accomplish before that happened?

It is not the life we create that makes us amazing souls. It is the life that we allow God to create in us that makes us all amazing and part of God! When we see God in the eyes of every person we meet, we will learn to see ourselves more clearly.

When you allow yourself to bloom where you are planted, to do what you can with what you have and where you are you, you will begin to grow. Deciding that you have power and authority over an illness or any situation in your life will cause you to be healed to the degree that you allow it. The illness will either kill you or make you feel better, stronger, and certainly wiser. If it kills you, you have no problems.

This book shows you how to integrate the lessons of your life with the lessons required by your soul. The reasons that you choose to be in your body in this life must be honored. You came here for a reason. Perhaps it was to suffer some rare, incurable disease or to have an illness that makes you very dependent on others in order to appreciate what true dependency and love are really about.

When you are being present and share the love that God gave you, it allows you to heal others. Simple touch and smiling, bringing provisions and love can heal as greatly as anything else can. When you have faith in the provider of the healing, when you trust God to give you the power, then healing, peace and comfort result.

Being told that you are good enough, smart enough, or strong enough, or simply being patted on the head as a child or getting a pat on the back, makes a big difference in life. Humans need touch. Hugs, holding hands, holding another person, looking into a baby's eyes - all of these things bring life renewal to you. Many people also gain this from their pets.

It is integrating your health with your attitude that will save you many painful moments. When you have that low point where you are sick of being sick or abused or oppressed, you simply need to proclaim to the world, **"I AM MAD AS HELL AND I AM NOT GOING TO TAKE IT ANYMORE!"** Just like the character, Howard Beale, did in the movie "Network."

When you radiate the love you have inside to yourself first, you will begin to heal. When you radiate this love and the feeling of health and love to those around you, they will heal. It goes on and on and on. When it goes out to the people around you, you will find that your vibration frequency, your radio wave or station, is increased in amperage. You are able to attract more like-minded people and tolerate more people who need to be exposed to all that you have to offer but may not be ready for all the truth that you share. It is important to: *radiate love without concern for results.*

This is how God works miracles - through His people here on Earth. I am a miracle worker and so are you.

You can be a conduit of this energy of love and healing when you work without any expectation of return or reward. This is really what unconditional love is about - loving another person and expecting nothing in return, no money, sex, power or position. When I do healing work, I do not charge for the healing. I charge for the cost of my time while doing the healing. But I do charge for my time, because I could be doing something else instead of doing the healing. When you do this, you are able to love yourself more and are able to plant seeds in other people - the seeds of faith, love, hope, understanding, compassion and acceptance.

*Three grand essentials to happiness are*
*Something to do,*
*Something to love*
*And something to hope for. – Joseph Addison*

(Note: He does not say "someone" to love.)

So make a plan! Seek out what you are to do here. If you remember that life is not about the destination but about the journey, you learn to treasure every moment, because in the very next moment it can all go away.

It's prudent to save money and make plans for your future, but not at the expense of having some JOY today. Why dream of world travel when you are old and wealthy but may lack the energy and health to travel? Never put off until tomorrow what you can do today. Love someone and tell him or her so. Be the best friend or supporter you can be. Be happy and let the world feel the glow you put out there from that.

Many people want to do huge, wonderful things in their lives and start an effort to achieve them. Through a combination of cosmic circumstances, they end up not only failing, but also feeling worse about themselves and more depressed than they were before they started. I am sure that this has happened to you. It is so painful to them and to the rest of us.

That is why I find that building a network of like-minded people, friends and advisors will allow you to grow at the pace you set for yourself. As you look at your old life and release what no longer serves you, you will find that everything will start to change. You just need to start. You may have to leave behind or limit contact with old friends and even family simply because they get on your nerves, or you cannot relate to them anymore. Discordant energy causes people to separate.

Spirit tells me that we just need to believe that there is some power higher than ourselves, some mysterious strength that loves us, supports us and wants the best for us, and wants the best from us. We need to believe that when we allow the energy to move within us, our lives can change in an instant. That is the reward in believing that we are more than our body and mind.

This connection to Universal Love is easily accessed simply by being still and allowing it to move within us - to reinvigorate our spirits and to allow for direct connection with the God energy. It can come from holding someone's hand, enjoying a bottle of wine, meditating, laughing or sitting in the sun. It is not important how you define the God energy, it is simply important that you are open to receiving that energy that is at a higher frequency than energies we have here on Earth. We all have a radio receiver and we just need to listen to hear God.

Believe me, this is very hard to accomplish. I was never aware of how controlling, manipulative and stubborn I could be until I had to confront my own demons. As you rise and grow spiritually, the things of the past may no longer serve you. It was normal in the IRS to act like I acted. But I found that I could do a difficult job without those feelings if I just used love, understanding and compassion.

We all have many demons if we allow them, whether it's lack of self-esteem, lack of self-confidence, unworthiness, anger, fear, worry, resignation, or just plain lack. Finding demons and allowing them is the easy part. In life, many people have not been gentle, nurturing, or loving to you. Few have tried to understand you and fewer still have loved you unconditionally. So I am not suggesting that you do not have good reason to have demons. I am merely offering you the chance to get rid of the demons and all the negative energy that surrounds you and seeks to destroy you. I pray that you will be healed completely and instantly just from reading these words and receiving the intention of wellness that I am sending you right now.

God cannot be explained to you by words written in a book, by a great speech, or by touch. God can only be experienced in your heart and spirit and soul. This can only happen when your mind and ego and body allow it.

Mind/ego does not understand this spiritual connection and fears it. In fact, mind/ego is all about control, fear, worry, and anger. This is why it is so difficult to even contemplate beginning your spiritual journey. That journey begins with hope, is guided by faith, and is fed by trust. All these things must happen just to start the journey. It is very scary. Believe me, dark forces will conspire to prevent you from going down this path. Most of the dark forces are already contained in you - the fear/anger/worry combination in you makes for a good host.

So I hope that these words will resonate with you and cause you a moment of peace and comfort.

If we think that we do not need our fellow man, that we are able to live a good and rewarding life without others, without serving others and without experiencing the joy of being with another person, this is the worst behavior we can have. You will get sick from your aloofness, your arrogance, your greed, your obsession with how you look or where you live. None of that matters. What matters is what you did for other people. That is what benefits your soul. What you do for others you do for yourself as well.

So it is important to get back in touch with yourself, the reason for you being here in life, and identifying your mission. You will set your intention to be healed. This allows you to also heal others. The gifts of Spirit as outlined in the Bible include hands-on healing, emotional healing, spiritual healing, knowledge, wisdom and discernment. This path is so amazing and so fulfilling. Let's begin!

# CHAPTER 9

## *Why You Are Sick and How You Can Heal*

I am a healer and medical intuitive. I am not a medical doctor, psychiatrist, psychologist, social worker or mental health counselor. I am not particularly interested in organized medicine, but I am very interested in healing and allowing circumstances for healing. My passion is to help people help themselves using the energy already available to them and teaching them how to access it. I look into the eyes of every person I meet and see the Light of God. *When I love myself, first, best and always*, this allows me to love others. From this love comes healing and miracles.

Every client that I work with is a witness to the power of this love. It is the love energy from God. Defining its source is not important since so many people have various, limited perceptions of "God" and what and who God is. That is alright and will not be debated here. Simply believing that there is a power greater than you, a positive energy that is in control of the Universe, allows great things to happen. This energy is what I call the Creator of the Universe. We are talking about believing that you can be healed and allowing the healing to take place.

So many people get hung up on their idea of what God is. How can you know what is unknowable? You can only sense God through His creations, other people and the Earth. A friend of mine, who is Native American, tells me that when she sees a tree she sees God, the Creator of all of us. Some Native Americans use the term "Great Spirit." We know that we ourselves did not create the seed, the dirt, the water, the climate and the atmosphere that contribute toward causing that tree to grow. Simply said, there is a Higher Power than you. Accept this and you are halfway to healing.

Healing can come from Light or Dark energy. Energy is just energy - it is not good or bad. The Bible gives a good example of this when it explains that dark angels can appear to deceive you as angels of Light and present you with half-truths, lies and deceptions. The Bible talks about recognizing the difference (discernment). There are angels and fallen angels.

Did you know that Satan was once an archangel until he had a falling out with God and took one third of all the angels and left Heaven? In the Hebrew Bible he was "The Opposer of God." Satan had a place under God and he brought into life the negative energy or lessons that you need to learn in your life. He challenged good. In the later Christian interpretations, we find Satan identified as "the prince of this world" in the *Book of John 12:31, 14:30*; "the prince of the power of the air" also called Meririm, and "the spirit that now worketh in the children of disobedience" in the *Book of Ephesians 2*:2; and "the god of this world" in *2 Corinthians 4:4.5.*

Clearly God approves of this dark energy as a part of the team. Good versus good just does not sell any tickets. God and Satan seem to have an arrangement where you are offered many choices in life and you make all the decisions and choices. Think about that; you make all the choices, not God or Satan.

So discernment is important. The devil is all about deception. He can appear in many ways and through people, friends and family. Dark forces tried to scare me away from my gifts. When we start to wake up, we have many challenges as we begin to allow the connection to God to come to and through us.

It is very important to determine where you are receiving the information from. In the initial stages of clairvoyance and intuition, you will attract many lower spirits/demons who will bring you deceptive messages. Some may be coated with truth but with a bad intention. So always ask, "Does this information bring me enlightenment and peace, or stress?" Any spirits that come to you can have influence over you. Beware especially if a spirit comes to you clothed in the body of a deceased loved one. Things are not always as they appear. Some spirits will use this to plant incorrect information in you.

Discernment is one of the spiritual gifts and is essential in determining if what you are receiving is good information for you. Discernment is easy; the information you receive will always direct you to something good, positive and pleasing to yourself and others.

> *1 John 4 says: Beloved do not believe every spirit,*
> *but test the spirits to see whether they are from God;*
> *for many false prophets have gone out into the world.*
> *By this you know the Spirit of God; every spirit that*
> *does not confess Jesus is not coming from God.*
> *And this is the spirit of the antichrist,*
> *which you have heard is coming;*
> *and is now already in the world.*
> *Little children, you have conquered them;or the one who is in you*
> *is greater than the one who is in the world.They are from the world;*
> *therefore, what they say is from the world*
> *and the world listens to that, but we are from God.*
> *Whoever knows God listens to us and*
> *whoever does not is not from God and does not listen to us.*
> *From these we know the spirit of truth in the spirit of error.*

Now this is a very limited perspective but still good advice. If you look at the term "God" which is all encompassing and more than the word "Jesus", which is more defined, you will see what I mean. Remember, this book is about recognizing truths that I have learned in my life. One truth is that you don't throw the baby out with the bath water.

Otherwise this is like saying that only one type of bird is special, or only one religion or one race is special. This is not what I am here to share with you.

We must use our spiritual gifts to help ourselves and others, or we start to lose them. So when you share what you receive from spirit, do not say more or less than what you are told. Do not lie or embellish either. Simply state what you are receiving, then leave it up to the listener to determine if that is accurate in their life.

When you believe that the illness or pain that you have experienced in life is an important part of your life, then you can learn from it. Then you can learn how to live without it. Then you can examine what lessons you learned from it. The energy to heal yourself always comes from within you. It is supported by the energies available from the Universe.

## Being Born Again and Again and Again

Why do we get sick in the first place? Why do good people have horrible diseases? What sense does that make? Why? We look at the lives they have led and the thoughts they have had and usually can find no reason for an illness to attack, and sometimes triumph over, them. In western Judeo-Christian culture we are encouraged to think that you have only one life which is the be all and end all for our souls. This could not be further from the truth. In fact, Jesus came from a people called the Essenes (through his mother Mary's bloodline) who taught and believed in reincarnation. They understood that there is a reason that things happen. The Christian philosophy is that bad things happen to people morally, spiritually, emotionally and physically because we are all "sinners" and somehow deserve it. When horrific things happen to innocent people we are told by priests and ministers that "It is all God's plan." What? It is God's plan to kill innocent children or kind old people just because? What kind of plan is that?

When we look at the pain and brutality of the illness on the victim and family, it seems too horrible to believe. But if we look at that life as just one life in a string of hundreds of lives and see that the soul of that person could gain greater compassion, empathy, knowledge and wisdom from experiencing the illness and the effect, then at least we have some small explanation and partial understanding for why the illness occurred.

Life is all about balance and opposites. Illness strikes people who are good or great, bad or evil. It does not care. It merely serves God and the person. It is part of their contract. It is a blessing in disguise. We are here on Earth to learn, share and grow, and to experience and understand. When we die, the truth of that and all previous lives is made clear to us.

It is through life's experiences that the lessons are learned. All of our experiences, joyous and painful, are learned and recorded by our soul. Spirit has shown me that it is written in this huge book called "Your Soul's Life", and this life is carefully woven into all the other lives and life plans that you have had. So once we have experienced it and recorded it, we are free from ever having to learn that specific lesson again.

Thinking that people or things offer some permanence, we find disappointment when those people or the power, position, money, and things, are lost. Many clients that I have worked with want a closer connection to God Energy and they want it right now. They seek connection through other people or the things they can lose. Some have killed themselves seeking it right now.

Many clients sense that they are missing something huge in their lives. They yearn for connection to something greater than themselves. But others are afraid of what their ego does not understand, so they seek to diminish this yearning with sex, drugs, alcohol, excessive exercise, excessive work and a big spoonful of denial. Do you deny what you cannot deal with? When you sense you are disconnected from something and seek it in the ways of the Earth, this is part of your natural "fight or flight" instinct. You will not find connection when you are giving in to this instinct.

To get what you need you must *"Become One with God."* To do this, you need do nothing except allow God back into your life. Turn off your brain, and minimize your ego. Stop and listen. Allow the God energy to come through you.

## Pray, Meditate, and Shut Up and Listen

I had a hard time with this. I was a Type A-workaholic who thought that I could control people and situations if I just worked hard enough. Having German blood and working for the IRS did nothing to dispel this fantasy. It is all really a big trap that your mind/ego creates. If you are so busy working on "something or someone else" then you will find that your goal will remain forever just out of your reach. In fact, it will move further away from you.

Accessing the power of God requires little study. You just need to be aware that there is a power greater than you and allow it, experience it, and enjoy it. Have some fun in your life (Go *with the flow!*).

There is power in action and words, and also in contemplation and silence. As each situation presents itself, decide which works best at that moment and then healing will result. People process healing, knowledge and growth at their own pace. There is no race here.

When we try to freeze, or silence, our brains for even a minute, then true healing can come through. This is the *"Just be"* part of the saying, *"Just be and Allow Joy into Your Life."*

This is easier said than done, but so satisfying. My whole life has been on the go, learning, growing, and just trying to keep up. I wish that I had had more time to be more developed or polished or perfect in whatever I did but I have learned that God does not care about details, just results. My whole life has been a series of events.

When I was too rushed, God slowed me down or stopped me, usually by making me sick. The way that I learned about this was that God made me sick on many occasions. I went to medical doctors and received a diagnosis and prescriptions and MRI's and x-rays and therapies and recommendations for various surgeries and therapies. This is my medical history.

## Medical Intuition

I am ready to share the truth about how medical intuition, healing and remote healing work. I make myself available for people to contact me who seek assistance in these matters. They come, we talk. I talk at length sometimes and they listen. Then they talk at length sometimes and I listen. Hopefully, they learn and I learn. Then the healing begins. Sometimes it comes through my hands, my fingers, my words, my heart, my body. Then, if they are open, they are healed. It is by my intention to help and heal, so I allow myself to be the conduit of the higher power's positive energy. A few seconds or minutes of just being and allowing will change how the rest of their life goes.

Healing can happen spiritually, mentally, emotionally and physically. Usually the hardest healing to accomplish is physical healing. The easiest is healing emotional/mental wounds. Those have the deepest scars, but when a person is ready to forgive, healing comes rapidly. Some are healed mentally and emotionally but still die from their physical illnesses. When my clients have discovered or sensed that they are not well, they start reading quasi-medical information on the internet and may diagnose themselves. Or they may go to a medical doctor and turn their whole life over to this person that they do not even know, and expect the doctor to find something wrong with them, mentally or physically. Odds are good that the doctor will find something; that is what doctors do even when there are no symptoms or apparent disease. Neither of these approaches is helpful for healing.

So some people follow the doctor's advice and get well. Some follow the advice and show no change, or even get worse. Then they may start to seek alternatives like natural medicine or a consultation with someone like me. Many people listen to what they want to hear and if they think being sick suits them, they will grab on to the illness and give it emotional support which encourages it to get worse. This happens because when we enter a medical establishment we are herded around like sheep from the consulting room to the labs and the MRI, CAT scans and x-ray rooms. They keep going until they find something. But when we switch back to ourselves, we say, "Hey! Wait a minute! I do not want to be sick! I do not want to cooperate with this illness that wants to disrupt my life! Hell no! Disease out!" When we remove anger, worry, fear and anxiety from our healing process, we are left with facts and things we believe to be facts. Then we can start to seek the true alternative and allow for healing from Universal Love Energy of God.

When I am working with a person who is ill, I pray that the illness and its causes will be revealed to me. I pray that I can recognize the God energy already inborn in that person and revive it, and I give unconditional love, encouragement and empowerment to them. When they allow it, reconnection to their higher self, to their God self, will result.

Some people accept this instantly and others are fearful, which slows healing down. Each is given the opportunity to allow and receive healing.

When I first received this gift, I learned I cannot choose who gets healed. It is not in my power. I am just the conduit of the healing energy. Knowing this keeps me humble. It also caused trouble in my personal life when friends or family would come to me and I was not able to do anything for them, not because I didn't want to, but because it is not my power to direct. I only receive and conduct the power; I don't own it.

I give everyone I see all the energy coming through from God. Some need a great deal, some very little. Most are healed or changed in many ways. Physical, mental, emotional and spiritual healing happens suddenly or for many months afterward. Sometimes it takes years for them to experience the change. I do my best work with them and then let them go.

*Radiate Love without Concern for Results*

## Why Are You Sick?

The healings are amazing and some people are healed instantly. They learned what they needed from the illness and now they are ready to move on. It can be so simple and so instantaneous that it is amazing. I think it is amazing how each person receives the exact healing they need, whether they knew this is what they needed or not. There is nothing that God does not see and respond to when asked.

I have also seen when one disease is healed but is replaced by another, six months or a year later because we have not gotten down to the root issue of the disease. Why is it needed in order for this person to learn or grow? This is the important question. Why do they choose to be sick? What do they still need to learn? The disease is not as important as the lesson it contains.

The most important part is to come to the client where they are in that moment. No pushing, demanding change or forcing healing or treatments when they are reluctant. They must consent and be comfortable.

What I have learned in my spiritual counseling could help you also:

1. I meet the client right where they are in life, without judgment or criticism, and I determine what support I can offer.
2. Everyone processes information differently and on their own timeline.
3. Don't push too hard. But don't be afraid to push when needed.
4. Do not push anyone beyond their comfort zone.
5. The briefest touch or moment can provide them with healing if they are open to receiving healing.
6. Release the need to rush or control the healing.
7. There is power in silence.
8. Radiate unconditional love and healing into every reading.
9. Radiate healing without concern for results.

One lady I worked with was fully healed of breast cancer and then got pancreatic cancer. But she was happy because she said at least her daughter would still come and see her every Sunday and help her out if she was still sick. She admitted to having been a difficult person in the past whom the daughter did not want to associate with. So she used illness as a way to trap her daughter back into her life. This is sad, but educational.

We are all human beings; in the end we die. We need to determine what it is that we are on Earth to do in this life. It seems that so much routine bullshit is allowed to happen in our lives that has nothing to do with the reasons we are here. Where is the fun? Where is the joy, happiness, and ecstasy of really allowing ourselves to feel good about our lives and what we do? We allow ourselves too few moments of silence, joy, fun and adventure.

Seek and ye shall always find that what you seek is just around the corner. Stand still and when what you seek walks around the block it will find you. Set clear intentions and boundaries, and peace, wellness, love, success, and money will find you.

Much of life is still lived at the level of the caveman. We get a little something — knowledge, a job, money, food, position, housing or other creature comforts — then we go into our little caves and bar the door to protect what we have. The richer you are the more this happens; you just have more caves but you find that you are still alone. Money and these needs are all lower chakra energies.

The place you are protecting is still being controlled by fear, anger and worry. You are getting your share before others get theirs and you have somehow justified in your own mind that that is okay. In fact, in a capitalist society it is noteworthy and honorable.

Remember, we came to serve others, not to be served. Let every rich man be servant to another person and it will increase his wealth. I have seen many times when I work with poor people that they share what little they have of their food, resources, shelter and love. Sometimes people with money want to argue over my fees. It is a crazy world.

## The Source of Illness

When we seek to determine the cause of the illness or affliction we must not look at any one section but at the body as a whole. Everything that affects one part of the body affects all of the body. When walls of defense break down it is either because of situational karma, past karmic debt, or current life events and it stems from spiritual, mental, emotional, and physical upset and abuse. A person simply loses their will to fight whatever it is anymore. They give up and lose hope and get sick.

People that would appear most likely to be sick do not get sick, and other seemingly strong people do get sick. It can be mind over matter. Your mind will gather the resources you need to carry on. Form follows function. Your body will do whatever it can to carry on and sustain life. You choose the level of life.

When you stop buying into illness and your diagnosis, and the fear that the medical establishment seeks to inject into you, then you can begin to see around the problem of the illness to the solution.

When you see that you are involved in every situation you are in, you learn you are at least 50 percent responsible for everything that happens to you, with you, or through you in your life. Then you can make reasonable choices on how to resolve those situations and circumstances.

There is a great quote by Viktor Frankl that applies here:

> *"Sometimes pain is unavoidable,*
> *But your response is what*
> *Determines how much you suffer."*

I am sure that you know some people who embraced their illness and moaned and bitched about it for the rest of their lives. Then other people, who were gravely ill, had a positive mental attitude despite the deterioration of their body and the pain they were subjected to.

That is to say that good things can come from bad. Healing can come along with the illness and pain.

Don't work at treating the illness. Recognizing it only gives it more power in your mind and body. Prevent it by keeping your attitude - your vibrational energy - so high that you cannot be attracted by the illness. Unwelcome your illness. Bless it over and over again and command it away from you. Use this affirmation or make up your own. Say, "I am healthy and strong. I am fine."

When you make peace with your enemy, whether it is a person, an illness, or a situation, you take the enemy's power away. You are not feeding it with your energy anymore. This does not mean that you ignore problems and not seek medical attention as needed.

The first thing that you need to determine is what is draining your power and energy? Because you are experiencing disturbances in your energy and that slows your body's ability to recharge its energy. Address that and you will heal. Embrace your illness and it will eventually embrace and conquer you.

It is a fact that people don't wake up one morning and say "I want to get cancer today!" or any other illness, accident or disease. We do not long to be disabled by some intruder. They sort of fall into illness after prolonged emotional neglect, self-abuse, self-rejection, self-denial, self-hatred, depression, anger, frustration. This is sometimes mixed in with emotional, mental and physical abuse. So find the cause and you are halfway to finding the solution.

I have always thought it was strange that in Western Medicine, there are many doctors for each section or organ of your body. But all of your parts are connected. What happens to one part of your body affects the rest of your body. Healers come in many forms. Try to find one that looks at your whole being - body, mind and spirit - and then ask them for help in guiding your healing.

Throughout this book I talk about not being attached to results, so do not attach your thoughts and feelings to the results of your illness or the remedies and healings that you experience. Sometimes you will get better, for now, but then again you will still die in the future. Sometimes you will die now. But you will have learned volumes about yourself, other people, the illness and what you needed to know to grow past it.

In Western society, so many people are isolated and do not feel like they are part of the whole society. Their isolation makes them unhappy; they feel unloved and alone. This hastens depression, illness, disease and death. Most people are living too much in their heads and need more time being outside. They need at least 20 minutes a day in the sun and walking in nature, for example. We all need at least 20 minutes of "me time" a day.

When I have faith in my message, then I have faith in your mission. No one can heal, help, save, rescue or change a person who does not want the gift of healing and support I offer them.

## Intuitive Scanning

I think it is amazing how each person receives the exact healing they need, whether they knew this is what they needed or not. There is nothing that God does not see and respond to when asked.

When I put my hand on your forehead (third eye), I am able to feel your energy, to go beyond the walls of protection you have constructed around yourself and to see the "you" behind the façade that you project to the world. I feel the God energy coming in the top of your head. I start moving my hand about three inches over your head and face and find old thoughts, mental issues, brain problems, eye problems, nasal issues, hearing problems, infections, or dental issues. They may be things you may have lived with for so long that you forgot they existed, or blocked them out.

I am always amazed at what information Spirit is showing me. I scan the whole body like this. Many times women have their throat area clogged. They do not say what they need to say in situations where they need share what they are thinking or feeling. They often think that they are helping or protecting someone else if they do not share what is on their minds. In reality the unsaid words become a poison to them.

Most clients want to help people. I feel enormous pressure on their shoulders like they have been carrying all the worries of the whole world on their shoulders.

Many clients have swallowed their own words and feelings and emotions for so many years that their throat and esophagus are lined with old crap. This continues down to their stomach and intestines; it causes clogging in the gallbladder/liver area as well. This includes unresolved arguments, past fights and life situations where long ago they chose to "grin and bear it"; now these situations are blocking them up. They are simply unable to absorb any more. Then they become angry at themselves for staying in situations and relationships that no longer serve them. Perhaps they were going to "change" someone or help them or heal them. This rarely works on people who like being who they are just fine and are glad to find someone who they can abuse.

Abuse can go from mild to extreme, but if the person putting up with it is afraid to talk, then the feelings and emotions have to go somewhere. So, in my experience, they are simply swallowed. The intestinal tract is lined with unspoken crap. So the first stop is the stomach, where we often sense ulcers, indigestion, acid reflux and other problems often addressed by medical doctors. Anger, fear, resentment and worry line the intestinal tract as well, leading to all sorts of disorders, and sometimes ending with colon cancer.

After this, I scan the heart chakra area. The heart is in the upper left side of the chest but presents as being more centered below the throat. Often real fatigue is present here indicating a giving up and a sense of lack. Hopelessness and disappointment are also here. I have never found anger, fear or worry in the heart region.

Often the heart will present itself as grey, cut and bloated, ill with scars, many very deep. It is a wounded heart that trudges on. I break up this old heart energy and always behind it is a healthy pink heart with a small heart of gold behind it. It is important to break up the broken heart matter and dissolve it. I direct energy specifically to that area and it acts like a laser to dissolve the energy there. This matter then leaves through the intestines. Also I scan the breasts, upper back, lungs and bronchial tubes.

This continues down stomach, liver; words caught in the throat chakra will often cause issues in the gallbladder, spleen, pancreas, and kidneys. This is where unresolved arguments, past fights and life situations where they chose to "just grin and bear it; "now these situations are blocking them up. They are simply unable to absorb anymore. Then they become angry with themselves for staying in situations and relationships that no longer serve them. Perhaps they were going to "change" someone or help them or heal them. This rarely works for people who like being who they are just fine and are glad to find someone who they can abuse.

Much emotion like anger, anxiety and frustration are often hidden in the organs in this area. I direct energy into that area and try to break it up if they are ready to release these energies. Half of my clients have already manifested liver, intestinal, gallbladder and blood sugar disorders because of the emotions that are clogging their vital organs. What is really cool is that even if an organ has been removed, it still radiates its energy on the system. Then I detect how the intestines and colon are functioning – looking for any energy imbalance.

I continue down to the sex organs. If there is energy left from the present life or past lives of abuse, mistreatment, anger, and resentments, it is sure to be found here. In a female, we can determine how many babies she will have or has had, and how many miscarriages and abortions also show up.

In a woman I scan the ovaries, vagina, and uterus, and in a man the prostate and testes and bladder. When I am in the area, I also pick up hip problems and lower back issues.

Depending on what I find from a frontal scan I may also scan the back. The front is your current life and your future, and the back is your past in this life and the past for your soul. Many times on a back scan I will point to a place and ask if the client has a scar, birthmark, mole or large freckle right here. This usually indicates where they have suffered some physical trauma in the past. It may have been unresolved karmically so it is also affecting the current body. Usually this is from past life traumas such as being stabbed with a knife or shot. This especially applies to neck/shoulder, spine and lower back problems and hip problems.

I scan the arms, hands and legs and look for any disorders. Often twisted ankles, broken legs, etc. will all appear at this exam. Some may have happened over 50 years ago. Often clients will call me the next day and tell me how I was right, that they had forgotten about various physical ailments and healed bones because they happened so long ago, or that they had simply learned to live with the affliction.

Some clients have foot problems like cold feet, ankle pain, arch problems, bone spurs and knee problems. This frequently occurs when they are "too much in their head or spiritually connected." This means that they are not supplying sufficient energy to the bottom of their body so that it can function well. I instruct the client on how to drag their energy back down and tuck it under their feet. Then I rebalance them and tell them how the energy circuit works. It always travels down the right side, grounds into the earth with both feet then up the other foot and then back up the left side their head it makes the spiritual energy connection. Round and round it goes.

After I have scanned the whole body, then I go back and target certain areas where disturbances were found or energy imbalances caused my hand to tremble. Sometimes I can see inside with my closed eyes and actually address the ailment and ask why it is there. Usually the answer comes from some emotional issue in the present or in prior lives. It is important to locate and present this information and ask if they want it removed to speed healing. I always ask my client's permission to remove the energy imbalance.

In the scan we sometimes find negative energy that can be scary. This is when a person allows their own anger, worry and fear to be fully present in their life at high and unhealthy levels. This can also represent unworthiness, low self-esteem, and low self-confidence. We all need these emotions but not when we allow them to control us. These can become your own personal demons. Other negative energies may also be located at this time. They are removed with permission, as well.

I have to be very careful not to plant or encourage the growth of illness that may already be stuck in certain places in the physical body. Many people love to focus on illness and then make it their own disease. You may have cancer but you should not identify it as "my cancer". Reject it as a foreign and offensive stranger. Faith, confidence and good intention will bring healing. Fear and a scary diagnosis will just bring more illness. I offer hope, compassion and understanding. I believe, and have been shown, that if a person is given a medical diagnosis, or even words to that effect by a spiritual reader, it is like giving the body permission to allow the disease to flourish if it is truly present.

Finally, I direct intense energy into the person through the palms of my hands — sometimes for minutes, sometimes for hours — praying all along that they be healed on all levels. I am told it is very electrifying and intense and lets them be at peace and relaxed beyond what they have known before. It also allows them a moment to make that energy reconnection with God.

When I am through, I scan them again and make sure all the energy is clear, flowing in from the top of their head and exiting out their feet. I explain how to stay grounded. It is like an electrical circuit, or a big circle of energy, being picked up from the air and down your right side, some exiting into the earth and then picking up the grounding and balance that they need as it continues up their left side, and again to the brain, either pulling in new energy, or allowing old energy that is no longer needed to exit.

This cycle of energy keeps you alive and allows your body to be constantly refreshed. It allows healing and happiness to flow through your veins allowing for peace and joy in your life.

One of the best methods for healing is to evaluate your own life and the actions you have taken for and against yourself and others. Did you love yourself? Ever? Do you always, or just sometimes? Then assess the impact those actions have had on you. Did your actions hurt or help you? Did they provide you with experiences that allowed you to better understand and love your fellow man? Then you must decide if you want to go through those same experiences over and over again, or if you have learned everything that you need to know from them.

Depending on what I find, or do not find, in the scan we may do the Disconnecting Cords Procedure, which I briefly mentioned earlier. This allows you to peacefully settle old relationships and old karma. This can be as simple as you want to make it. Basically, you think of people who have used or abused you and whose presence in your life is no longer good for you. This can be your spouse, lover, family, friends, neighbors or business associates.

# CHAPTER 10

## *Have a Relationship with Yourself First*

*"Energy is everything and that's all there is to it.
Match the frequency of the reality you want
and you cannot help but get that reality.
It can be no other way. This is not philosophy, this is physics."*
*–Albert Einstein*

The theme of this book is that you should *Love Yourself First, Best and Always,* which is easier said than done. In this chapter, we will be looking at how you can do this. We will be looking at what makes you – you. How you're different from other people and what you have in common with other people. You were born preprogrammed by genetics and God into your life. Then you were influenced by the people around you, where you lived, their economic status, their religion, their culture and customs. You were told what to do and what not to do. What to think and how to feel. This all created your persona - that public image of yourself you show to the world.

Still, even with all that, you were already a complete "you" before you were born. Your spirit/soul existed before you came into your body on Earth and it will exist after you leave your body here on Earth. It is very easy to become disconnected from who we were and very difficult at first to remember who you are.

You may have forgotten where you came from; it is like God wipes clear our memories so we can start life fresh. But you are still aware of other senses that you still have connections to. You get gut feelings, and "sense" when something is wrong with a situation or a person you are around. You know stuff that you would otherwise have no way of knowing. It is difficult to blend these - the spirit/soul part of you with your body (mind/ego).

You need to figure out who you currently are, and how you got that way, before you can have a relationship with yourself. That is done by evaluating everything you are doing and thinking in your life, and seeing if it is helping you make emotional and spiritual growth and progress or if it is hurting your growth.

We are each like our own television station. We are sending out a signal that other people can pick up ("your vibe"). When you pick up signals from a Russian-speaking channel but do not understand Russian, you can watch the picture but not understand what they are saying. You can, however, discern the energy that the actors have by the tone of their words and the looks on their faces. You may not be aware of it, but you are picking up their vibrational frequency.

Basically it means that when you are connected to something you are passionate about, let's say your passion or your mission, then you are producing energy different from what you were producing before. This is your vibrational frequency for that activity. You may like to take walks, create things, or read, and that pleases you, so everything associated with that will raise your vibration when you focus on it. The excitement of anticipating it will get you ready for the activity. You will feel good doing what you love to do. When you are doing what you love to do, you will feel good about yourself and your circumstances, at least in that moment.

When you are able to do an activity with another person, perhaps playing pool for example, and the other person is delighted to be play-ing pool also, then you have clear energy of a certain vibration. Both of your energies are attracted to that thing you are passionate about. You may also be attracted to the energy the other person is broadcasting that day.

Each of us has one primary signal – our own. For example, we can call mine Radio Richard at 105.7 FM. Under my frequency there are many sub-frequencies. I am a man and that is a frequency; I was a government agent, I was a tax collector, I am a psychic medium, a son, a husband, a father and a friend. Each of these roles or activities is generating a vibrational frequency. They are all just attributes of the range that is within my 105.7 primary frequency. One might be 105.71a, another 105.72b, and so on. They can all be classified and analyzed. The best friendships and relationships are those that have matching as well as opposite frequencies.

Your overall signal can be very weak or very strong, depending on many things. This includes what your situation in life is, how you feel about your situation, life issues in general and the people in your life in particular. When you seek something to do, something to love and something to hope for, you are paving the way for a new tomorrow. The fact that you are focused on your passion/mission instead of your own wants and needs in life is a sign that you are starting to *Love Yourself First, Best and Always.*

This higher frequency within you attracts more approving thoughts and feelings, first towards yourself and then to others around you.

You have to go through all your old thoughts, beliefs, feelings and emotions to determine what still meets the vibration that you want to become. Then you can use the Disconnection of Cords Procedure to release those things that you no longer need or want in your life.

You have to try to know yourself, understand yourself, trust yourself, and be compassionate with yourself (love). This is usually a process that can take some time, but you will grow lighter and lighter as you continue through the process.

Your good feelings about yourself will generate a new and improved signal. When you do not care about what people think who seek to define you, limit you and judge you, then you will rise even higher in frequency level. When you stop caring if people will like you or not, whether they will find you attractive or want to be your friend, lover or partner, then you have opened the garden gate to your ability to attract the partner that you may desire in your life.

This is when kindred spirits and like-minded people are attracted to you. This is when your new life begins because other people will be attracted to the vibration you put out, whether it is playing a game of pool, doing your work, working on a project or helping others. It is so easy and, yet, so hard because the world is busy trying to define who you are, what your skills and education will be, and what you can and cannot do.

Many people are searching for acceptance, understanding, warmth, support, emotional connection, and sensual/sexual connection. They may have found some of these qualities with some relationships and friendships, but rarely will they find all they desire in any one person. Some people do not wish hard enough for the best person to walk their path of life with them. Old thinking causes them to settle for less than everything they want in a relationship.

When you send out a new, positive frequency, you will be able to attract a whole new life. Let's be clear; even if you are moving ahead, each new level brings with it new situations, new problems, new pains, new opportunities and new joy. The Universe is set up so that we are always in motion. There is no standing still or hiding out in your castle and just watching the rest of the world change around you. That is living in a prison of your own creation, self-sentenced by fear, worry, uncertainty and anger.

This vibrational energy can increase or decrease in various areas during your life. You may have loved some activity at first and then gotten tired of it. Now, you just like it. You are always emitting a vibration with your thoughts, ideas, dreams and desires. This vibration can be also brought about by negative thoughts, feelings and activities. Most people who lead frustrated, depressed lives are operating at a lower energy vibration. If they *"go with the flow,"* (*Let Go and Let God*) they can emit a charm, beauty and glow that other people can perceive.

I do not believe that, short of Divine Intervention, you can learn about love without having first experienced love. By love, I am describing compassion, acceptance, nurturing, understanding, and warmth, plus all the regular expected necessities of life, like food, housing, clothing. You learn about love from being loved by someone else first. Sometimes people do not experience this love; some parents or others who did not receive it themselves really don't have a clue as to how to give it to their own child. It is sad. Some parents "over-love"; this means to smother their child with so much love and advantages that the child does not benefit, because it is deprived of events in its life that would serve as valuable lessons. There is a middle ground between both of these places.

A child who is loved will feel free to explore the people in their lives without fear and worry. Such a child will radiate love to those around them and the whole world. Their eyes will glow with love.

Since kindergarten we have been taught how to love others first and take care of ourselves second. We do not love ourselves first and that is why the world is the way it is. I'm not speaking of loving yourself in a selfish, greedy, narcissistic way. When we recognize the gifts we bring to the table while being taught to recognize that society has greater gifts, then that knowledge allows us to connect with the energies that will guide and support us.

## To Find Love, Look in the Mirror

People who do not receive this love must work harder to first learn about it and then allow it into their lives. When you don't feel good about yourself, or when you don't care for yourself or love yourself, you are sending out a signal to others who feel the same way about themselves. They are attracted to you because at least two confused, incomplete people are not as lonely as one.

If you are so starved for love that when anyone pays you a little attention, you fall madly in love with them, this is inappropriate. It is not good for you to accept and eat the first thing that comes along for you, as a starving person would do. However, this is usually great if you want to learn hard lessons quickly. Giving your love away to a person can seem magical, but can quickly exhaust you if you have to spend so much time and energy feeding the flames of the fire.

If you could just be patient for a little while longer, God has so much more in store for you. I want you to be able to look in the mirror every day, look into your own eyes and say *I love you*.

Consider this; if you are needy and feel incomplete within yourself, and knowing that "like attracts like," why would you want to attract another person like yourself? How can you give your partner love, nurturing and acceptance if you don't already feel that within yourself?

## Relationships with Family

Some relationships you can choose, some you are born into. Now you ask - how does this apply to my family? I can only say that families are all selected by you and approved by God and you, before you even come to Earth. To this you might ask, how can this be? I have poor or even horrible memories of growing up with my parents and family. Why would I ever choose them?

And then I would tell you that it is a combination of past life karma set up so that you can learn and grow from the life you were born into. Family is always chosen to benefit you, although you or they may get hurt in the process. Some family members treat each other wickedly; relationships in families can be passive-aggressive, mean and nasty, or loving, or calculating and manipulative. Family connections are always important, simply because you have the same blood in you. You may also have legal and moral obligations to your family and sometimes you may dislike, or even hate, them.

## Negative Past Life Relationships

Relationships I identify as **negative past life connections** are very common in family situations. This means that in a prior life, you had a connection with a person and it did not end well. Perhaps you killed or stole from the other person. This created a karmic relationship. God reconnects you together life after life until you resolve your old issues and come to love and bless the other person and leave them in peace. This happens in family, work and romantic/physical relationships. Sometimes people will come into your life and be host to mental issues like depression, or have psychopathic or even sociopathic tendencies mixed in with too many legal or illegal drugs and alcohol. It is trouble for all involved. (See Appendix for more information).

God has reconnected the two of you to give you both the chance to get back to each other and resolve old karmic issues. Then you can leave one another in peace, or build a new life in harmony. In romantic relations your amazing relationship can start to turn bad within 4-6 months. All the good things start to turn out to be bad and drive you crazy. You see their insecurities and fears as annoying and troublesome. You see their questions about what you have been doing or thinking about as intrusive, controlling and manipulative. At some point you begin to view them as a pain in the neck, creepy, scary and unworthy of your time. The feelings of possessiveness, jealousy and craziness also start to show up and they become critical, sarcastic, and unpleasant. Many people try to stay in the relationship for the sex, but that will fade as well. Sex at its lowest level can also be about power, manipulation and control. But the sexual rewards are not worth the pain of the spiritual/mental and emotional reconnections.

We cover romantic/physical relations in depth in the next chapter. But it is much more difficult when you encounter such people in your family.

## Changing Family and Friend Relationships

It can be very difficult to be in a family that you do not like or get along with. In order to survive, you need to know that they still have things to teach you. You will both learn from your interactions with each other. When you have identified the behaviors of the other person that you need to learn, then you can do so and move on. The Disconnection of Cords Procedure is one method to use with friends and family.

Another method is what I call "nonattachment." This is used when your life gets really stressed and there is nothing that you can do to get out of it. Children may try to run away from home, but that is not usually a viable solution. I learned this from my daughter Jessica when she was a toddler; she had a firm resolve to do things that may have not been good for her. So I, the parent, had to step in to stop and protect her. This usually involved many tears on her part and much stress and frustration on my part. It was very hard for us both. Then, as I marched off to a separate part of the house to recharge and feeling my blood pressure rise, about five minutes after our episode she would be talking or singing or playing with a friend. She went through the experience and then just like that Disney movie "Frozen" – she was able to "let it go." That is when I figured out how to still be the parent in charge if I pretended I was an actor going on stage to play the role of the disciplining father. I too was able to do what I needed to do to protect her, but not carry the stress for the rest of the day. It can work in any situation.

When your parent or sibling still has a strong role in your life, then you may have the issue of that relationship being stuck in the past. It can be unpleasant or even ugly. What I advise clients to do is to determine what the current status of the relationship is, and then change it to one that is more appropriate. To explain this, I talk about the stages of relationships. When you were a baby you had a parent-child relationship with each parent. It was helpful and appropriate to you. But as you grew up and became an adult, you had different needs and that old relationship may embarrass or anger you. You need to change the relationship to adult-adult.

This is the kind of relationship that two consenting adults would have, perhaps as friends or work associates. You know that friendships can end based on the bad behavior of either friend, but in families that is often harder to do. It stops needless emotional pain when you are allowed to view your parent as another adult with all their good and bad features. Then in time, they may be able to see you as you really are now, as an adult.

The same thing also applies to a brother or sister, growing up the sibling-child relationships to adult-adult. In order to do this, you should accept the other person with love and then let them go. That is what the Disconnection of Cords Procedure does. It allows you to say good-bye to the past relationship and leave the door open for a new, more appropriate relationship.

Another method that some adult children use to change their relationship is to write a note to each parent and thank them for creating you, birthing you, feeding you, protecting you and then letting you go. You can write this in a card and then give it to them or, if they are deceased, burn it.

Even in a family, you may have relationships that are not healthy and hurt you. You can love those people eternally, but cannot stand to be in the same room with them. You might find energy vampires as relatives; these are people who will use your energy to recharge their own energy. They will deplete you and move on. Start every new friendship and relationship (especially with family) with the knowledge that you cannot change, save, perfect, heal or modify the behavior of any other person without feeding it with your own energy. God will not fuel you with energy to feed your own self-destruction. You can, however, be supportive, helpful, loving, sympathetic, adoring, compassionate, and willing to support any positive attitudes or changes that your friend/relationship desires.

No one will be able to change any behavior – quit smoking, gambling, drinking, drugs, cheating on you or anything else – just because you want them to do it. They must want to do it themselves or the odds are high that they will either relapse into the old behavior or resent you forever for making them do something they did not want.

When you begin to see people as they really are and not who you wish them to be, your life becomes much easier. Sometimes the hardest part is being able to release your past with another person.

If you have children, understand that you will always have a family relationship, and that you will always be the mother or father to them. That connection never goes away. Hopefully, the dissolution of the intimate relationship can be handled with compassion, forgiveness and respect.

When you are doing what you came here on Earth to do, you will get what you need to survive and thrive.

When you embrace the principal to *Just Be and Allow God to Work in Your Life,* many new opportunities, both physical and karmic, will come to you. When you open up to the Universal Energy it will empower you for the rest of your life.

Every human being requires connections to at least one other person - someone who will respect them, advise them, guide them and make them feel that they belong on Earth. If you are lucky you get that from your mother at birth. But for too many people this feeling wears off. They become like corks floating in a wild ocean of life. They are disconnected and feel lost, alone and lonely. So instead of seeking a great connection and understanding with themselves, they seek connection with the "perfect man or woman" who they believe will give them great sex, love, family and life circumstances.

That never works because, really, who would want to be with a person who feels this way about themselves? The veneer always wears off and they find themselves feeling empty and alone again. Never look for love, acceptance and support from another if you cannot first find it in yourself. Reach out to God and know that the love energy never left you. You had it the whole time. You just forgot.

When we allow people, places and events in our lives that do not nourish our bodies and emotions, and do not make us feel loved, cherished, accepted and adored, we must decide how long we need to stay in those relationships to learn whatever we need to learn. If we stay too long, we begin to believe the thoughts and opinions of others who do not have our best interests at heart.

Most people have already forgotten who they were in soul form. They were born and then suffer a lack of communication with their own self/spirit/soul. It is just too much. It is harmful to them. You can read self-help books until the cows come home, but until you raise your vibrational energy you can expect more of the same. You will always fail because you are coming from a place of want and need because you do not believe in "*you*" the way God believes in you.

So what do you do when you find yourself in a relationship that is growing, but drives you crazy sometimes? A relationship can feed you emotionally but also sometimes drain you. You could get mad and attack everything you do not like about your family member, friend or partner, but that usually does not change them. When you maintain who you are, your inner peace, your goals, work and mission, then you can say what you need to say. Do not scream out in anger or frustration what you wish you could say. Keep control over your tongue, your actions will follow. When you focus on the many good things happening in your life - your work and your mission - small impurities will not disrupt your relationship. As you appreciate what is good you will seek to speak up about what you think needs work. Seek a counselor if you have reached a road block. Respect the differences that people in your life bring to the table. Life would be boring if everyone was just like you. All the energy in the Universe has its opposite; otherwise life and relationships would be boring and tepid.

You should not expect others to provide joy and ecstasy to "light your fire" and make your life amazing, filled with growth, learning opportunities and joy. But you can expect that for yourself. What can you do to recognize how amazing you are so that you can love yourself?

Stop looking outside yourself for happiness. *Love Yourself First,*

*Best and Always*, then recognize that God already loves you as you are. When you are full and complete, take your act on the road and you will be amazed to meet people who are somewhat similar but also vastly different from you.

Love people as they come into your life for as long as they are there. Do not seek to make people stay in your life longer than they are supposed to be there. When you find love, find it in each second of your connection, because nothing lasts forever.

## Listen to Your Words

Did one of your parents ever ask you that question? To show you just how rude, selfish, mean or stupid something was that you had just said? It is hard to listen to what you said when you meant to hurt another person. It is harder still to have that thought analyzed by other people who might judge you.

You need to know that the Universe regards every word, thought and feeling you have as a request or a work order. Prayer works the same way. When you turn your dreams into intentions and goals, you begin to allow them to manifest in your life. The Universe does not judge the right or wrong of your intentions. It just seeks to provide you with what you are calling out for. I have found that people who serve others or even those who serve themselves, such as being very rich or successful or good, are frequently rewarded more quickly than people who muddle through life with no dreams, no goals, and no deliberate intentions toward anything.

Your mind/ego likes to control everything you do. Relying on some unseen force like God or the Universe is incomprehensible to mind/ego. Worry, fear, guilt and unworthiness stop many projects before they ever start. I remind my clients that they have the power to make the request to the Universe and then healing and fulfilled dreams will result. Have hope, trust and faith in some positive energy higher than your own.

How you feel about yourself changes every day depending on your health, what you ate and if you had enough rest. But what is also changing is how you see yourself. Somedays you will not feel well so you will look in the mirror and not think you are amazing. That is to be expected. Do not raise the bar too quickly when you are making growth in your life.

If you believe you are worthy, so does God. But if you believe you are unworthy, this is not what God feels. He/She/They/It never gives up the hope that you remember who you really are at your soul level. Stop acting like the victim, always wounded and unsatisfied, always waiting and yearning for love to come your way, because that just brings more waiting. Enjoy each day. Find some part of each day that really turns you on. Find something about yourself each day that comforts you and something that you enjoy being around or doing.

# CHAPTER 11

## *Romantic and Physical Relationships*

Most of my clients seek a connection to another person that is sincere, meaningful and loving—one that nourishes their soul. They want the relationship of their dreams. Yet they come to me because they feel a lack of desire, or feel physical and emotional desolation. They may have money, career, positions of power, and many possessions but they are in, or have been in, unsuccessful relationships. They all seem to yearn for the perfect connection to another soul in spirit, mind, heart and body.

When you imagine that a person of your dreams has already been created and is waiting for you, then you are ready for them to appear in your life. It is almost like there is a door in your house that you have walked by thousands of times, but have never seen before. Now it is time for you to open that door and it will take you to a new level in your life.

Many movies have been made featuring women who search their whole lives for the perfect man, the most amazing lover, their soul mate, a friend, and a partner. These films are mostly fantasies, but they are very popular and sell very well. There are television shows that feature matchmakers (who mostly appear to be single) who apply their magic to finding the perfect partner for their clients. It seems like this is usually a rich man who mostly wants a sexual relationship with a woman who is half his age.

Then there are the Disney, MGM, Hallmark, and Lifetime Channel movies that offer another version of relationships and romance: a man comes to rescue a single mother, usually around Christmas. I am not saying that magic fairytale romances cannot develop into productive, long-term relationships, but it is rare for anything in life to work perfectly according to some plan you made up. When you decide what you want in friendships and relationships, and allow it to be created in your life, then you must raise your vibrational energy to match the person coming your way. Movies are great at portraying that perfect first kiss where butterflies surround you and romantic music plays in the background.

I love to watch those movies that show the woman being kissed, then clicking her heals together and having everything turn out wonderfully for the rest of her life – or at least until the end of the movie. Who wouldn't want that perpetual feeling of butterflies in the stomach? Or that tentative and growing passion and desire that comes from a new connection with another human being? Love can be lovely, but it can also be short-lived if you rely only on the love and sexual connection to sustain you years from now.

One good friend of mine whose partner had cheated on her numerous times said, as we discussed her relationship, "Maybe I don't love him anymore. I still love him as my daughter's father, but I don't think I am in love with him. I used to feel amazing just being with him. I loved him so much and then he killed my butterflies."

I have counseled many clients who have accepted relationships that they intuitively knew to be wrong for them when they entered the relationship. Many clients admit that, armed with enough love, they thought they could change or heal the person, or that the person would come around. So many times it rings in my ears when a client, usually a woman says, "But I love him!" This is unfortunate, because love alone is never enough!

Many times my client then follows it up with, "I don't want to be alone!" This even occurs in situations of infidelity, immorality, adultery, or physical, mental or sexual abuse, because the client is afraid of being alone and continues to suffer with the wrong partner.

Most of us have been in love, or what we defined as love at the time. We have had soul mates that seemed perfect for a while and later turned out to just be sexual connections filled with pain and bizarre emotional overtones.

My friend Michele Fancher shared her thoughts on this: "Sometimes we are in love with an illusion, and we delude ourselves into believing that someone is something other than what they truly are. We are, in essence, falling in love with a person who simply does not exist. It can be a deeply painful experience and we do it to ourselves."

My own personal relationships, while an excellent source of life lessons, are hardly something that would qualify me to advise anyone. Instead, I offer what I have received from my spiritual communications. I am told that when I do relationship counseling the advice I bring is accurate, profound and helpful. So I offer the following for your consideration.

## LOOKING AT YOURSELF FIRST

I counsel my clients to make a list of the 15 things they like about themselves and then the 15 things that they do not like about themselves. It is usually more difficult to come up with 15 good things about yourself! Then hang that list on the refrigerator and look at it for 30 days. Edit as needed. During that time evaluate what you can do about those things that you do not like and how you can use what you do like for your greater benefit.

My clients are also advised to make a similar list for their ideal partner. This is fun and challenging. I think that people usually hold self-limiting, unrealistic expectations. We simply are not in the habit of dreaming BIG!

Many people do not like themselves; some even hate themselves. They feel unworthy to receive love. They feel insecure. This can cause cling-on behavior as they desperately try to attract or keep a person in a friendship or relationship. Sometimes they debase themselves to do so. Some people have trust issues, abandonment issues, or, for women, Daddy issues (I have seen this so many times). When you put out unworthiness, the Universe will hear that you feel unworthy and you are concentrating on your unworthiness so it will send you people who will be unworthy of you, or not honest, or respectful. In a relationship when you lower your needs in terms of what is being offered by the other person, (if they are on a lower vibration than you) then you are not *Loving Yourself First, Best and Always.*

When you have taken inventory of yourself and others, I then ask my clients to burn the list. Forget about it. Have faith that if you are supposed to meet another person for any type of relationship, then it will happen right on schedule, when you are truly ready. Otherwise you are likely to limit your supply of both friends and partners.

No one is perfect; everyone has their own thoughts, beliefs, understandings, habits, wishes and desires. That is what makes life exciting. Otherwise, if you merge your life with a clone of yourself, that is as boring as two pancakes stacked on top of each other.

When we have faith and trust that God will bring the right person to us, it makes a great difference as to who arrives. When we actually *allow* that person into our lives, it is huge. The most important part in my experience is that the people we have attracted or chosen in the past simply were not good or not good *enough* for us. We are choosing someone while we are still in the darkness of our past. When we have been reactivated, we are in a much better place to allow what will be a positive connection in our lives.

An important question is, "Does this person have their own life, their own interests, and their own dreams?" You don't want to have to be at their beck and call all the time because it will suffocate you.

"Does this person have their own occupation and interests?" Define what you like. Do you like being with them all the time or some of the time? Boundaries help each of you to feel secure in the relationship.

Then as you become better friends, lovers and companions, you can expand your horizons.

In many relationships people lower their expectations in order to enter the relationship; then they find that they must manage their expectations about what to expect from the relationship. Then they find that they are soon attracting people who want to be in relationships where there is "no expectation." You are worth more than that. Don't fall down that slippery slope.

## To Find Love You Must First Be Loved

If you want to attract love, you must first know how it feels to be loved. A candle is no good to you if it cannot be lit. For some people this love and nurturing comes from their parents. That is also where they learn to trust another person. If you did not receive that love early in your life, then you must *Love Yourself First, Best and Always.* Because if you can't love you, how can someone else love you in a healthy way?

Many people are searching for acceptance, understanding, warmth, support, emotional connection, and sensual/sexual connection. They may have found some of these qualities with some relationships and friendships, but rarely will they find all they desire in any one person. Some people do not wish hard enough for the best person to walk their path of life with them. Old thinking causes them to settle for less than everything they want in a relationship.

## Looking for Love

If you are looking for or waiting for a partner to arrive, this chapter was written for you. Have you been looking in all the wrong places and are not finding what you seek in a relationship? Have you in the past, or are you now, settling for less than everything you want in a relationship? It's healthy to want to share your life with another person or people. It is not healthy to need another connection so badly that you sell yourself short because the person has some of what you want.

We are all born perfectly as God created us. We join the world seeking a reiteration of the love God gave us on the other side. Sadly, when we are growing up, many things happen to diminish that beauty, that knowledge that we are all connected to God. We seek God in our relationships with other people and, while we have good times and great connections, no one person can provide you with this same feeling as the "The God Connection."

Many people spend their entire lives waiting. Waiting for someone to recognize them for who they are, for someone to recognize they are different and special, and a person that will still like and accept them. Waiting for someone to recognize that they have spiritual gifts and recognize the beauty beneath the façade that they have on the outside, someone who will look past their social class or their financial standing, or someone who will see them for who they are. Often clients become impatient waiting, waiting, waiting. So they allow themselves to fall into a place of pain, and accept their life and the people or circumstances that do not help them, do not nourish them and do not provide them with love and comfort. They live like they are already dead, yet yearn for a lover's breath to come near them and awaken what has been dormant for so long.

I think we are on Earth for learning and growth, and we should not expect some perfect person to be along with us for the ride. Make progress, not perfection, your goal and, in the long run, both will be accomplished.

True love seems to come when you are busy doing other things with your time and attention.

I have spoken with many clients over the years that are waiting for Mr. Right or Ms. Right, but because they denied themselves love they often suffer many years of pain with Mr. or Ms. Wrong, or Mr. or Ms. Abusive, or Mr. or Ms. Not Quite Enough.

Do you walk around day to day waiting to be recognized? Always judging yourself? Wondering why, if you are so damn special, nobody else can figure it out? Do you want acknowledgement, a pat on the back, approval or unconditional non-sexual love? I suggest that you buy a dog. Pets can teach you a lot about love.

**Deli Order**

If you are serious about attracting someone special into your life, you can remember the example of a person going into a deli and ordering a sandwich. They order everything they want, never mentioning what they do not want. Then they have faith and confidence that after a wait while it is being prepared they will receive their lunch. This is the same for telling the Universe what you want in life - after you have made your "deli order," then just release it to the Universe. Let it go from your mind - a watched pot never boils. Then go do what you enjoy doing. Perhaps your future friend or partner will also be doing that same activity and you will meet there. One thing is sure, if you never leave your house, you have very poor odds of ever finding a relationship.

This does not mean to downplay the importance of social media, especially Facebook. It gives many people the opportunity to safely share their innermost feelings with a member of the opposite sex without any physical or sexual connection implied.

Often, if you can extract yourself or reformulate the situation that you're in, because you are learning to respect yourself, love yourself, and are cultivating the desire to get closer to higher energy than you currently have around you, then you have begun the climb to reconnect with your spirit/soul. You will attract like-minded people as you nurture the higher energy.

**Evaluating and Receiving a Friend and Partner**

You will find that if someone does not want to raise their energy you cannot do it for them for very long. It depletes you even with the Universal Energy access that you enjoy. Otherwise, the energy vampires will use you up, deplete and depress you.

Many people pass up the opportunities of their lives because the people that they meet are not as the entertainment media told them a loved one should look. They may not be pretty enough, not sexy enough, not thin enough; they are bald, or too hairy. Looking at the body is poor criteria for who that person is. When you look at a person's eyes you can see into their soul and, if they are open to you, you will know it.

People pass over potential partners who are attracted to them, because they do not have money, education, good jobs, or assets. Even worse, they block a relationship because the partner does not meet some obligation that they are told they must fulfill in the relationship. This might be marrying within their own religion, race, nationality, or of similar, or even opposite, sexual orientation.

If you are looking for a man or woman to complete you, save you, rescue you, or in some other way make you feel valid and whole, then stop reading; I cannot help you. This is never the way to move from an attraction into a successful long term relationship. You are already complete, exactly as God made you. You are already perfect. Perhaps you may think you are perfect in your imperfections. No matter.

The only person that you are responsible for is you, and the only person your potential partner is responsible for is themselves. Start doing what you can with what you have where you are. Develop yourself, improve yourself. Love yourself. If you do not recognize the beauty within you, how can you expect someone else to recognize it? Sometimes the only way to change others is to make a change in yourself first, and you cannot help others until you help yourself first.

In *War and Peace*, written by Tolstoy, a heavily pregnant character tells her husband that he cannot love her now because she is so unattractive. He says that is ridiculous. "It isn't beauty that endures, it's love that lets us see beauty." Relationships can be frustrating for this very reason; you are different from your partner, but love will win in the end. But love needs to be fed daily.

## What Do You Seek in a Partner, Friendship or Relationship?

Is the person fun and funny? Do they enjoy whatever they are doing? Do they laugh? Do they talk to you about anything and everything? Are you able to discuss, argue and fight with them in a respectful manner? Do they value something? You do not need to value the same things; it is the valuing that is important. Do you feel like sitting next to them on the couch after a great meal and reading together or watching a movie? You do not need to touch because the energy between you is so strong people will actually comment on it. The silence between you is a sign of the strength of the relationship. Do they have their work and their mission, their passion in life figured out? Are they available and willing to support you spiritually, mentally, emotionally and physically? Is there growth potential for this relationship without you having to heal, repair, fix or change the other person? You see, there are so many factors to dream about.

You goal is to seek a person who will love you unconditionally, facilitate your spiritual and emotional development, and compliment your energy as you compliment their energy.

## Is Sex Love?

Sex can be fun, but sexual intimacy is amazing and builds on itself. Many people have experienced sex, some in great abundance, but have not necessarily found happiness or even fulfillment. Sex without emotion is usually about power, control and manipulation. In your heart you know that sex should be spiritual, mental and emotional, in addition to the physical connection. Many people are so desperate for love that they send out the emotions and vibrations of need and want. This does not serve their best interest. If they would simply be open to attracting a partner from the crown chakra down, great things would happen and much sooner. There is a saying, "Man Plans, and God Laughs." If you look back at your life and realize that your best laid plans have often led you astray in the area of sex, then I'm sure you will agree that it is difficult, but essential, to begin operating from the crown chakra.

*"Sexual love makes of the other person an Object of appetite," said German philosopher Immanuel Kant in 1780. "After the act has been done," he continued, "the loved one is cast away like a lemon which has been sucked dry."*

Marilyn Monroe said that *"sex is the opposite of love."* When we look at sex on these terms, this is really separating what may be happening in a person's life versus what would make them feel good sexually and emotionally in that aspect of their life.

## RECEIVING A FRIEND/PARTNER

### Soul Mates

Many people talk about soul mates and twin flames. These are people who are kindred spirits to you. They are your best supporters and advisors, and they will bring you many lessons. The people who hurt you the most in this life are the people that love you the most on the other side (in Heaven). They are also soul mates. They love you enough to come and create difficulties and mess up your life so that you will learn some lessons you need to learn. Please read that again. *The people who hurt you the most in this life are the people that love you the most on the other side.*

Twin flames, or twin souls, are what some describe as the other half of your soul that you were split from. This is confusing to me. Spirit has shown that you can also have many twin souls because your soul is your Master Self and it is incarnating in dozens, or hundreds, of bodies all at the same time. This life you are in right now is just one of the lives. This has also happened in your past lives. You actually have an unlimited number of soul mates and twin flames.

According to the book *Soul Mates & Twin Flames* by Elizabeth Clare Prophet, "Soul mates are not necessarily a romantic partner. Soul mates can be anyone who comes into our life to help us learn our soul lessons whether it be our mother, father, brother, sister, children, a friend, a teacher, etc. However, twin flames are also known as twin souls, souls that were created together that are two halves of a divine whole. One of the twin flames is of the masculine polarity and the other is of the feminine polarity. This does not refer to the actual sex that they are in this life." When you have a connection with a soul mate or twin soul it will affect your life in many ways. The part that I have gotten that is different from common thinking is that your Master Soul has been in many incarnations. These attributes, or threads, of it match the threads of people who come into your life.

To reunite with the full soul self would cause you to die. You would lose interest in life as you knew it because the desire to reconnect on all levels would destroy you. That is why my experience with twin soul relationships showed me that they are very intense, life changing, move very quickly and then they are over.

## EVALUATE YOUR RELATIONSHIP

Never settle for less than everything that you want in a relationship. At the same time, do not paint yourself into a corner with a list of demands and characteristics that make it hard even for God to provide the person you are ordering. Believe me, none of us are perfect.

You may think that you have found completeness, so then you have sex or become friends and you think this is so great – for the first six months. Then you begin to not feel good about yourself, or care for yourself or love yourself, except now there is another person just like you in the room. Then you really start to feel empty and alone. You feel anger and, eventually, hatred for the other person.

# RELATIONSHIP STRESSES - ABUSE/PERSONALITY DISORDERS/NEGATIVE PAST LIFE

## Past Abuse

Many people carry around memories of past sexual abuse. The person who has committed the abuse has moved past it, but the victim cannot. The victim still feels powerless day after day. It is as if the abuse just happened, and is continuing to happen. It can ruin their life, relationships, friendships and intimate connections with their partner. When they are offered the chance to disconnect from people who have used and abused them, they finally feel empowered to stand up and say, "I am not going to take it anymore. I am strong, I am powerful and no one says or does anything to me or touches me without my consent." It does not matter if the abuser was ever punished for what they did. What matters is that the scar they left on your spirit can now be erased simply by forgiving them and turning them over to God. I have counseled people who have had years of therapy and they are still not able to release the abuser. My method gives them the power to do so.

I have worked many cases where a client is still suffering emotional and mental damage from various abuses committed on them in childhood or their teen years. When a person wants to date, or be in a relationship with a person who has been sexually or otherwise abused, everything must be done slowly. Your partner may have already been touched, used, abused and disrespected. They don't need that coming from you. Your partner has been waiting a very long time for someone to love them unconditionally. They have been waiting for a person who will be honest, supportive, patient and understanding of what they have experienced. When you first make connections with your partner, seek to go to the highest spiritual place you can go. Then connect, make the great mental and emotional connections. If you really want a real relationship, it might seem like you are being tested every day. You may feel angry and like you are about to explode. Your partner would expect that from you, and then you would be frustrated and go away. This is what your abused partner would consider to be normal behavior. But if you *radiate love without concern for results,* without some timetable as to when you have sex or a relationship or whatever, then you will have the greatest friend you could ever imagine. This is not easy. Your partner is not like a candy machine; they are worth more than some "hit it and quit it affair." If you are meant to be together it will all come in due time. Patience is its own reward.

## Abuse in the Present

Catering to people who abuse you usually does not work. The abuse gets progressively worse and worse. It can grow from emotional abuse to sexual abuse to physical abuse. Abuse grows on abuse. Standing up to your abuser or even suggesting counseling can also get you hurt. Sometimes the only answer is to build your own castle walls higher and do your homework about jobs, income sources and social services that can guide and protect you. Every abuser needs a person to abuse, so if you and the kids are out of the picture, they will find another person who is sending out that energy vibration asking to be abused. I suggest that the best time to leave your abuser is the day before he or she physically harms or kills you.

Abuse is part of your past; you don't need any abuse in your future. Abuse breeds more abuse. It does not matter if it was spiritual, mental, emotional, physical or sexual. Many people carry around memories of sexual abuse from 20, 30 or 40 years ago. When you decide to do the Disconnecting Cords Procedure, you are standing up for yourself, taking control of the situation and saying "no more - go away from me forever." Whether the person was ever punished or not for the deeds that they did against you, it does not matter. What matters is that you are now in the power/control position and you are choosing to have mercy on them. You may find that if the abuser cannot be punished, you end up punishing yourself. By packing this all up and turning it over to God, we must have faith that God will take care of it. Whether God judges or punishes or hits them with a lightning bolt, or grants them mercy, that is not important and that is not your business. It is the releasing of your negative feelings, and the harm and suffering, that will free you and offer the promise of a new life.

## Negative Past Life Relationships

Relationships that I identify as ***negative past life connections*** are usually with people who are sociopaths, psychotic or narcissistic. In many relationships, oftentimes it appears that everything is amazing and perfect in the first four to six months. The two of you are so very much in synch, in love and however else you describe a relationship that makes you feel wonderful. The other person tells you how much you have in common, how amazing you are, how beautiful, how smart, how sensitive, how you share the same strengths and weaknesses, and how they have waited forever to meet you. You are both glowing and the emotional, mental and physical/sexual connections could not be stronger or better. You are sure that your relationship is meant to be, ordained by God and karmic fate — that is, at least for those first four to six months.

God has reconnected the two of you to give you both the chance to get back to each other and resolve old karmic issues. Then you can leave one another in peace; or build a new life in harmony. Usually, in the seventh month, all the good things start to turn bad. You see their insecurities and fears as annoying and troublesome. You see their questions about what you have been doing or thinking about as intrusive, controlling and manipulative. At some point, you begin to view them as a pain in the neck, creepy, scary and unworthy of your time. The feelings of possessiveness, jealousy and craziness also start to show up and they become critical, sarcastic, and unpleasant. Many people try to stay in the relationship for the sex, but that will fade as well. The sexual rewards are not worth the pain of the loss of spiritual/ mental and emotional reconnections.

## When a Relationship Produces Children

When a relationship produces children, whether or not the couple stays together, it must be clear that each parent forever remains a father or mother to the children their union produced. There is always a family, and divorce or disharmony does not take that away. The looks and habits of both of the parents, as well as grandparents and other relatives, are sure to turn up as the children grow older, serving as a reminder of the relationship. Attachment and partnership combined with respect and understanding can make this family unit work even if the parents do not live together. Just because you may not be having sex with your former partner, the father or mother of your children, it does not take away your responsibility to provide some stability to your children's lives. Otherwise, you are being very selfish and damaging to the children. Love has nothing to do with it. Of course, you also have legal, financial and moral obligations that you must take care of.

## Evaluating Where Your Relationship is Now

We have come to a place where a client can look at their present relationship and decide if it is still the right thing for them. Some people will no longer feel fully attached to their marriage or relationship, at least on whatever the original terms of it were. They just don't share the same spark anymore. They don't have the same magic they once had. They still "love" the other person but are not in love with them. Often clients will tell me all the good things about their partner – the person is attractive, has a good career and income, they'll talk about what a great parent they are — but they do not want to be in the relationship anymore. I counsel them to determine exactly what it is they are lacking and then seek to renegotiate their arrangement. They have invested so much time into their partner that maybe increased communication, work changes or other changes will light a new fire beneath their relationship. Many people have the idea that the "grass is always greener on the other side of the fence" until they are on the other side. Then they feel angry, resentful, empty and alone.

Sometimes they can negotiate within the arrangement to try different life pursuits, define new missions, or try new sex habits. They do not want to disappoint or hurt their partner, or any children, but usually the longer they stay working under the old rules the worse things become.

When they decide, through self-examination, that settling for some parts of the relationship is not good for them, and have tried to do everything that they could to redesign and renegotiate the terms of their relationship, then they must decide if staying in that relationship is *Loving Themselves First, Best and Always.*

Sometimes they can continue in the relationship if they are more involved in a career or their mission in life, or if the emotional/physical part of the relationship is not as important to them as it was when they were younger. It all comes down to talking, understanding and re-negotiating their relationship with their partner. A relationship is a constantly changing thing. No one is the same person they were 30 years ago when they first got married, and the relationship or the partner is not either. But when one is honest with themselves, then it is always good to listen to the heart.

Leaving may come with costs but there may be great benefits. Walking away is sometimes easier and many choose that. Staying and working on a strong friendship or relationship takes work but that too can yield great benefits.

How do you know when it's over? You know you are in a bad relationship when you wake up in the middle of the night and realize that being there is not about *loving yourself.* You feel drained and stupid, you feel bad about yourself, sucked dry of love and your power. Fear, anxiety, resentment and anger are what you sprinkle on your cereal in the morning. You realize that perhaps whatever you described as love is gone now.

Other signs that the relationship is over are that you are self-medicating just to get through the time you have to spend with your partner, or you are overweight, sexually frustrated, eating, drinking, and smoking too much. In later stages you will actually get physically ill because the emotions of your relationship will plant the seeds of illness in you.

Take control over those things that you allow to control you. I like this old quote "Make liquor your slave, never your master." This can also apply to drugs, food, or exercise - anything that you do in excess that controls you.

See people as they really are, and not as you wish that they were. Trust the gut feelings you have. You may listen to what your partner is saying, but your gut feelings are telling your something different. Always trust the gut feelings over another person's words.

I remember a story my Uncle Bob told me when I was growing up. It was about a snake and a mouse. The snake was caught in a trap and could not escape.

The snake asked the mouse to open the door of the trap. The mouse said "No, if I do that you will get out and eat me." The snake asked ever more sweetly and said no he would never hurt the good little mouse. The mouse sensed this was a trick. He had a gut feeling he should run away. But the snake knew he was a good mouse and appealed to him on a higher spiritual ground. He told him if he released him from the trap, he would go out and eat bad snakes and everyone in the village would benefit. The mouse opened the door to the trap. The snake came out and bit him. As he was dying, the mouse was mad at himself for not following his gut instinct which was to get away from the snake. He asked the snake how he could even think about biting him after he had saved his life and the snake said, "That's what snakes do; we bite people and eat mice, and everyone knows that." Then my uncle said "Never trust anyone in life and you will never be disappointed. Always trust your gut instincts."

## Ending a Relationship with Love

When I do relationship counseling I say that when it gets rough, one party may want to hide out for a day, go into their man cave, or on a shopping spree. Leave them to make their way alone. If you feel you don't want to talk to your partner for three days, it is time to schedule a talk about your issues. If after seven days you still do not want to be around them, it is time for someone to walk. The walk may be to a counselor, a lawyer or a new life. Each step allows you complete choice; just take care of your obligations before you go.

Coming to terms with the fact that a relationship is over is very difficult and many people delay it for years. But then they get mental, emotional and physical problems because they stay. When you have done all you can to help another person, you must surrender and let them go. It is best for both of you. Otherwise you will just end up torturing yourself and getting nowhere in life.

Trust your gut and decide to live again - to love again - and yes, even to get hurt again. Have faith in yourself and your future for even a second and it will change the rest of your life. That momentary act of faith will guide the rest of your life. Your life will instantly start to change just on your act of faith. Forgive and bless those who hurt you and turn them over to God.

I like to think of a successful relationship model as being where each person is independent and *wants* to be with a partner, but does not *need* to be with a partner. I don't know where this saying came from, but I like it: "Let us grow as trees next to each other, but do not crowd the growth of the other. In the morning my branches and leaves will shade your roots, and in the afternoon your branches and leaves will shade my roots; and the leaves and acorns that I drop will fertilize us both and we will make new life."

You should never rely on another person to provide for you what you cannot provide for yourself (or at least have attempted to provide). Romance and falling in love is fun, inspiring and a good learning tool about being intimate physically or emotionally with another person. It is only an opportunity to get ready for real long-term intimacy, the meshing of your two spirits, your minds, your hearts, and the physical/ sexual connection. Usually most people have had enough improper intimacy by the time they seek a long-term connection. Don't expect another person to provide you with what you lack; it puts a burden on them and the relationship, and over time they will get tired of it.

When you yearn to rest in the warmth of another person's soul, this is a prayer that God responds to. But don't waste a lot of time yearning! Make your intention known to the Universe and then have faith and trust that it will be delivered. Then, get going on other projects.

Wishing, hoping and praying for love is fun. When you find a person who wants to love you, it can be very hard to release and trust that person without attempting to control and direct them. The more you learn to love yourself, the better you will be able to receive the love that you desire.

Release the need to dictate every circumstance in your life. Let people come and go. Love people as they come into your life and love them if they leave. Do not seek to make people stay in your life longer that they are supposed to be there. When you find love, find it in each second of your connection, because nothing lasts forever except the love that goes out from you.

Sometimes love comes in passing, when you are making plans about what you want in your future. When you are projecting lack and unhappiness, love will pass you right by. Don't say you never meet anyone who is right for you. Perhaps you just don't recognize them when they appear because your model of the perfect friend or partner is flawed and incomplete.

I also talk to my clients about the male and female energies that they have. Some of these attributes may be male: strength, action, force, ego, and some female: compassion, nurturing, sensuality, allowing, giving, intuition and spontaneity. These are stereotypes. It is in discovering what you do not have, or do not have much of, that you will discover gifts other people can share with you. Sometimes sexual orientations come up in a reading. Sometimes clients' relationships are affected because they are sending out mixed signals about what they desire and from which sex.

To make the necessary changes in your life to include a partner, you must first give up ideas, habits and behaviors that no longer serve you. Some of these include negative thinking, self-abuse, the need to control other people, and the belief that you can fix other people. Forgive and bless people from your past and present. *Radiate love without concern for results.* You will find that you have planted a trail of seeds of love that will sprout all around you. *If only you allow it.*

It is difficult to not want a relationship with a person who may be wrong for you. It is hard if you want a person so badly that you sell yourself short. It is hard if you push away people who could love and support you. Sometimes you need the lessons that the person who is wrong for you can bring. Sometimes you are not ready to see what is best for you.

When counseling a client going through a breakup, I said, "I know it's hard. You loved him with everything you have. And it did not work out! Your fault? His fault? Who cares? It's over! Now you swear that you will never be loved again or be in another relationship. It is like that song: *No, No, No, don't mess with my heart.* The song plays over and over in your head. There is a quote about this I saw on Facebook, *When someone hurts you, cry a river – build a bridge and get over it.* (Author unknown)."

I continued, "You still want someone to come and rescue you, to appreciate you, to acknowledge you, to know the innermost parts of your being, to make love to you from the depth and breadth of their soul, but every new person who comes into your life looks just like the person who left you, who hurt you. In fact, every man or woman who has ever hurt you appears before your very eyes. No one can climb over the walls of protection that you have built to protect you. No one can pass the tests you devise. So what do you do? You can continue to hide and hurt or you can face the pain and conquer it."

**Let People Go**

When you learn to "let people go," you will learn how that is loving yourself also. The Tyler Perry character, Madea Simmons, had some extremely valuable information about this in the movie *Madea Goes to Jail*. She said, "If somebody wants to walk out of your life, let - them - go!"

> "Some people are meant to come into your life for a lifetime, some for only a season and you got to know which is which. And you're always messing up when you mix those seasonal people up with lifetime expectations.

> I put everybody that comes into my life in the category of a tree. Some people are like leaves on a tree. When the wind blows, they're over there... wind blow that way, they over here... they're unstable. When the seasons change they wither and die, they're gone. That's alright. Most people are like that; they're not there to do anything but take from the tree and give shade every now and then. That's all they can do. But don't get mad at people like that, that's who they are. That's all they were put on this earth to be. A leaf.

> Some people are like a branch on that tree. You have to be careful with those branches too, because they'll fool you. They'll make you think they're a good friend and they're real strong, but the minute you step out there on them; they'll break and leave you high and dry.

> But if you find two or three people in your life that's like the roots at the bottom of that tree, you are blessed. Those are the

kind of people that aren't going nowhere. They aren't worried about being seen; nobody has to know that they know you, they don't have to know what they're doing for you, but if those roots weren't there, that tree couldn't live.

A tree could have a hundred million branches, but it only takes a few roots down at the bottom to make sure that tree gets everything it needs. When you get some roots, hold on to them, but the rest of it... just let it go. Let folks go."

I want to add that you can also "let shit go." Whatever shit is to you. Old thoughts, situations, dramas – Let them go! If you have a lot of clothes that don't fit, or "stuff" in your house, that "stuff" is no longer needed in your life. Get rid of it.

A person who plants seeds of love and hope also knows they need time to grow. You cannot keep digging the seeds up and checking their progress, or the seed will die. You must have faith and confidence that what you have planted will bear fruit in your life. Allow the future as you dream it to unfold. You need do nothing other than dream and then allow your dreams to materialize.

*It is easy to take off your clothes and have sex; people do it all the time, but opening up your soul to someone, letting them see your tears, thoughts, fears, future, hopes and dreams – that's being naked. - Rob Bell*

The important thing to remember with relationships is not to want or need another person. Want and need are words that indicate lack. I use the example of a circle which is your life. Within your circle, you are a full and complete person able to take care of your work, your life's mission, cooking, cleaning, paying for your residence, taking care of yourself sexually, and all the other things that make you – "*you.*"

You are full and complete just as you are, but you may desire a companion or a partner to walk the path of your life with. Yet, you do not want a person to smother your spirit, either. You want a person who is also full and growing and then, just like a Venn diagram, your two circles may intersect. In the connection is your reward and the joy that this relationship brings to you.

*"The connection, if right, is so instant, so perfect, it draws you in. If it's not there, it's not there. You can't make it come; it either is or it isn't. If it's not there, don't waste time – move on to your future with someone else." Cathy Hill (A wise friend of mine)*

Allow yourself time to imagine, to dream, and wonder what this person will be like, or if you need another person on a more intimate level at all. Then just make your order with the Universe. God will usually give you all that you wish for and sometimes more, if that is your faith in this life. If you are meant to be alone in this life, it is still good, because once you *Love Yourself First, Best and Always* you will never be alone and unloved.

# CHAPTER 12

## *Disconnecting from Your Past*

Relationships are only dangerous when one person meets another person and tries to dazzle and delight, capture, confuse and control, distract and deceive, and then abuse and leave. When a person does come into your life, you need to use your natural gut feelings (intuition) to discern why they are there. Ask yourself, "Will the relationship produce good in my life, either in the short term or long term, or will it produce something bad?" Not everyone who comes into your life is good for you, but you have probably already found that out. Still, they may bring you valuable life lessons that will enrich your soul experience. Some people seek love where love is not to be found. Love cannot be found where it does not exist. There is a difference between being patient with someone and wasting your time.

In life, we all experience strong connections to other people and then we find that those connections/relationships do not help us, or no longer serve our highest good. Often those relationships were set up as ways to resolve past life connections so that you can settle old karma. You can usually tell when a past life connection has been made. Often the first time you touch that person or they touch you, you feel a shock - not a tingle, but a shock, like electricity just passed through you. Other times, when you first look into the other person's eyes you will feel like the world has stopped and it is only you and the other person, you are so captivated by them. This always indicates a negative past life connection that has come back to you to resolve.

When we speak about etheric cords, the connections that you cannot see but a gifted intuitive person can see; these are invisible connections that you have with other people. You can also be corded to feelings and emotions, to houses, businesses or occupations. If you are in any connection that would be viewed as codependent in any of those situations, then it's time to cut the cord with them. Usually the attachments are heart to heart, but they can also be spirit to spirit, physical to physical, physical to heart and physical to mind connection – all with the same person. There are connections that we all have with people which are called cords – karmic cords and emotional chords. Physical and emotional connections can be great blessings or they can be a call to pay back karmic events. It is as if God puts you back together with people that you knew earlier to make peace and resolve your old karma. Often I find that people who have made these connections and have these joyous reunions are usually rewarded with about four to six months of amazing connection on all levels. This is the time God is giving you to resolve old karmic issues you have with one another. To make peace, respect each other so that you can either stay together or you part.

As the relationship starts to fall apart, or cave in on itself, there may be fights, ugly incidents, painful words and much unpleasantness, all increasing as time moves on. The problem that a lot of people endure is that instead of seeking to resolve the old, through love and forgiveness, they incur new karma and karmic debt with the other person. Instead of resolving the old issues that come from some past life, they have the old debt plus the new debt that at some point will need to be taken care of and resolved. It is by your intention that you are able to resolve karmic debt.

I use the example of a person who may have robbed you in a past life. So you went over and got your money back, killing them in the process. This was a negative end to their life connection and it produced negative karma. If God were to present this person back into your life with this knowledge, there would be more negative actions. You would avoid them or be repelled by their energy. That is why, when you meet them in this life, they seem so attractive. God is sprinkling magical pixie dust all over everything and making them look very good. So, God is constantly reintroducing people into your life that you need to settle your karmic debt with.

Remember you might also have karma simply because of what you did or failed to do in a past life. For instance, if you were a German citizen who did nothing to aid people being prosecuted by the German government during either of the World Wars, you share in that situational collective karma. Or if you were a part of slave culture and oppression in America, you share in that racial karma. You do not always have to be directly involved, or have initiated the event.

You also have cords with people who nourish, love, support, and protect you in your life. It is important to recognize the circumstances and which relationship is which. We have many connections with hundreds, or thousands, of people in our lives. You must recognize that the relationship will either bear fruit in the form of good things happening for both of you in your lives, or it will yield pain, suffering and regret.

It is important, even within your family relationships, to have connections with the person who is really there now, not the memory or the spirit of the person you knew in some distant past life.

Disconnecting cords can lead to new relationships within existing relationships or it can lead to those old relationships breaking up. It allows you to see the other person as they really are in this life and allows them to see you as you really are in this life. Cutting cords helps you to keep from getting involved in a 30-year marriage with what should have been only a brief love affair. Some people come into your life for a moment, some for a day, some for a year, some for many years. That is how life works, but it gets messy when we get confused about how long and for what purpose they are in your life.

In order to dissolve cords, connections or other attachments that you have with a person in your life that is harming you, makes you feel sad, depressed angry or is driving you crazy, first you must be willing to forgive them and their conduct towards you. One of the important indicators of a relationship that has negative cords is that it drains you. A positive cord with people sustains you. It refreshes your energy at a very high rate. It gives you life. When you have a positive connection, it will lead to an exponential increase in your energy.

I can see connections that people have with each other. They are like long cords, or even chains, that attach sometimes heart to heart, mind to mind, or sex organs to sex organs. Some cords are no larger than threads. My procedure for disconnecting cords is outlined below. It is a procedure for spiritual healing that allows you to release negative emotions and relationships that no longer serve you. Many people have ended relationships with swear words and threats, orders of protection, and lawsuits, but find they are unable to get away from the person they no longer want in their life. This procedure is a way to remember and express the love that you once held for the person you are dissolving cords with, and it offers an opportunity for a clean, new connection, while releasing you from the bonds of the past and the chains of misery and suffering with that person.

Disconnection of cords is essential when a relationship starts to go bad. It allows each person to be reintroduced to each other as they really are in this life, without animalistic lust or codependent bondage that you might otherwise feel. You know what I'm talking about — that crazy in love feeling that yields you nothing but pain and suffering.

You can make cords with people from hugging, kissing, sex, talking and touching. These cords can be spiritual cords as well as mental; they can be emotional and physical. Many of the cord disconnections that I've done have been between dating couples and married people, and also between adult children, their parents and ex-spouses. You know you need this if you still think about a person or fantasize about a person who is no longer in your life, or you miss a person who has mistreated or abused you.

Some clients have also had success doing the Disconnecting Cords Procedure with new friends, and potential partners and lovers, and have felt great benefit from it. This allows them to see the new person as they actually are in this life, without any of the mystery or fascination that might be left over from past lives. It allows them to build a trust-based relationship early on.

Since we each have our own vibrational energy, we will attract what it is we need to attract from other people. But these cords always trip us up. If you're corded to someone who is not at your same energy, or is stronger than you, then you may be connecting with an emotional vampire, a person who will suck up your energy and use it to strengthen themselves. Disconnecting cords does not relieve you of legal or moral obligations you have with someone, though.

No matter how much you love the person you want to disconnect with, if the connection is bad, then it will stay bad. You are not the savior of the other person; you are not the person who can heal them — you can only save yourself or support change in others. There is a line in the disconnecting cords procedure that we add at the end, "and any men or women who have used or abused me." Sometimes it is not that the person is purposefully cruel to you or seeking revenge on each other, but that you are both actors in a play. You are together to learn lessons or resolve old karma and that is it. Anything else is extraneous.

## Disconnecting Cords Procedure

One of the greatest gifts and blessings you can do for yourself and for another person is to disconnect spiritual, emotion, mental, physical and ethereal cords with them. This allows you to see them as they really are in the present life. It resolves old karmic connections and debt, and has been known to change people's lives and relationships for the better. Disconnecting means forgiving them, praying for them and turning them over to God with love. You can also disconnect with your old self, your old emotions (self-defeating habits, anger, worry, fear, depression and anxiety) and people who have used or abused you.

Over the next three days you will see the person you are blessing in the Disconnection with new vision that will allow you to see who they truly are in this life. You will release old feelings, allowing for a fresh start in the relationship, if you choose.

Begin by asking God to bless and protect all involved in this process. Then say:

"Please come here in Spirit, _____" and read your list of names. You can call them out in spirit since spirit is not attached to their body.

The person or persons you are blessing will gather in spirit on your right side. On your left side is the Golden Doorway to Heaven.

Then say:

"I'm doing this with the Love and Light of God.

As I set you free, you must set me free.

No two spirits should hold each other as we have.

Now it's time to let go.

I undo all that I have created in you.

I owe you nothing and you owe me nothing. All is forgiven."

Then tell the person you love them and bless them, and anything else you want to tell them.

Then say:

"I dissolve all cords, contracts, commitments, agreements, vows, spells, curses and all other karmic connections with love. All connections between me and _____ (read your list) are null and void.

Remove any resistance and help us to let go.

You are no longer allowed in my energy on any level of my being unless you come with the Love and Light of God."

"Anything you do in any way to harm me or those around me will reflect back to you, and you and that which stands behind you will absorb all karma.

Whether it be by your actions or the actions of others created by you, you and that which stands behind you will absorb all karma."

Then say:

"I let you go, and now undo all that I have created in you. I set you free."

Then say:

"God - I give you _____ (read the list) – He/She/They are no longer my responsibility.

Take them where they need to go, to heal and grow.

I will not hold you anymore.

I set you free.

Go into the Light!"

When you feel this has happened, say:

"Amen" or "So Be It" three times.

Then envision a giant bubble around you that protects you from any reconnection. Stay in the bubble for seven days. Do not discuss past or emotional issues with the person you are dissolving from. This will let you decide if you want them in your future.

The cord cutting gives you an opportunity to speak to the person safely and truthfully, without fear, while they are in Spirit form. You can say what you need to say, release what you need to release, express your love for them, and then turn them over to God. It is important to forgive the other person for whatever they have done against you. I used to tell people that they needed to forgive, not necessarily forget. However, that was short-sighted advice because while the forgiving part usually comes along, it creates another cord. We want to get rid of *all* those cords. This is important because once you release, it will not come up in your memory and is simply becomes part of your past.

The result of not disconnecting cords is what I call baggage, such as old pains and abuse that you continue to carry around into every new situation in your life. When I talk about disconnecting from those old events and leaving all your baggage for God to store and deal with, you would be amazed how quickly you forget and grow. God can handle the baggage that you have carried for so long.

# CHAPTER 13

## *Other Healing Exercises*

Another procedure that is used in readings is what is called the "Elevator Exercise". This is where my soul joins your soul and reviews your present life in the body you are in on Earth. We take the elevator up many floors to see what you have learned and experienced, and, also, what you have denied and the pains that you have hidden away. This process must be experienced. Visualizing and dreaming is why prayer and direct revelation, and the elevator exercise, are important. They reconnect you with who you are at a higher spiritual level.

The elevator exercise guides you to get into an elevator and rise to the third floor. Then you look down and see yourself in the body that you are in. This is a good exercise to do with another person who has already done it, so they can guide you and verify what you are seeing. At the third floor, as you look down and see your body; you are a being now at the soul level. As your partner in the process I will ask you to describe the life of the person you are looking at (your human body), offer advice to them, tell them what they need to know. You are at the soul level looking down knowing everything that has ever happened to that person in their whole life. It takes a few minutes to recognize that you are still in your body, but part of you is away on the third floor. As you relax and trust, you remember that you are more than a body with a soul, but a soul currently in that body. You begin to receive more and more self-evaluation and wisdom.

You may continue to rise to higher and higher floors on the elevator, going to see people and places where the person may have experienced joy, pain, comfort and also hatred, pain and misery. There is also usually a floor where old memories of good and bad events in their lives are stored. Then as we climb higher and higher in the elevator, we find we are rising to higher chakra levels as well.

Clients have shown me floors where they are at the beach or a mountain top where their spirit can escape to be alone and meditate. Other floors are places to go dancing, sing and have fun. Some floors have dark energy, old memories of stored pain and regret. The vibration of those floors is oppressive.

On some floors you will see old friends, loved ones, people you, as that person, knew in school or jobs throughout this life. Many positive and negative emotions arise as we continue the elevator trip upward.

Often you will find yourself in a village full of angels. We go into a shop and I will tell my client to ask the clerk if he can tell us where God is. We need directions. The clerk will laugh and smile and point directly at my client. We are both confused at that point. We exit the shop and walk down the street and usually we find a homeless man (Jesus) who is happy looking and very friendly – very cheerful and happy we are visiting. Sometimes we also see a beautiful older woman (Mary - Mother of Jesus) who is glowing. She always has some message to share with my client. The best part is how empowering this is for my client. I am not telling them what anyone is saying, they are telling me, because they have allowed themselves to access that soul energy.

Then, at the top, we find a mass of all the spirits and souls (the collective consciousness) that have ever been or ever will be. We see loved ones, feel peace, and know that we are part of a much bigger picture, a much bigger production than we have ever imagined before. When we look up, we usually see three bright stars or lights that many describe as the male God energy/the female God energy/and the Holy Spirit (Triune energy). The Jesus, Buddha and Muhammad energy is found, of course, under the male energy. The person begins to see everything with a new pair of glasses. It is a very powerful exercise and can be life changing.

It will allow you to see that you are not alone in the world and that you never have been. It will also show you your connection with God and all the other souls on Earth. It can be a very moving and gratifying experience. Often deceased family members will present themselves and embrace my client and me. Every person or soul that ever was or ever will be has origins in this place. This is the Source Energy.

Miracles happen when we access energy that is higher than our own energy. If we allow ourselves to become a conduit of this healing energy of the Universal light, we find an inexhaustible supply of energy always available that supports healing and changes in ourselves and other people.

When we are able to make a reconnection with God and the infinite power of God, our lives can be changed in an instant. When we allow God closer to what we can see in the world, we become closer to God; we recognize the energy of God within us. God is never far from us. God is never further than our own shadow. You do not need to learn anything, profess anything, feel anything, do anything, or go to any building or place. Simply turning around, you will find God, if that is what you allow.

*To get what you need, you must become one with God.*

When I first received this from Spirit years ago, I had no idea what it meant or how I could do it. I began to read, study and learn more about the gifts of Spirit that I already had and had long suppressed.

Our linear mind/ego demands that God not only present himself, but identify himself and his qualifications to be God according to our own limited knowledge of what God is and what God should be. Many people just expect God to show up at the 10:00 a.m. service every Sunday and then that is enough God for them for the week. This will prevent them from seeing that God is with you always wherever you are. Nothing can ever sever the love, understanding and connection with God.

It truly requires a leap of faith for people to find God. If you only seek God in a Bible, a spiritually-inspired book, or a prayer book, you may never find Him. It is only when you open your heart that the connection can be made. Don't get me wrong; you can find God in organized religion but often you have to swallow so much religious dogma first that it dilutes the "God" that you are finally allowed to know. In every religion there are amazing rabbis, priests, ministers, and religious and lay ministers who actively bring people to this realization every day.

When you allow for spiritual connection, and seek and allow healing, it will come in one form or another. The healing is a gift to you from God. It is not given because of who you are, or because of mercy, nor even of grace; it is a gift of pure unconditional love.

Miracles are great for getting people's attention; big miracles like producing fish and bread loaves, or the wine at Cana, or parting the sea are very impressive. But every healing is miraculous to the person who is healed. When you realize that there is a higher power interested in your well-being, you truly open the door to God.

I figured out how to use mediation and prayer to keep my mind/ego busy as this allowed God to reconnect with me. The more I was reconnected, the greater my life became and the greater my abilities to share, care and support other people became. When I did healing from my own energy, it made me sick. When I learned how to conduct energy through me from a higher source, it gave me hyper-energy, and made me happy and healthy and even more sexually connected with myself. My daughter Jessica calls me "the energizer bunny" because I keep going and going and going. I felt more connected, not only to God, but to my own body.

Many people who are healers complain about the trials and struggles they have gone through in their own lives, but fail to recognize that those trials and lessons were what made them qualified to do the work that they are doing now.

Other methods to connect with God are meditation, guided meditation, grounding, chanting, prayer, and organized prayer - such as the rosary, or prayer beads. I have found that these keep my mind/ego busy, and I am able to reconnect with God very easily. I regard my mind/ego like a three-year-old who is very curious but also wants to control every situation. If I can find him something else to do, I can enter into a meditative state, at least for a while.

It confused me when I first started doing readings and healings how people were so greatly affected by the actions and words that came through me from Spirit. I just delivered what was given to me and it affected other people's lives profoundly.

People come to my door looking for God. All they find is me sitting in my chair, so I have the duty to act in the place of God and counsel them with unconditional love, conducting the energy of God that comes through me.

At first, I did not feel worthy of this energy that God chose to send through me. Then I learned that I should just *radiate love and healing without concern for results*. My intention that people be healed allowed healing. Opening my heart and allowing energy to come through was enough for some people to receive healing.

Many people I see have suffered mental, emotional, physical and sexual abuse. I meet them where they are. No judgment, no criticism. I just love them unconditionally. Through my gift of seeing the issues that have happened in their lives, I am able to support the change that they seek. This is also called reading their soul or reading their hearts.

The result of any abuse is pain and memories. The reaction to abuse continues to occur sometimes decades after the abuse. Some people have resolved some or all of it. Some have thought they resolved it but if I am still able to pick it up, there is more left. Often the abuser just did what they did and went on their way in life hurting dozens of other people as well. The victim still suffers and the abuser probably can't even remember the events or totally denies them.

I think it is amazing how each person receives the exact healing that they need, whether they knew this is what they needed or not. There is nothing that God does not see and respond to when asked.

## Exploration in Life

The surprising thing is that once you decide to give everything up and follow God, sometimes, disappointingly, God doesn't want you to go anywhere or leave anyone or change anything because you are where you are supposed to be. God simply wants you reactivated as a member of the team.

When we allow God to use us for healing, planting seeds or building bridges, we find growth can be rapid or very slow, but at the same time healing is coming through us and it is happening to us. It is like an onion. There are many layers, not just of the person being healed, but of the healer. Often God will send people with problems and issues – physical, mental, emotional, spiritual – that are also your problems and your issues. Sometimes you will never solve them for that person, but something in you will be resolved.

Think about Judas Iscariot, the apostle who betrayed Jesus Christ to the authorities, which led to his arrest and crucifixion. Judas was a valuable part of the Jesus story. Another interesting part of the story is the Apostle Peter who denied Jesus three times, yet Jesus forgave him. Peter ended up being the First Pope of the Roman Catholic Church. If everything went perfectly in the ministry of Jesus we probably would have never heard of him.

Our souls are continually being refreshed and refined to bring us closer and closer to the energy of God. That is the goal of all life - to reach for and be in line with the energy of love that emits from the Creator God and to take that and share it with those around you. Closer my God to Thee pleases me.

Every time we come into a body there is pain, suffering, joy and happiness. We cannot know one if we do not have its opposite for contrast. In my experience, it is rare to find people who are doing metaphysical work or healing work who have not suffered in their own lives. It makes them the best teachers. It can be very frustrating to be different, to be intuitive and be called to be a healer. Being spiritual in the real world is not is an easy task.

# CHAPTER 14

## *What Happens After Death*

Many clients come to me seeking to communicate with dead friends and family members. Some are so sad, so depressed, so lost that they're having trouble coping with their day-to-day lives. Instead of remembering the blessings of having had the other person in their life, they remember the illness, the process of dying, and the emptiness in their house and in their lives.

I'm always able to tell them what the status is of a loved one - if they have crossed over into Heaven, or did not feel worthy and have consigned themselves to a purgatory-like holding place. Some are in Hell and those who killed themselves are in a self-created exile. But none should lose hope.

The first thing the deceased does when they die is to see and feel loved ones (could be family or friends who preceded them in death.) There is also their guardian angel and the angel of death that will accompany them and guide them to the Light. They are all in the place where death occurred. They will feel the vibrational energy and unconditional love coming from each of these spirits.

I am sure that you have heard the story before about there being a long black tunnel with a super bright white light at the end which is the way to Heaven. This is what I have witnessed also, in my personal life and in my readings. The Light is the entrance to what we call Heaven,

Nirvana, and Paradise. When they get there, they feel the hugs of unconditional love energy. It never stops. It is awesome and amazing. Then, as I mentioned before, you wait your turn and, with God next to you, you watch a movie of your life on a huge IMAX theater screen. You cannot say anything, but you must decide if every action or word said in your life either hurt you or helped you grow spiritually, or hurt or helped another person to grow spiritually. No excuses or justifications. You can only observe, assess and then address remedies with thumbs up or thumbs down. This is a just assessment of your life actions. There are angels there that will counsel you as to what worked and what did not and what you can do to resolve karmic issues that you created or failed to resolve.

No judgments are made. The angel/counselor will help you plan other lives to resolve those issues that caused you to harm yourself or others.

First though, you must rest and slowly drop your physical body. If you were sick for a long time, especially with a lingering disease like cancer, you need a longer time to recover so your first stop is like a giant Intensive Care Unit where you are surrounded by friends, family and loved ones who have already passed over and completed the process. You generally stay there for one month to three years. You are bathed in love energy. The faster you accept it and allow it, the quicker your spirit/soul is healed and replenished. The memories and attitudes you had in life slowly fade away, but the feelings of love that you had in that life follow you forever. Your love will change you and the fate of your loved ones. Your love will allow you to return to one another.

In time, you will start to sense the activity all around and feel the unconditional love. When you leave this resting area then you are free to make Heaven whatever you dream Heaven is to you. You are also free to come back and forth from that side to this side. Then we can feel your presence and love around us. It is very comforting, but as I said, first we need to let you fully surrender yourself to God.

There are times when we can lose touch with people that have crossed over. They leave their body behind but have not gone into Heaven. This is for people who are in what Catholics would describe as Purgatory. It is a halfway station between Heaven and Hell and is a place that each person has created because they do not feel worthy to go to Heaven.

Some people fantasize or wish for death or think that death will be a great blessing and get them out of their current situations. But when they do this, they are putting out an energy that prevents them from living. Killing yourself is selfish. It is a coward's way out, no matter how noble your intentions.

When you first kill yourself, you feel pretty good; you are finally out of that body, that life, that emotional state that was so horrible that you could not live with it anymore. You start to feel positive as you rise up in spirit to Heaven. But it is only a temporary "fix." You wait in line at Heaven's Gate, then you are reviewed, your life chart is reviewed and they tell you that you are not supposed to be there for 31 more years, 4 months and 12 days. (That would have been that person's natural death date.) Then they send you back to Earth. There are valuable lessons to be learned for the person killing themselves, and also for everyone connected to that person. In the many lives we have over the ages, I am told that it is a normal part of everyone's learning experience. It is an educational experience in what not to do in future lives. When you experience the pain of being a suicide victim, you probably won't want to do it again.

What Spirit has shown me is that God is like the manager of a baseball team; He put you into the game of life and He, only He, decides when to remove you, so suicide is shown to be a major deal. It is measured in part by the intent of the person. Since there is social stigma attached to suicide, many cases are not reported that way. For example, with drug deaths from heroin, the intent of the person may have been to get high, but the fact is that they were so high that they caused their own death. God decides on those cases.

Most suicide cases are easily identifiable to me when I do a reading.

The person who died is in a jagged-edged bubble/aura about three feet off the ground and next to the person that I am reading. Spirit tells me suicide is a selfish act that affects so many hundreds of other people. These include the parents and siblings, aunts and uncles, cousins and grandparents of the suicide. It also includes every other person that the deceased would have affected in their lives, if only they had not chosen to kill themselves. It includes the people they would have married, and the children they would have had. It continues with all the teachers and students, the employers and co-workers. One person's life does affect so many other people. Just like the movie *It's a Wonderful Life* showed.

I am told that God notices this especially when the suicide of the person is under the age of 70. This may be because they had such great plans and potential when they co-created a life plan with God before they were born; suicide was listed as a possible choice in the life, but one that comes with many painful consequences.

A person who has died by their own hand is usually denied the ability to communicate with people who are still alive. They must be present to witness how their friends, family and loved ones respond to the news of their death and the suffering it causes them in the future. This lesson is repeated over and over so that the suicide victim completely understands the ramifications of their single selfish act. When they acknowledge this, then they can ascend to whatever their idea of Heaven is. No further judgment or review - just unconditional love and acceptance. This occurs when they forgive themselves first.

Now, you may ask: why does the person who committed suicide show up at the reading also? It is because they affected the life of the person that I am doing the reading for. They must witness everything they caused to happen in the survivor's life, the tears, anxiety, pain, regret. They must feel everything that they caused. Now here is the amazing part: God splits their spirit into as many parts as needed so this happens in the life of every single person that was or will be affected by their suicide. Losing one person changes the life plans of many other people.

I have been shown by Spirit that all suicide victims will stay on Earth until what would have been their natural death date. Then they automatically go to Heaven. If they realize the consequences of their actions on other people, then they can go sooner.

A praying person can appeal for suicide victims to hasten their journey, and that will help them to realize the consequences of their action. The Family Healing Prayer (appendix) works for this.

In those readings with survivors, I spend most of my time listening to the horrible way that the family was treated after the suicide - the ministers and priests will not allow them to have services in their churches and not allow them to be buried in the consecrated ground of their cemeteries. I hear how they were told that their loved one will be in the flames of Hell for eternity. This is so damaging. If I were looking for behavior to describe as a sin, that is what I would call that behavior. So wrong!

Suicides and people who die sudden unexpected deaths bring the same result for those of us who are left behind. You don't have time to say or do anything about it. You cannot communicate with a dead body. It's just not possible. But they will be around you in spirit. People who die sudden, unexpected deaths often do not even know that they have died. They may stay in the place where they died and try to communicate with people there. Some call those places haunted. But they are not really. It is that their energy is caught up in the moment of death and they cannot believe it. Even worse they cannot talk or touch anyone who is in their area. You would be doing them a great favor to pray for them and then explain to them what happened. This is the normal process that you and other survivors will go through. These are called the "Stages of Death" by Dr. Elisabeth Kubler-Ross. These include learning about death due to accident or whatever causes it and then:

- Denial/Questioning (Why did this happen?)
- Anger/Regret
- Aggression

- Depression
- Confusion
- Early Bargaining
- Continued Anger & Denial
- Bargaining
- Acceptance

When you explain how you felt and reacted, it will also help the deceased come to terms with their death, helping you both.

You can also recognize these stages if you have lost someone and have survived. You may go through the same stages. Eventually you will realize that the death happened, and you will understand that you can do nothing to change it. Whatever you did or did not do for the deceased in their life is all in the past. When you forgive yourself, and accept the death, then you can move on to your new life.

You need to know that it makes no difference where a deceased person is at in spirit/soul. They can hear you. So always talk to them. Often when they are in the process of crossing over and dropping their bodies they will not be able to respond back to you except with the aid of an angel. Any response that you receive will be short, because at that stage they just don't have much energy to communicate.

## Dead People are the Same as They Were in Life

When someone dies, those left behind tend to forget the bad/sad times they may have experienced with that person. They usually recall only the good qualities the person possessed, and they tend to elevate them to a level far beyond what they actually were in life. In truth, the deceased person had good and bad qualities in life and they pass to the other side in that condition – no more, no less.

Some survivors hold so tightly to the memory and spirit of their loved ones that they do not let them peacefully pass to the other side. They are being selfish and making it all about the survivor now, not the deceased. Spirit calls this "tethering" the deceased to Earth.

When a person dies they are in spirit but may still have the body attached to them. There may be much grief, sadness and worry for the survivors, but the one who has died is not sad. For them it is like going to sleep in the body and then waking up outside of the body. They are elated to lose the dead body and be free to travel anywhere or to many places at the same time. They are free and sense the unconditional love that God is offering them if they just go into the light. Most will stick around for 7 to 30 days and see how people are coping and dealing with their passing. They watch the funeral and any religious services and celebrations and wakes. This is the time, most often, when loved ones will experience visitations with them.

Some people, especially parents of young or disabled children, choose to stay near them as they grow up and cross over later.

This transition time helps them release the physical and mental connections on Earth so that they can continue on their path. This does not mean that they leave us. In every moment, when you have a thought about them, a remembrance, or anything reminds you of them, be it good or bad, they appreciate that acknowledgment. They will live again in that moment simply because you have remembered them. But they won't be able to come back to you (in spirit) in the form of their spiritual energy until they have fully crossed over.

Now this is different from a person who has died and neglected or refused to crossover themselves. I have seen this a lot with people who lived in fear in their life. They may be so afraid for the welfare of their children or grandchildren that they want to stay with them, even in death. It is very hard for the deceased person to sustain the energy to be able to do that, so they grab other people's energy.

Then there are the people who were addicted to drugs or alcohol; they hang around bars and drug houses and can get a fix off the drug just through the human beings that are in the bar.

People who were addicted to sex do the same thing. They find circumstances where they can witness, if not experience, sex. Advanced or very determined souls have been known to enter a living person's body to do just that.

Then there are the greedy people, the ones who want to take their wealth with them beyond the grave. They feel true pain when their assets are distributed after death - so they may haunt the people who received the money.

Whether death comes to a young person who has suddenly died or an old person who was expected to die for a long time, it is a blessing to them. To be relieved of the pain, heaviness and uncertainty of this world, and to be reabsorbed into the soul, into the essence of God, is the greatest blessing. Spirit has shown me that we all go to Heaven and Heaven is a 1000-story building. We all get in. Some might be in the lower floors, some in the penthouse and upper floors, and some might be in the sub-basement, but we all get in. Not all feel worthy of going in. That is their free will choice.

When we do well in our life we go to Heaven. When we do bad things in our life we go to Heaven, we just end up driving around the block 14 times looking for parking, but we still get in. God never denies His Own and we are all in the club - Catholics, Jews, Prot-estants, Muslims, Evangelicals, Atheists, Agnostics, and every other single person on the planet. We are all from one God - one Creative Energy. It takes some time for people to release their religious ideas. Ministers and priests seem to have the hardest times.

It reminds me of an old joke. St. Peter is at Heaven's Gate, and he quietly sees each newly arrived person. He then directs them to the Life Review and when they are done, those who most identified with religion in their lives, are directed to their own version of Heaven. He has a room for Jews, a room for Catholics, even a room for those 144,000 chosen Jehovah's Witnesses. Then they are all in their room only with members of their own religions, just like they always said it would happen on Earth. When he is guiding them, he is very careful to not let them know that all the "other people" who they may have thought would not get into Heaven also arrived and were welcomed.

## How We Can Help Through Prayer

When we pray for the dead, we must also pray for ourselves. I had a hard time doing this at first because I was raised in a culture and religion where it was holier to do things for other people than it was to do anything for yourself. So, it was holier and better for you spiritually if you prayed for other people, but it was selfish and evil if you prayed for yourself. This was confusing to me as I grew up. Now I know that prayer is simply talking to what I cannot see, only sense. It is sharing what is in your heart with a power greater than you, that you have faith and hope in. Your prayers are noticed and responded to but the answers you receive will not always be what you desire because you lack the perspective of the big picture. God is like a parent – sometimes He says "yes, maybe or no." Sometimes, He says "not right now" or "be patient." But it does no harm for you to ask and share your list of desires with God in prayer. You simply cannot know what is best for another, or yourself, in the context of the many lives and lessons and experiences that we must go through.

There is no reward or punishment for how you have lived your life. God simply reabsorbs you into the fold because the Creator God is the God of eternal, unconditional love.

Having been shown by Spirit how many times we have all died in past lives, I find it amusing that people get so dramatic when death happens around them. There really is no spiritual death. Your spirit/soul continues without your body. But since fear is what most people live with every day, it is not unexpected for them to fear death.

When we are born, we have no fear, only trust, comfort, security and love. We had to learn fear, anger, worry and anxiety, all things of this world. There is a great balance here between knowing something in spirit and actually living it in a body. That is where the lessons come in.

Sometimes, past life memories will affect how a person lives in their present life. They need to learn that whatever behaviors or actions may have affected them in that prior life will not do so in the present life. For instance, if you were intuitive in a past life, you might have been labeled as a witch and killed because of it. That is not going to happen in this life.

The lightness that comes from being without a body is joyous and free, very liberating. In spirit, you can be whoever you want to be, you can feel the people you are thinking about. Depending on the circumstances of the death, whether the death was anticipated or was sudden, or the person suffered a long debilitating, lingering illness, will dictate what happens after physical death. Many older people who have dementia or Alzheimer's, for instance, die and just sort of stick around for a while because they're still confused. They have not really been in their bodies for some time so they don't immediately recognize the difference once they are out of their bodies.

The same happens with people who are killed instantly in accidents or other calamities. Many times, they tend to congregate at the place where they died. They, too, are confused and often don't know that they are dead. So, they just hang out near the place they died. Our prayers can lift them from this confusion. We can do so much good for those that we love simply by sending love and prayer their way.

Unfortunately, many clients go into profound grief, mourning and depression and experience a sense of helplessness and hopelessness. That freezes them from healing and beginning the next part of their lives. Some stay there for the rest of their lives. That is wrong. The lesson is that you were born to experience these events and then move though them to the next lesson in your life. (See St. Germaine and the Violet Flame in Chapter 3)

Many people come to me to discuss their loved ones who have died and the best way to continue to love them. The best we can do to love and support their spiritual growth is to talk to them, pray for them, to send love to them, and to let them go. We can explain to them what happened to them and how we feel about it, but we need to let them know that we will be just fine. Don't make them feel guilty for leaving.

Cherish the time that you had together with that person. Know that there were both good days and bad days when they were in life.

Remember what you learned and what you experienced together. It is fine to miss someone for a while actively day-to-day, especially when you lived with that person. We do miss them when they are not coming in the kitchen, or walking down the hall, or sitting next to you on the couch. That's normal, but missing them too much will entrap them on Earth. What is the best thing you can you do for a loved one who may be stuck here on Earth or who may be stuck in a Purgatory or Hell of their own creation? Pray! Prayer is the single most powerful tool for helping people who have crossed to the other side. Praying for them, talking to them and telling them it is alright to move on to a good place is important for them and for you. It is hard, but it is the greatest gift that you can give a loved one.

When survivors experience loss, they should seek help to let go, acknowledge the death, anger, and frustration, then accept and bless it. People who do this can overcome their grief and resume their lives in six to twelve months. This will help in releasing the loved one who has passed. But some of my clients are still mourning people who died three, five, ten or even 20 years ago. That hurts everyone.

Not letting them go, or worse, making them feel guilty about going, is hurtful. This leads to long term depression and anger. The lesson in life is to cherish the time you have with a person and then, knowing that we all have to die someday, let them go and celebrate their leaving. You will be fine eventually. They will be fine eternally.

Some people are afraid to die because they were dishonest or adulterous, killed people, raped, or did other acts that they believe put them outside this place of love that God creates for us all. But God especially welcomes "all lost lambs" back into the fold.

When they are in spirit form and have fully crossed over and dropped their body, they are free to come and go. Releasing their spirit to God is to release any cords that you might have. Because of your own selfish needs to have that person still in your life, if you create a guilt or blame situation then that person cannot move on. You don't let them move. It's essential that they cross over into Heaven so they can rest and lose the rest of their connection to physical body.

The faster they shed their body, the faster they reconnect in spirit with their own soul and with the Creator God, the faster they can come back and forth in spirit to be around you forever, if that is what they choose.

I have had many cases where my intuition has revealed that husbands and wives who are deceased regularly come back to be with their spouses; sometimes they still have sex with them also. This was so bizarre when I said it to a young widow – I thought that I had gotten the message wrong. But she acknowledged it. She said he made love to her in death like he was "Superman." Needless to say this was not helping her to move on in life or for him to move on in death. I had another widow and widower who also verified this information. They were as shocked as I was that I had access to such information.

This sounds fantastic on many levels, but it is not good for either person. The person left in body needs to let the deceased lover go. The spirit needs to go and be with other spirits.

When we are in body, our primary concern is taking care of the body, getting food, shelter, clothing, warm, cold, drink, physical pleasures; all of us have the same needs. We also have the need to find a way to pay for our needs. That usually involves working and relationships which can create a life of drudgery and boredom if you are not happy in your circumstances. When a person is dead, they no longer have to worry about any of these things. They have time for feeling and thinking and learning and experiencing thoughts and ideas that they did not get to learn about on Earth.

When a person dies, it's like they had been wearing an overcoat in life and now they are free to take it off - they are free and light and happy. Now they can focus on spiritual matters, such as spiritual growth, learning and doing what is fun for them.

## Negative Spirit Activity

Death does not suddenly make the deceased a good person. In death, they are what they were in life. They are unchanged - no better and no worse. I was told by Spirit that some people are so bored when they die that they seek to reenter a body almost immediately because they are so attached to the world, their worldly goods and physical pleasures, and they do not want to participate in spiritual, mental, or emotional growth. Or they just don't want to leave.

Some people do not cross over, because they are connected to physical states that they are afraid to leave. They may be addicted to sex, smoking, drinking, money, power, control or drugs, so they wait around people who practice those habits and partake with them in Spirit, sometimes overtaking the bodies of the living person. When you are drunk or high, you sometimes turn over your physical body to whatever spirit wants access, and they come through in whole or in part, using your body to cause trouble in your life or in other people's lives. These spirits choose to stay on Earth instead of completing the cross over to the other side. Sometimes a person who is mentally ill also will be able to channel these negative spirits, because they have impaired ability to resist outside spirit activity. If you die and you're closely associated with your body due to vanity or various emotional/personality disorders, like narcissism or borderline behaviors, you will have a harder time leaving Earth and shedding your body.

I have witnessed a spirit's face about one inch in front of the body of another person they have overtaken. The words are coming from the spirit through that that person's mouth and body. The message will be out of character with the person. That is one of the clues. You can always determine who is speaking because this message will be angry, hurtful, damaging and belittling, and may provoke physical violence.

Troubled spirits may come to you to scare you, watch over you or seek your assistance in a matter that is unfinished from their life. This does not make them bad or evil, just troubled, in need of assistance.

Many people have experienced this, but it is not normally talked about. With any spirit who is harmful to you, or troublesome, because you are in your body, you always have the power to say "No – Get out of me and get away from me!" This is what we call "commanding out." You have the power to protect yourself. You can limit or shut off the access of any spirit to you, good or bad.

Some clients that have moved on and perhaps remarried or have new relationships have reported they have seen their deceased loved ones watching them having sex or doing other tasks. It gives them the creeps. Ask them what they want and then respond to it. Be aware that the dark side can create the deception of your loved one bringing you a message, but it will really be from the Dark Side, not your deceased loved one. The devil is all about deception. Discernment is always essential in any communications with spirits. One method that I use in discernment is to test the spirit and I say, "Is Jesus Christ the King of the Universe?" If you get a yes, you go ahead. Your body will feel good and that is another verification. If you do not get a yes, then bless the visiting spirit and say, "I am turning you over to God Our Father with love and my blessing." Truly dark spirits detest that and move quickly away from you.

Some might only move three feet away and taunt you, but you can use Holy Water to encircle you and they will always go away. Some will also try to come back with their buddies if you do not keep yourself strong with good thoughts and prayers. You could get angry and command them away from you in fear and with great anxiety. I have seen people do that and it is quite theatrical. But it does not work in the long term. Remember that then you would be coming from the negative energies of fear, anxiety and worry. We do not want that for you, we want you to come from the Light, giving blessings and love to all spirits. Unless they are in the middle of attacking you, of course, then that is a different matter.

## Symptoms of Negative Energy or Spiritual Attack

Some symptoms of negative energy or spiritual attack on you are:
- You have 3 a.m. nightmares/dreams and sleep paralysis
- You feel drained after talking to or being around people with negative energy
- You may be talking to people and be yawning uncontrollably
- You are attracting people who say strange things to you
- You notice that people are trying to manipulate you
- You have visions or thoughts that are not usual for you and could be self-destructive
- You are suddenly having mental confusion and loss of memory
- Spirits appear as angels of light but lie to you or deceive you
- Getting a sudden cold feeling. We used to say it was like "someone just walked over my grave"

You can stop any of these by thinking of God, love, Jesus, the cross, or the crucifix or calling out to St. Michael the Archangel (the one who carries a large sword). Like I said before, it does not matter if you are Christian or even believe in their ideas. You are using symbols that pack power over spiritual oppression. I keep a spray bottle filled with Holy Water next to my bed. I have a crucifix in my room, a large wall hanging of Lord Ganesha and a Buddha and a Quan Yin statue. Seems to work - it allows me to sleep soundly every night.

When you get chills, goosebumps, heat flashes or tingles, electric feelings, or the hair on your neck or arms stands up, this can be either good or bad. The higher the spiritual energy around you the warmer you will feel.

When you experience the feeling that something is wrong, trust that and figure out what caused that feeling.

When a person first dies, it is generally difficult for them to communicate. They are exhausted from the transition. But if you ask a Higher Power (angel) to energize them, it is amazing what wonderful loving messages they will have to pass on. The deceased loved one is already in the process of dropping all connections to the body and the connections that they had with the illness. They are processing the lessons that they learned from having the illness, as well as reactions to circumstances that happened around them, to people who were caregivers and to those they left behind.

We all have an opportunity for spiritual, mental, emotional or physical growth in bodies here on Earth. Many times we did not allow ourselves to take full advantage of the opportunities, so in response, some people lead lives that may be more empty, pointless, and frustrating than other people. That is their own choice.

Some people get stuck here on Earth due to their own fear or feeling of unworthiness. They fear going to another place that they comprehend would be bad for them, such as Purgatory or Hell. They judge themselves and think they are unworthy to be in the presence of God as defined by whatever religion.

I rarely advertise this, but by the Grace of God, I have done a lot of work helping clients reclaim their lives when negative energy has attacked them. I have also worked with Catholic priests who were also doing this. It all comes down to this; the person who is being negatively attacked must want to be free of the negative spirits. They must want to resume full and complete control of their own bodies, mind and spirit. I do this without fear, knowing that good always triumphs over bad in the end. I have faith that the Love and Light of God are the only tools I need to command and compel the negative spirits out of my client. It always works.

I admit, I was sometimes terrified when I started learning how to do this. But then I remembered that I was not doing it, but God was using my voice and my hands to direct the process. This process usually involves intense prayers before and after with me and my client. I also use a lot of Holy Oil and Holy Water in the process, and some techniques I learned studying under a Hopi Medicine Man. So scary became the routine.

I proclaim that God wants the person who I am working with to do His work here on Earth. No matter what religion the client was raised in, or even if they have no background in religion, I ask Jesus to be my guide. At several points, I say, "I command you in the name of Jesus Christ and God Our Father to leave this person." Or, "I compel you by the power of Christ to go into the Light of God." The key here is to give the negative energy a place to go so they don't return to the person. I bless their forehead and the palm of each hand with Holy Oil and then have them say the Miracle Prayer (see appendix). That will keep them connected to the God energy as they transition to the next place they are supposed to be.

I strongly recommend that persons who are attempting to do healing and spiritual work read both of the following books cover to cover. They will help you a lot, and also the people you are trying to help:

*Protected by the Light-The Complete Book of Psychic Self-Defense* by Dr. Bruce Goldberg
*The Practical Psychic Self Defense Handbook- A Survival Guide* by Robert Bruce

The dark energy is always making demands and threats. In fact, when I was first starting to write this book four years ago, before my two IRS books were even thought of, I was warned. In a dream I had a vision of Satan who came and said that he did not want this book written at all because it would take power away from him. Because I advocate unconditional love and acceptance, meditation and prayers; no, he did not want me to do that at all. Finally, he said, "What do you want to not write this book?" And I answered simply as though I were still a child, and said, "I want nothing from you. God gives me everything that I need or desire." It was terrifying to me and the clients that I have done it on, but now it has become easier.

## Pre-Death (Exit) Counseling

When I have done work with a client who knows they are dying, it is very important that I explain to them that they will never be alone in the process, and that angels and spirits will be close to them the whole time. They will see and feel loved ones who have already passed and feel the spirits of those people still staying on Earth. Basically, it is similar to a cylinder-shaped tunnel that begins at the Third Eye and projects out into space. At the end of this tunnel is a light so bright that it is hard to look at, at first. The higher your spiritual energy, the easier it is to see into this light.

The most important part of counseling someone before death is to let the client know about the tunnel, and tell them about the light at the end of the tunnel. Let them know that God and unconditional love await them at the end of that tunnel. Assure them that all will be well for them and their loved ones.

When you leave your body in death you will do much the same; there will be a life review with God standing next to you. As I said before, you will review your life and you will judge your own actions simply by putting your thumb up or down when asked if those actions caused you to grow or shrink spiritually. There is no talking - it is all mental communication. You do not have a chance to offer any excuses.

It seems that people who keep hanging on to the past are the same ones who hang onto those who have died, who hang onto emotions and circumstances that they should have let go of a long time ago. You cannot rewrite the lessons you and your loved one have gone through. They are already recorded in the book of your soul. How you react to those things that happened to you is what makes the difference. Forgiveness, compassion and understanding go a long way.

Know that it took two people in every situation and you need to take responsibility for at least 50 percent of what went wrong. You always had the choice to leave, no matter the hardships that leaving might have caused. At the same time, we have karmic connections, karmic debt, and other situations that arise in our lives that cause us to do things, say things, and make things happen that are not in our own best interests. All growth is absorbed and recorded by your soul.

Putting down the emotional/mental baggage that you carry is the most important thing that you can do. I have a short prayer that I like to use to help the process:

I love you God
I love you unconditionally,
I am of God.
Please let my loved ones go into the Love and Light of Heaven.
I release them.
All is well.

Death and loss have no power over you. When you were born, the person who birthed you knew that someday you were going to die. That is no surprise. The lessons of death are to live in every moment of your life, share love and compassion with those you find along your path and say what you need to say so people don't walk all over you. Start to have fun and happiness will begin to surround you.

# CHAPTER 15

## *Abuse and Empowerment*

Many of my clients have experienced abuse. It might be physical, mental, emotional, or sexual abuse. Spirit has given me a combination of methods to help my clients who are ready to let past abuse go and move forward to a new chapter in their lives.

The circumstances of my life provided me with a wealth of knowledge and information about abuse. Sometimes abuse was being directed towards me and sometimes I was sending it out. My whole life I have witnessed or experienced abuse. For instance, it was considered normal and acceptable to be spanked with a wooden paddle at home or at school. I cannot remember how many times I saw adults backhand their kids, or kick them or beat them up. It was not regarded as a big deal. Corporal punishment is no longer legal in schools in Illinois, but still legal in homes. All the experiences in my life that diminished my spirit prepared me for a 33-year career at the IRS.

In the IRS, I suffered abuse from some managers and fellow employees who were psychotic, mean, obsessive/compulsive and had sociopathic tendencies. They delighted in punishing and abusing delinquent taxpayers, and generally treating people like shit. I had a great deal of power and authority over thousands of cases that affected people's lives. I used that power to hurt people for about half of my career; to advance myself and the goals of the IRS. I see now that I was the abuser and the abused depending on your viewpoint. The power of the IRS comes from fear and intimidation. I was a foot soldier in an army of fear.

Abuse goes both ways; the IRS abuses, but it is also abused. Being an IRS employee is not easy job on the best of days. Think about it. It seems the whole U.S. population hates you.

I wondered why I would be selected by Spirit to talk to people about abuse. I did not think of myself as being abusive. Then I remembered all those years as a tax collector at the IRS. I became the abuser of taxpayers during my time at the IRS, until I stopped. One day I realized that because of my time in the IRS, it made me a perfect person to talk to people who had been abused.

**What is Abuse?**

Abuse starts off with intentional disrespect and disregard for another person's feelings or personal space. Some abuse is hardly noticed, such as being cut off when you are speaking, being interrupted, being criticized for your thoughts and opinions, being condemned for being yourself, being told to shut up because you are stupid, fat, ugly, or different. Anyone who finds fault with any of your personal habits or ideas, or who seeks to control you is skating on thin ice. It is wrong to shame, belittle or tease another person. It is wrong to make another person feel put down, feel bad, guilty or stupid. This includes ignoring what someone is saying to you, inappropriate touching, tickling or threats of same.

Abuse can be active and loud or quiet and benign. Both have the same result. They leave you feeling depleted instead of empowered. Anything that anyone does to you that insults you and makes you feel small and insignificant is abuse. Anyone touching you without your consent is in your space and should be told to stop. You should feel empowered to tell them to stop and not expect any repercussions for it.

## Spiritual Counseling Session

Abuse usually leads a person to more abuse. Abuse in any form disables, depresses and destroys the lives of the one being abused and the people around them. As a spiritual counselor and medical intuitive, I have access to information that can speed healing and identify the causes of distress.

The best part of my intuitive gifts is that I am able to see inside of my client and actually feel what they feel now or felt in past situations. I am able to trigger enough from them to allow suggestions for change to happen for them in the present. Traditional counseling does not usually allow for this. I do not ask you "how do you feel about that?" like a therapist does. I know how you are feeling, I only need to verify it with you as we talk and move forward.

So many people have been abused and carry it with them every day. Abusers have taken away their victim's trust, hope and the respect that they once had for themselves. I create a safe space where healing can begin. I establish clear boundaries and explain that while the subject matter will be intense and intimate, we will not have any connection outside of the reading/healing process. I have heard of and witnessed other healers who manipulate their clients for more power, sex and money. I don't work like that.

I have heard so much verbal abuse. Repeated verbal attacks cause my clients to lose the ability to even think of themselves as able to stand up, fight back or leave the abuser. Sometimes the abuse only stops because the abuser is sick or dead. Since the abused person did not end the prior abusive relationship, they do not know how to go on in life. Sometimes they allow a new person to abuse them simply because they don't know what a normal healthy friendship or relationship looks like.

When you have been abused it is traumatizing and life altering. Many people do not talk about abuse, but they suffer silently like they somehow deserved it. They try every day to contain the anger, hate and rage that is just below the surface in their lives. They often feel powerless and dominated by other people. Many numb themselves with drugs, drinking and sex, and become chronically depressed. They suffer with low self-confidence, low self-esteem, fear and rejection every day of their lives, even decades after the abuser has moved on. They may have many relationships and marriages, but they are always seeking what was taken away from them in the earliest abuse situations.

Sometimes when you look back on your life you will discover overt and covert abuse in many forms. When parents or caregivers who are supposed to be responsible for you allow you to be abused and do nothing about it, it is almost as bad as the abuser's actions. There can be primary and secondary abuse. If you were directly abused or if you were present when abuse was taking place - it is all abuse.

Many abused clients feel like they are unworthy of love, or friends, or a healthy, balanced relationship. It does not matter what type of abuse my clients have suffered. All abuse is damaging to them in body, mind, heart and spirit. Being dominated by another person takes away their hope. Over time, prolonged abuse erodes the inner you, zapping your energy on a daily basis.

Many clients have repressed the memories of abuse. It is just a faint memory that they cannot deal with, so they don't. Many people have gaps in their memories or they cannot remember before a certain age when they were growing up. Painful memories need to be brought up and released. Learn the lessons of your afflictions and then learn how to move past them.

To help my clients release abuse, Spirit gave me what I call The Empowerment Method. This allows my client to recall past abuse, forgive the abuser and release the pain and suffering to a Higher Power. This method is a combination of the Disconnecting Cords Procedure, the Family Healing Prayer, past life hypnosis, inner child healing and my intuitive ability to see what the client may have forgotten, blocked or denied. To me, I am the guest you invited into your house to help you get organized and I have free access to every place in your house. I am going through closets, opening drawers and closets and looking under your bed, searching for those old carefully-hidden file boxes that contain the details of your past and abuses you have suffered. Then, <u>with your permission</u>, I have the Hoover vacuum sucking all those memories out - making your space spotless. The importance of this method is that the client is always in charge. I am only opening doors; they decide what to keep and what should go. This is part of empowerment, having authority to make your own decisions.

A psychologist reviewed my process and said "Your book is fabulous. The chapter on abuse is so helpful. I have experienced horrible life events that I have only recently been able to release and I just got my Ph.D. in Psychology. I think if a person would read your book with an open heart, they could save years of therapy. Your method is so loving, and yet so direct, that it has changed how I see my life."

Sometimes full stories of abuse come out as the client tells me their story. Sometimes only partial recall is needed for them to want to resolve the past.

Sometimes they know "something" happened, but cannot stomach the details. Some are ready to acknowledge that "something is wrong" and work to let it go. Whatever works for the client works for me. The stronger they are motivated to seek change the faster healing can occur.

When a client is empowered, then they are able to find their own voice. When a client can identify when they lost their power and who took it away from them, it is very empowering. Knowledge gives them more power. It speeds healing.

## The Desire to Change

It's important to decide that whatever you have tried to do to get the abuser to feel your pain, to be sorry and to apologize is a waste of time. Forgiving can be the hard part; wanting to be heard and relieved of the messy memories of the abuse is the easy part. If a parent, partner or authority figure in your life tells you that you are ugly, fat, stupid, or unworthy, you will start to believe that and put out a signal (a vibrational energy) to the Universe which will attract other people who will treat you like that. This leaves the door open for more emotional, verbal, physical or sexual abuse. It is easy to be angry, fearful, and resentful, and to use distractions such as drugs and drinking to hide from your past. I know that trying to extract yourself from that mess of emotions is hard to do by yourself. That is where the Higher Power comes in, an energy that is someplace above where you are that is able to hold out a hand and help you up to the next step in life.

It is easy for others to tell people to change, and easier still to encourage and direct yourself to change. But when you seek to rid yourself of unworthiness, low self-esteem, low self-confidence and many other issues that may be related to all different types of abuse, you cannot do it yourself. You should seek help and support. Part of you may even hear these words, "You Deserve More!" But inside the abused person, who has lost faith and hope in anything, the mind/ego, is saying, "I am unworthy and I don't deserve it."

My friend Franklin Matthews said, "It is easy to change your mind but it takes some work to clear your soul. The work is clearing all those emotions, experiences and thoughts that occurred as a result of your childhood emotions of unworthiness, and so forth. The childhood emotions created a spider web of events that are all attached to the original unworthiness emotion. This spider web then catches all the events that trigger a feeling in us — anger, fear, worry — that tells us that the original emotion is still there. The spider web is like a radio antennae picking up signals from our environment." This explains why people find themselves in the life situations that they are suffering from, with people who are not right for them or, worse yet, are abusive.

## Learning to Love Yourself First Best and Always is Hard

I think the hardest things we ever say are:
I Forgive Myself.
I Forgive You.
I Am Grateful for the Lessons of my Life.
I Am Sorry.
Help Me.

The vision that I often have when I speak to clients is that they are dressed in fine clothes wearing expensive shoes or high heels, and they are standing in a pile of their own shit. They keep looking down, crying and complaining about how their beautiful shoes and clothes are ruined. They wonder why no one cares. But even those who care and love them are unable to stand being in the stench of the shit for long. Healing can only come to the abused person when they look up and ask God for help. Immediately an angel is sent to lift them from that mess. Then the healing can begin. As they are lifted up, and declare that they are done with that shit, it falls away from them. They are able to see more clearly. They are supported by people and circumstances around them that will allow them to heal and grow. When they have love and mercy on themselves, it becomes easier to forgive and forget the past abuses they have suffered.

*Many people will try to dominate*
*and kill you in body, mind and spirit.*
*Some will succeed. But none will kill your soul.*
*Your soul is eternal and is your God connection.*

Many clients are tired of giving their energy to old self-defeating ideas, self-abuse, and self-hatred attitudes that they may still be carrying around years after the actual abuse occurred. Even though it is painful, it is familiar. But the pain of past abuse is not over until you say it is over. Some clients I have worked with were not ready to confront the abuse and let the abuser go from their minds.

I remember one social worker who had been married five times and she admitted all of her husbands were just like her father. She said that all of her marriages were abusive. I was getting from Spirit that her father had been emotionally and sexually abusive. It was coming through very clearly to me. But she adored her father even 60 years after the abuse had occurred and still worshipped him. I had to just let her go, unhealed and unhappy. She was just not ready to acknowledge that the abuse had even occurred; of course, I did not bring it up and share it with her. She just was not ready. It was easier for her to blame the problems of her life on her abusive husbands than to see a pattern that attracted that sort of partner to her.

Change is also hard because abused clients have to recognize that they need help. Many try to do everything themselves, because they have a hard time trusting other people. Imagine that you are driving your car on a muddy dirt road and you get stuck in the ruts of the road. You cannot get out of it alone. You need help and support; you need to let someone else in to help you get out. The hardest part is that you will have to trust yourself and you have to decide to trust another person. If you can, in this moment, put out the signal or the intention, and you will find that help and support will start to come to you in the form of other people.

Believe me! Trust this advice. When you decide that you are *mad as hell and not going to continue the daily suffering in your own life*, then people will appear in your life to support your intention of freedom from the past. You will be flooded with opportunities to let your past go and let those who have hurt you go. It is such a burden to you to carry around people who have hurt you so many years after the actual words or acts were done.

No one wants to suffer anything, ever. All situations in our lives are meant to guide us to greater empathy, compassion and understanding for ourselves and our fellow human beings. When we forgive, and have mercy on someone who has hurt us, it means letting them go or letting some situation around them go. Having mercy and forgiving yourself is often harder.

Often the victim remembers every detail of the abuse whether it was one time, dozens of times or hundreds of times. The abuse can play over and over in their heads like a movie. Even when my clients have suppressed these memories, when I sense abuse I always ask this question, "Do you remember any traumatic things that happened to you when you were growing up?" They usually say yes and just start talking and sharing strange thoughts and memories from growing up. These usually lead to memories of abuse. The important part of this is that they are telling me, I am not telling them. It is so empowering to them to be able to dictate their own healing, with me serving only as a guide.

**Body Scan**

When I scan a person's body I can feel the abuse, and I need to determine if it happened in this life or if it is left over from a past life. I see what my client can see.

The peculiar part is that no matter how reserved or professional or composed the client was a few minutes earlier, they always remember things, or at least suspect that things happened, and have vague memories or feelings. If they do not recall anything, I ask about their relationships with family members. I will ask, "Do you feel creepy around any friends or family? Do you feel uncomfortable to be left alone in a room with someone?" Usually that releases even more.

Then I may also ask, "What is the earliest memory you have in your life? How far back can you go?" Most abuse victims cannot remember anything before the age when the abuse began. They have blocked the memories. They often deny what they cannot deal with on an emotional/intellectual level. If I sense current life or past life abuse, I ask a series of questions to uncover their story. I never tell what I see in these abuse cases. I do not want to introduce what my client may have suppressed. I can only confirm what they remember. It is actually not important that they remember specific words, emotions or physical touch. It is allowing for the possibility that things happened to them without their consent, that they may have been used or abused.

Then I will ask, "Do you remember any friends, family or neighbors that made you feel scared, uncomfortable or creepy?" I also ask, "Is there a person or persons that you would not like to be left alone with?" I don't press them for details, they usually just start to come out and the client thinks and remembers long forgotten things. There is no need to go into the details unless they want to. I tell them that now as adults they are in control and need never suffer that person or persons again.

This often involves some "wounded inner child healing" as well. The adult tells the child who was harmed at specific ages that they are grown up now and will protect the child that they once were. They give permission to the child to go out and play or do whatever it is that a child that age would like to do. Just go have fun!

At this point, we discuss the power of clearing those old harmful memories and give them the information and access to the universal energy of love which gives them the power to forgive and turn the offender over to God to be dealt with. All the pain and suffering they have experienced, and all the hate and resentment they may feel towards the offender may not have really caused any pain to the person who harmed them. Even if the offender was charged and went to jail, they do not care. The offender did not get any true punishment from what they did. They may deny it even happened.

Every child should be taught what is appropriate touching and affection, and what is not. Acceptable and unacceptable patterns of behavior are instilled in us early in life. Learning to distinguish what is acceptable in the society we live in is a lifelong chore.

One man, who was connected in a sort of spiritual bondage with his father years after his father's death, talked about his situation after

I sensed he had been abused. He said, "Daddy never laid a hand on me. He just would not talk to me for weeks at a time to show his disapproval and disgust with me. I didn't know that was abuse - it was just the way Daddy was."

Another man told me that his alcoholic father would punish him for whatever displeased him – it could be striking out at little league or failing to get all A's on his schoolwork. His father would urinate in the toilet and then push his son's head into the toilet and tell him what an idiot he was. He did not see that as abuse, he really thought he deserved it because he thought he was an idiot.

Sometimes there are improper connections that make up abuse or 'friendly' abuse. It might be from a friend, cousin, or babysitter who is exploring their own sexuality and wants to explore the victim's as well. Again, many people have described this to me but even as adults still did not think it was improper or abuse. Some even looked at me questioningly like I was off the mark, suspecting otherwise. They just accepted that this was part of growing up. Many also told me that it felt good physically so they did not think more about it until much later.

Sometimes abuse is discreet and quiet, even consensual, because the victim is accepting it as love and attention from the abuser or does not know any better. In cases of family incest, many times the victim's perception is not that there was abuse. One woman, who I sensed had been abused as a child, when I explored the subject said, "Uncle Charlie always liked to rub me. He rubbed all the girls -our backs, our chests and he always made us sit on his lap. It actually felt good when he rubbed my chest and privates. I did not think it was abuse then or even now at the age of 40. I thought that that was just the way Uncle Charlie was."

Much of the abuse that I have talked to my clients about seems to occur because there are already abusive relationships going on in their own homes or greater families. Generational incest is also something that families know happens, but do not talk about it. In many cases the abuser was abused when they were young. The Family Healing Prayer found in the Appendix addresses this also.

Many families I have worked with just accept various types of abuse as part of growing up. One or both parents may have been abused and it is like a rite of passage. Sometimes the abuse would start with one relative. Then the victim would be passed on to other family members and sometimes to outside friends as well.

By the time clients come to me, in most cases the abuse had already affected their adult relationships and marriages. They claimed various sexual dysfunctions but could not determine why.

When a victim does recall that there may have been some sort of mental, emotional, physical or sexual abuse in their house growing up, they often remember it happening to someone else first. They do have a deep suspicion that it may have happened to them as well and it is very often never discussed. Other family members will deny the story and condemn the victim which leads to greater confusion for the victim.

In many of the cases I have worked, at least one of the parents or caregivers knew of the abuse and quietly allowed it. Shame and fear kept the stories from coming out. Usually the accuser was accused by other family members of being a promiscuous, lying, crazy person and they end up being shunned by the rest of the family. The shunning becomes a second level of abuse that they suffer.

When I do the body scan we often find that some clients have done work to release the past trauma and abuse. If I detect it still in them, though, it is not totally resolved. The only way to completely clear them of their karmic connection is by using the Disconnecting Cords Procedure.

Many clients are happy to turn over this baggage to God. Some like to imagine that they are filling an ornate box with all of the memories and feelings that they no longer need, and then they wrap it up for God to hold.

When they confront their abusive memories and fear, they have two choices: either continue giving the person or the memory their power or not. If they choose to not give the memories and fear power, then they can surround the abuser with a bubble and fill it with love, understanding, and mercy. That usually has a much greater impact on the abuser than by being abusive back to them. The greatest thing an abused person can do against those who have used and abused them is to pray for them and then to turn them over to the Light (God). Some clients imagine filling a hot air balloon with all this and releasing it to rise ever higher into the sky, until it finally disappears from their sight and mind forever.

However, fear prevents many people from confronting their old memories. This is very sad because if they do not deal with the fear, they will continue to attract more fear and abuse into their lives. Old injuries cause painful relationships and marriages as the client is unable to trust, believe, respect, care for, or in many ways, connect with other people.

If what happened to you 30 years ago in your youth is still affecting your life today, you either must want it there or just don't know how to release it. This is fine if you like to display all your abused trophies on the shelf or if you want to be thought of as a martyr that no one understands and no one cares about, let alone could love. But my methods offer my clients a way out. Spirit tells me that when you are ready, we are here to serve you.

## One Example of Healing

Angela knocked on my door exactly at noon for her reading. When I opened the door, I saw a young woman who had beautiful eyes that were filled with sadness. For about three minutes as I was entering her energy, I had to fight the strong urge that I had to just hug her and tell her that everything was going to be alright. At that time, I had no idea why she sought me out or what I was supposed to tell her. I just felt this profound sadness and resignation coming out of her energy.

She was an introvert and very quiet, but I was not having any trouble picking up her vibration. She said that a friend told her to come see me, but that she did not even know why she bothered. She gave the impression that everything in life was a burden to her.

This was a person who was so sad; she just did not care anymore. She was beyond depressed. She had an air of melancholy that filled my office. I asked her what made her happy and she said that it was her ability to work and work hard all the time. That was all she had.

As usually happens in a reading, other spirits that were connected to Angela were alerted that she was with a person who could see and talk to them and receive messages from them. I told her that her beloved grandmother was present and was showing her rocking Angela as a baby. I could feel the love that they both felt for each other. Even in death her grandmother was her guardian angel and protector. But the grandmother had the same air of sadness, fear and resignation. She was careworn from her life, but she was not going anywhere until she knew that her granddaughter was protected.

I asked her about relationships and at age 33 she had had none that lasted over six weeks. She said, "I get a guy when I need one. And then use him until I am through with him. Then if I want another I go back on Tinder (a dating site)." I picked up a very strong bisexual vibe while doing the reading and I asked her about that and she said sometimes she "likes or thinks about other women." She also said that she gets "girl crushes" sometimes. I asked if she had ever explored this side of herself and experimented and she said, "No."

I asked her what she did for a living and she said she was a counselor and she "just wanted to help people and to protect them from themselves, from their demons".

I asked her how she protected herself from the energy that her clients were sending out. She said that she just listened and then followed the protocol to help them. But she never let herself get personally involved.

I shared messages from her grandmother - memories of happy times, people they knew, messages of encouragement. I shared career advice and future impressions that I was receiving about what she would do in the future, where she would live, how successful she would be - or not, depending on the choices she made.

We talked about my *Love Yourself First, Best and Always* idea and I offered her unconditional love and acceptance and expressed it to her. I asked her how she felt about that and she said, "What am I supposed to say?" I said, "If the energy feels good you can receive it, if it does not you can reject it. You are the boss." I told her that unconditional love is exactly that – unconditional. She did not owe me anything for that.

As the reading progressed she was more comfortable and her sad eyes turned to me now with a look that seemed to be saying, "I implore you to help me." It was getting really hard to hold my boundaries. I felt like I had known her before, some past life connection, perhaps. I felt like I owed it to her to do something to help her or support her in helping herself out of her present condition. So, the hour turned into two hours and, then three, and then four. She did not say much, but she was listening and nodding her head; sometimes she gently cried. She said that she never cried. She said that "only people who were weak - cry."

In our talk, Spirits said that we had "plowed many fields and planted many seeds that would blossom in her future." But they also told me that although she now had an arsenal of knowledge to protect herself and connect herself to a higher sourced energy, that we had not reached the core issues that brought her to see me.

We scheduled another appointment to do a past life hypnosis since we had established what she said was a "safe connection." I invited her to bring a friend during the hypnosis, but she said she did not trust anyone enough to do that. A song played on the radio that included the lyrics "safe and sound." I like those little coincidences.

A few days later, we did the hypnosis process. It is really just a matter of trust, comfort and relaxation. Deep, deep relaxation. My hypnosis technique is based on training I received from Dr. Brian Weiss, a well-respected psychiatrist who opened the door to a new generation about the healing power of past life hypnosis. My favorite script is found in his book *Messages from the Masters- Tapping into the Power of Love*. It is Meditation 1: Through the Door into Past Lives.

The hypnosis process was very empowering because she was able to tell me what was going on in her visions. I was guiding her, but she was in charge.

Angela focused on her breathing - deep breaths in and out. When she was in a deep relaxed state, I began by asking her which past life she wanted to start with. She received many messages from her past. In one life where she had suffered an unhappy marriage and life, she said, "Allow yourself to love – stop punishing yourself. Allow yourself to be loved. You have trouble trusting in love. You are more afraid of life that you are of death."

In another life, the advice she received was that she should "just feel the love around her and then it will come to her."

In a third life, she was a female who was married to a man who was physically, sexually and emotionally abusive to her and their four children. She said that they had a very comfortable life but – "We are not happy. We smile like it is OK, but it is not." The husband in that life was the same soul as her father in Angela's current life. She said, "I failed to protect my children." Her husband in that life abused the children in the same ways that he abused her. In her Angela life, those four children are her sisters and she is distant from them all. She said that has been the way it was since she was born (she is the youngest). It was like they "resented her from birth."

Then she abruptly changed positions on the couch as if she were trying to hide her face in the pillow. Her breathing became heavy and when she turned over her face was contorted in pain, like she was witnessing something so horrible she could not even find words to describe it. She started sobbing. As the hypnotist, I was able to lift her up to a higher level where she was just observing, not feeling or expe-riencing whatever it was that she was sensing. I asked her to describe what she was seeing, but she said nothing. She said that the scene had gone black in her eyes. She settled down and resumed shallow breathing. She seemed calm.

Then Angela was asked what else she was receiving from the spirits and lives that she had access to in hypnosis. She spoke directly to me, and said, "Rich, you need to help me find love and be happy. I need to learn how to trust and learn how to be loved and I need you to do that for me. I will let my guard down and let you help me. I trust you." She added, "Rich, there is a rough gentleness in your healing work, and it is not easy for you or the person that you are working with, but it works so well, because you come with unconditional love and acceptance."

Then she directed the comments she received to herself. "Angela has used her weight, her looks and her attitude to keep people away from her. When she stops seeing herself as less than perfect and learns to love herself, then she will learn that there is no part of her that is not from God", addressing herself in third person. She added, "Stop wearing a mask; if you are not happy with some situation, say so - no matter what the consequence. Just say the words you need to free yourself." Many people wear masks all the time to hide the deeper parts of themselves. When you learn to feel comfortable taking off the mask, you gain a new life. (Google – *The Picture of Dorian Grey*.)

I concluded the hypnosis and brought her back. She seemed happy and rested. It was about nine o'clock at night, there was huge full moon right behind her close to the horizon as she got in her car and headed home. But, I still did not think that we were done with our work together.

The next day was a Saturday and the call came early; she said that she needed to see me, that I would never believe what happened. She came right over. She was very shaken up. She said that just before she woke up, she had a dream that her father was molesting her from the age of 3 and up, just like he had molested and raped her four older sisters. She said that she woke throwing up all over her bed. She said that she could not stop gagging. The pictures flashed in front of her eyes, awake or asleep. Then she remembered hushed rumors that her sisters had also been abused. She had been able to block this memory even while under hypnosis. She was so shocked, because she adored her father. He died when she was 13. The abuse continued until that time. Then her mother married another man and he also abused her. She got as far away from her mother as she could on her 18th birthday, and moved across the country.

She said, "I thought that I had lost everything when I lost my father and when my mother remarried, I lost her also. I have been lost and alone and had no one to trust since my grandma died."

She went through all the stages of grief: anger, rage, denial, negotiation and then at first said that she hoped that her father, "the rotten bastard", burned in Hell for eternity. I explained how even that emotion makes a cord - the barest thread from her to him. In time, and after a great deal of conversation over many weeks, she was able to do the Disconnecting Cords Procedure. She disconnected from her father, mother, sisters, grandmother and stepfather. She reported that it was very effective and empowering.

She later verified that her sisters had also been abused, but were too ashamed to talk about it. She also heard of horrible abuse that happened to her mother. She realized that her mother was in some kind of strange Stockholm Syndrome situation. That is where an abused person bonds with their abuser and identifies with them and defends them.

She is starting a relationship with her mother and has discovered that she was also abused by her husband and that he was a drug user, alcoholic and womanizer, all behaviors that Angela had covered up in her memories of her father. She idolized him, maybe in part because she was so afraid of him.

Because Angela was strong enough to take the first step to healing, now this has allowed the abuse to not be a secret in her family any longer. Her sisters are now in therapy and so is her mother.

When she learned my techniques of how to protect herself and her client's energies, her effectiveness as a counselor increased.

Once we had identified the cause of some of the many issues in her life, she began to accept herself for the wonderful, smart, funny person that she was. A few months later she went to a lesbian bar. She explored that side of herself, found that she liked it and moved in with a partner within a few months. The last time I spoke to her she said that she was finally learning what being happy was all about. She had learned about *Going with the Flow* and what unconditional love was all about and practiced my motto - *Love Yourself First, Best and Always*, every day.

She later told me that she was suicidal on the day that I met her; she was just debating which was the most effective method because she did not want to be locked up in a mental ward if her attempt failed. She was thinking about jumping off the edge of the Grand Canyon, except she was so afraid of heights she did not get picture herself making a flying leap into the canyon.

## Just Start and Change Your Life

When you start to *Love Yourself First, Best and Always* then you will no longer be comfortable holding those memories of old abuse. Remember that fear, anger and worry are allowed by God to assist you in your karmic growth. When you learn the lessons abuse brings, the abuse will stop.

When I am reading a client I have to determine what has occurred, and to help identify who they need to release. The client needs to be motivated to change. They must trust me to hand them the keys to release them from the prison their life has become. I do not understand why so many of my clients have been abused, but I trust in God to guide me through their treatment. When they stop feeding the darkness, it will begin to move away from them.

The authority and control over their own life returns to them. They never really lost it; they just never knew they had that power inside of them. They always have the power and free will to change and to create whatever they want to see happen. But first, they must decide what that is. It is not hard to wish for change, or to acknowledge that you want to change, but it is so hard to cancel out and withdraw from old thought patterns and feelings. It is important to support people who wish to change. Otherwise they may fall deeper and deeper into anger and despair, and actually will attract that which they want release from.

Having a successful relationship after you have been abused is difficult, if not impossible, unless you have let go of your past. Talking and counseling is usually essential to this process. If you were raised with chaos or abuse you will probably seek it out in your adulthood because it feels familiar to you. It feels right even though it can hurt so bad.

Often you will invite people into your life so that you can save or help or heal them, because you failed at doing those things with the people who abused or neglected you. I cannot tell you how many times I have seen this. I've had clients who are reliving their past with new people; some are on their third or fourth marriages but still not happy.

Children may become so conditioned to abuse and neglect growing up when their parents don't care or don't listen to them or love them in the way that they need to be loved, that they expect nothing more in their lives.

If a child is conditioned to abuse, it is easier for education, government and society to continue the pattern of abuse. If you mix that in with low self-esteem and feelings of unworthiness it can take a lot of work to climb out of that hole.

You are putting out the signal that you want more abuse, more anger, worry and fear and, if you look at your life, you will find that this has been the rule, not the exception.

The negative feelings, thoughts, emotions and experiences you had in childhood will be recreated in your present life. You will create the world that you want or do not want. You may have behaviors or coping techniques you learned growing up that are no longer serving you in adulthood.

Children may go to school and be bullied and abused by other children if they are in any way different - too short, too tall, too fat, too thin. The other students can be mean. The teachers are often so overworked in a time-controlled situation that they cannot help.

Many of the abuse stories have so been shocking to me. When someone takes away your power, your hopes and dreams, it can break your will to go on. In fact, I have seen many people like this in my life. I call them lost souls. They are still alive, still beautiful and attractive but without roots to themselves.

Many people suffer because their throat chakra is 80 percent clogged. They do not say what they need to say. This can often be tracked back to when someone made them feel stupid or small or inadequate when they tried to say something and it is a direct result of this kind of abuse. They just have to say what they need to say.

I worked with a lady who had trouble with a throat chakra that was mostly blocked. She was afraid to say what she thought or truly felt which resulted in those around her being confused and angry at her. She reacted to the confusion and anger by pulling away and using only half sentences and silence, which made it worse. She needed to figure out what she wanted to say and then say it in a kind and respectful manner. This was traced back to the first time she remembered being told to be quiet when she really needed to speak up about her truth.

I teach that it is safe to speak the truth without fear or prejudice. In part, this comes from releasing the need to control others and, also, letting go of caring what other people think of you. When you stop giving away your power to those who seek to control, use and diminish you, your life will begin to change.

First, you must believe in yourself or you will be put into nearly impossible situations. People will attempt again and again through subterfuge, disguise, and force to make you submit, quit and/or die quietly inside. But don't, don't, don't.

"Nobody can save you but yourself, and you're worth saving. It's a war not easily won, but if anything is worth winning then this is it," said Charles Bukowski.

I always share with my clients that they are a creation of God and that they have a spark of God within them. By continuing with their self-hatred, low self-esteem and low confidence, and carrying the anger, pain and worry into every new situation in their lives, they are actually disrespecting God. This is true. Many clients do things for other people, but they lack the self-love and motivation to do the same things for themselves.

I tell my clients that if they allow the positive changes, then their children do not have to repeat the same agonies and pain that they experienced. Many clients are very giving to others and find it difficult to direct some of the love, care and affection back to themselves. I advise them to try something: every time they look into a mirror, they should look into their eyes and learn to see inside themselves, to make love to their own eyes in the mirror, to see their own soul looking back at them. This triggers happiness from within that can be allowed to come out, if they receive the proper support. Praying and meditation are one level of self-love. Counseling and caring are what I do. Allowing and accepting is what they do. But some are not ready, and I respect that also. Still, some refuse to bloom into the glorious creations they are and they stifle their own growth.

I have seen over and over that people with this God connection inside of them want to help others, even though they have not yet helped themselves. They have gone through circumstances that have tried their souls and they have survived. They are now worthy teachers. Now they want to reach out to people who are going through the same trials and pain. That is why I have written this book, to make it easier for people who are sensitive, empathic, intuitive and old souls to assimilate better into the world while still having access to their spiritual gifts.

When the healing is done, I remind them that now they are in charge of their own body and have full authority over who touches them. They have the power to say "No" or "Stop" or "That is enough." It is important to say what I am going to do instead of just doing it, because their space has already been violated many times during the abuse and by people doing things to them without their consent. It is important that they feel empowered and not ashamed to speak up to protect their own bodies and the space around them.

Then it is important that they do not attach anything to the response from the person they are saying "No" to. They should not judge themselves based on the emotional reaction of the other person who is seeking to come into their space. Giving them the opportunity to say "No" several times will expose them to this new power of having total control over their own bodies and space. After I create a safe space between us, I ask permission as we go along. Even when we are done, when I usually give a person a hug, I always ask permission first. Honoring and respecting who they are and who they are healing into is very important.

On the other hand, when I scan and address specific areas of the body that were touched inappropriately, it is important for the client to take ownership for those body parts. Often we address the sex organs. I will have the client tell those parts that he or she is an adult now, they are in charge and will not let anything inappropriate happen again. They have the power to decide who can touch them and when and for what purpose. This is part of the healing and releasing of the wounded inner child.

Even after the healing, it may still be difficult for them to say what they need to say, to give themselves permission to speak. In the past, they may have been slapped, ridiculed, blackmailed or threatened into not speaking or taking any actions at all. Their session with me is all about recovering from the trauma and illness of past events. This is no long-term project; you can heal minute by minute. Sometimes healing happens instantly.

Many clients have been sexually abused and, while it was sometimes forced and non-consensual, many have reported that physically it felt good. They might have gotten turned on. Later this confuses them when they are with a person they do consent to having sex with. Being touched in certain places on your body can feel good and still be inappropriate or wrong. Or maybe there were other issues like emotional connections (they said they loved you or that you were special) to the person. Or they felt love or approval or attention that they were not receiving from friends or parents or family. I have counseled hundreds of women who have been the victims of abuse. From the outside they look like everyone else. But on the inside they have been abused and lost some part of themselves.

Some clients like to be identified by their tragedies and my work seeks to give them new life goals to identify with instead.

The men and women whom I have worked with were violated and now they want to heal and give back, but still they carry the threads or chains of the past abuse. They want to help others to heal, but sometimes they have not been able to allow healing in themselves. Some respond by giving into it. I have seen many women who go from one sexually abusive relationship to another. This is because they want to be loved and do not want to be alone; the verbal and emotional abuse seems like love to them.

It is so hard to know how to get out of the box they have created for themselves. The coping strategies that worked to survive and get through their past traumas are still employed in their daily lives and draw people into their lives that will abuse them. Some are still the subject of unwanted advances so they tend to hide from relationships, connections and life.

**Physical Abuse**

Physical abuse is not as common in my practice, but it is always difficult to hear about. There are so many excuses about the other person being drunk or high, or that the abuser told the victim they were asking for it or deserved it.

Sometimes victims of abuse describe themselves as damaged or broken and are waiting for someone to recognize that they are not happy. They want to change and want someone to rescue them. They are lost and unable to connect with other people because they are unable to trust, respect and care. It also means they would have to accept that they need to love themselves, and to safely accept unconditional love and acceptance from another person who wants to support their growth.

Boundaries are important in life, but so is trust and respect. People need to know that they are not alone and they do not need to continue their lives unable to trust or rest, even for a moment in the warmth of another person's spirit.

Sometimes mean people have power over us. It just happens. We don't like it and usually don't yet have the knowledge or strength to keep fighting against them. We don't know how to make it stop. It is like the sibling who would tickle you endlessly, or after being yelled at by Mom for touching, she would then stand an inch away from you pointing in your face and yelling, "I am not touching you!" Why people do this is not a mystery. Often when we have emotional connections that are intense in this life, they are rooted in past life relationships. We do not understand why we do not like someone or why they seek to dominate and use or abuse us. These connections can begin with your parents, family, friends, or neighbors and they always are accompanied by intense and usually unexplainable feelings.

Sometimes you have legal or moral obligations to those who used or abused you or allowed it to happen. In this case, if it was a parent who abused you, I advise my client to do this exercise to reorder their relationship with that parent. They say or send a note or card with these words, "Thank you for creating me, birthing me, feeding me, protecting me (at least some of the time they must have protected you or you would not have survived, even if they did it so they could keep abusing you). Thank you for letting me go. Love, (sign your name)." If your parent is dead or incompetent, you can burn it.

In fact, this procedure can help in all of your relationships. It will help move you to a new status from your original relationship status.

Currently, you may be suffering because you have a "parent-child relationship" with one or both of your parents. That was wonderful when you were seven, but now at 40, it is not appropriate. You would be in a better place if you moved into an "adult-adult relationship" with your parents. You might take a lot of crap from your parent that you would not take from a friend in an "adult-adult relationship."

If you were, or are, abused and do not want to release yourself from those old ties, you will find many problems with this statement. But no matter what happened, they created you and you are, in fact, a gift to yourself and the world. "Thanks for letting me go." This is a sticky point. Maybe the abuse was so bad they never let you go and you never let them go. Now you are in a position of power over them, maybe regarding their residency, or health care, or life and death decisions, so you need to rise up and become their equal. Saying this or writing it to them in a note ends your "parent-child relationship." It creates your new "adult-to-adult relationship." Love your neighbor as you love yourself. This is very important because it allows you to access power to deal with people who used to have power over you and hurt you. When you allow yourself to forgive and have mercy on them and turn them over to God, you are in fact saving yourself, helping yourself and loving yourself.

Many times people that abused you many years ago will not remember it, or deny that it ever happened. Or even worse, they may have deluded themselves into believing that you in some way invited it or wanted it or, worse, deserved it. There may be so many other abuse victims that the abuser cannot even remember them all if they tried.

We all want acceptance and love, and for people to care for us and acknowledge us. We want to feel important to another person. We want what we think, say and do in life to matter. But first it must matter to ourselves. Then if we share it and we help others with it, that's fine; but we must stop giving away our power to other people who could care less what we think or feel.

The people that hurt you the most on this side are the ones who love you the most on the other side. Wait! What? Read that again. The people that hurt you here on Earth are the people who love you the most in Heaven? What? By this we mean that they love you enough to be a part of the lessons and opportunities that you will need to learn. They are in your soul group. They are just like actors in your play of life. Everything happens for a reason. Every painful, awful thing can give you lessons and growth. Knowing that God always loves you unconditionally means it does not matter what you have done in your life or failed to do in your life. It does not matter if you have experienced joy or suffered, it means that lessons came to you and you learned from them. Then that allows you to move away from them in the future.

When you care for yourself you will begin to respect what you are all about, what you believe in and what you want in your life. It is very important to like yourself and have a relationship with yourself. You deserve it, you are a survivor, and no one can touch you or take advantage of you anymore. You are an adult now and you can handle anything that comes your way. When you start noticing your intuition, it dramatically increases along with other spiritual gifts. In fact, the people you have around you may also change because you are now able to say what you need to say without fear of rejection or condemnation. You will recognize this spark of the Divine in yourself and it will attract new people to you. You will then see the spark of the Divine in them as well.

Sometimes in life, in order to *love yourself first, best and always*, you need to turn the other cheek and get the hell away from people that hurt you or do not respect you. It may hurt for a while, but it is the best thing you can do for your future.

Learning to love yourself is hard work. Learning how to create a new life with yourself despite your imagined shortcomings and faults is hard work. At the next level you will learn to ignore other people's ideas about who you are, what you know, and how you look. Do not believe what others have told you; do not believe even your own ideas about yourself, which are likely not correct.

There is a spark of beauty in each of us and when that spark ignites, great changes begin to occur such as self-love, self-respect, self-confidence and an increase in self-esteem. This also means the end to self-abuse, self-loathing, self-sabotage and self-pity. When you have mercy on *yourself*, it is the start of a whole new chapter of your life.

When someone has harmed you, bless them, have mercy on them, forgive them once, and forgive them 1,000 times if need be. It is good for you and lets you release yourself from them more and more until there is no longer any connection.

When I first started doing the abuse release work, many people could forgive but not forget. I thought that could work, but it does not. Not forgiving plants seeds of anger and resentment that silently grow over the years. It costs you nothing to release a person from your field who has abused you; you also release your internalized anger and resentment, which has been harming you, not them.

People may be strong at the start of relationships, friendships and in family situations, but when abuse and intimidation goes on for so long, they get worn down. Then the abuser assumes greater and greater control.

Sometimes, the abuser and the victim come to need each and rely on each other in some curious type of co-dependent relationship. This can happen even in the finest homes. Abuse is everywhere – wherever people do not feel empowered to say "NO."

The abused person may be unable to believe it because they do not have a history of hearing good things about themselves so they reject the message. They are often more comfortable in the dysfunctional, abused state. That is alright, it is their choice and not your business. As much as that might pain you as their friend you should have faith that there is something they need to learn from that connection. You cannot force someone to heal or seek help.

Some people developed methods to not suffer on the inside on a spirit level, adopting a mantra of "never give in - never give up." They have managed to save some part of themselves while suffering the abuse. They may have had no other choice but to endure the abuse.

However, the thick walls and defenses they built around them for protection now impair them in life. It threatens their physical and mental health.

You do not need to go back down to the abuser's level to free yourself from their abuse. Memories or visions of the abuse are hard to remember and can be even harder to erase if the Disconnecting Cords Procedure is not followed. It's important to know that they have all been saved at your soul level in case you ever need to refer to them again (maybe because you are counseling people). Otherwise, they are best gone. They are no longer needed.

After the release of the abuser a re-education process needs to begin for your mental, emotional and physical bodies. You will have to retrain and re-feel what you need to learn, think and know about yourself and your relationships with others.

Some clients are addicted to the pain, the abuse, and the drama. They have no sense of self-worth and, even when they are freed of the abuse and its aftermath, they refuse to believe that they have any value in the outside world. Some women become codependent on the men who abuse them. They may even financially support men who abuse them.

When any abuse situation is exposed to the light of day, when the abused shares their story with another person and plans a strategy to get away from it, then the power that the abuser has over them begins to weaken.

The best part is that when I am done counseling someone, I pray for them for a day and then it is like everything that happened is put in an invisible file and taken away from me. If they call, even years later, it is instantly brought back to my mind. It is so amazing and keeps me from having their energy affect my life.

# CHAPTER 16

## *Healing Stories*

This chapter will include stories of actual cases where clients experienced spiritual, mental, emotional and physical healing while working with me. I attribute my gifts to God and the Universal Energy of Love.

### When Healing Fails

I have had cases where my clients did not experience healing.

Healing fails because healing cannot be forced on someone. Each of us has free will and we can do whatever we want in life. It may be good for us or it may hurt us, but we always have that choice. No one can take that away from us. If a person has not learned the lesson of what is happening to them, or they are not ready to receive healing, the healing will fail.

There are many reasons that a healing will fail. Perhaps a person has karmic debt still owed to others. Sometimes they do not feel they are worthy of the healing, or the time for healing is just not right. That does not mean that it can never occur, just not now. When I first started using my gifts to heal, it would frustrate me because I often unconditionally loved my client more than the client loved themselves. This is frustrating to me because I want them healed, but it does not work. We are both disappointed. However, when I remember to *radiate love without concern for results* and give my client what I have to share, then it is up to them to use it or not. It is a lesson I had to learn – I could "lead a horse to water, but I can't make him drink."

When I first started healing, I wished to help everyone right here, right now. But that is not my role. I have dozens of stories of people who have tried to help their own families or friends with healing energy and failed. They feel abused and misled. One person was told by his wife, "You can help heal perfect strangers but you can't heal your own family? That's bullshit!" This can create bad feelings all around. Now I ask God to send me people who are ready for the spiritual gifts that I bring.

I have had clients who said they wanted healing, but there are various forms and levels of healing. I have often been told by Spirit that while I can pour some healing, love, and knowledge into someone, I must be careful to "not over fill the pitcher." Sometimes they are ready for emotional healing but not spiritual healing. Or they are ready for mental healing but not physical. I am often told to remind them that "progress is the goal, not perfection."

There is another group of people who want to tell God what to do, when to do it and how to do it. This simply does not work. Healing does not come to this group, either, because their ego prevents it.

I have to push my ego aside as well because the healing a person needs may only come when I do nothing. A wise elderly woman once told me "Rich! Shut the Fuck Up and Listen!" She said, "The healing will come just by you being present in the moment."

I often run into the problem of wanting to do too much before a person is ready. I need to remember that just because I have my healing gifts it does not mean everyone is ready for them. As I train others on receiving their spiritual gifts I remind them to respect what the client will allow. It can be too easy to overwhelm a person and healing will not occur at all.

Healing can be instantaneous, but it is more common for there to be degrees of healing. Most people have many layers that they need to release before healing can begin.

I use a combination of therapies and methods, but if you are not ready to let go of your anger, pain, fear and worry, and move to a place of understanding and forgiving someone or past circumstances, healing cannot occur.

Some clients are addicted to the drama in life and thrive on it. One client had been a hooker and drug dealer. She was drawn to the dark side, but had an attraction to the light as well. She said she liked to dance with the devil and the DEA. But she was also drawn to God. Fortunately, the God got to her first.

## Spiritual Healing

I have known and worked with many Catholic priests and nuns who have spiritual gifts of healing and have been forced to deny or use them for fear of being reprimanded. The priest who conducted the healing on me had been healed from blindness as a child by some miracle.

Another person, whose work has heavily influenced my life, is Francis MacNutt, a former Catholic Dominican priest who was ordained in 1956 and baptized his congregants in the Holy Spirit. This is something I do for all my clients today which you can read about in the healing chapter. He learned that his ministry was not compatible with the teachings of the Catholic Church. Perhaps the Church did not want to lose the control they had over its members by people who received direct revelations and spiritual information directly from God.

Francis' ministry was ignited from the Pentecostal Protestant movement and is now practiced openly in the Catholic Church as the Catholic Charismatic Movement. In 1980 he married, which resulted in his automatic excommunication from the Catholic Church. Then he received a dispensation from the Catholic Church and the marriage was celebrated by a Catholic Bishop. He and his wife were allowed back into the Church. The important thing is that he decided to do the right thing to help support spiritual growth in other people and it came at great cost to him. He chose to go outside the Church, but his practice has changed the lives of tens of thousands of people. I do work that he does as well. It may not be widely understood or accepted by the Catholic Church, but it is important and gaining recognition. God does not need the recognition of some church, though, to show his greatness here on Earth. He is in each one of us who seeks to love God, love ourselves and our brothers and sisters.

I feel that my work is much like Francis'. I am working outside of established churches to bring people back to the God already living in their hearts.

Doing healing work is sometimes about doing the right thing at the right time. God puts people in the places they need to be so that they can be conduits for the healing love energy that is available and abundant.

## Mental Healing

My clients feel they are different from most other people. I tell them they are in the five percent of people who are very spiritually connected and sensitive. I tell them that they should not compare themselves to the 95 percent of people who are have turned off their spiritual connection. They are not crazy, just wired differently from other people. This is such a relief to them when they hear that. Many tell me they had to always pretend to be who they were told to be because the real them was just not acceptable.

Some people start crying when they learn they are not crazy and that I recognize their gifts. Then we talk about finding soul mates in all aspects of their lives and how like-minded people are all around to help us out.

I have worked with Catholic nuns and priests from five different orders. Just because they are in the God business, does not make their lives perfect. They know that people look up to them, so they sometimes have lives of stress, trying to walk on eggshells all the time. The primary subject we talk about is how to continue to have faith and trust in something greater than themselves. It is like preaching to the choir, I thought when I first started. These people had taught me and I looked up to them. The first nun I worked with had stopped saying the rosary. She said that she did not know if she believed anymore, given the state of the Roman Catholic Church. Her faith had been tested and she was shutting it down. We did a reading to find that she had been under spiritual attack for some time and that it was depleting her. She had changed the lives of thousands of people because of her faith, so the darkness had targeted her for attack. I spoke to her about remembering who she was and what her mission in life was.

We also included some easy behavior changes. The Catholic Mass requires that before you take communion (the bread), you say, "Lord, I am not worthy to receive you, but only say the word and I shall be healed." The nun said she could see the truth of that once, but she questioned it now since she was doing good works 12 hours a day. What was making her unworthy between Mass on Sunday and the following Sunday?

Her attitude changed after she started saying, "I am worthy to receive you!" She saw how she could serve her fellow sisters and the people she worked with, and she did not have to feel responsible for or swallow all the other negative parts of the Catholic Church that were not under her control. She said she traded in her old life for a new life with the Living Christ, the Christ who helps people on the streets. She had to be discreet about it, but her life changed.

I have worked with a dozen religious sisters who were very intuitive, but when they talked about it publicly, they were shunned and made to take it underground. This is curious since the Catholic Church's saints were a collection of prophets, mystics, and others who had similar spiritual gifts.

## Sexual Identity

Many people have secrets when they come for a reading. They try to hide certain parts of themselves because they think that if others knew their secret they would not be liked anymore. Once you give a secret such strength, you empower it and it grows as a bigger threat in your mind. Your own secrets, and those that you keep for others, cause you to lose your power. Your own secrets can abuse you.

Secrets that come up all the time are the sexual secrets: what they have done, what they want to do with others, or how they want to be with people of the same sex. Spirit calls it the "bisexual issue." Each of us has free will to like or want to be with anyone we wish. If it is consensual and pleases you, then the Universe does not care about it. Often clients will be terrified thinking they might be gay or bisexual, and they will try to hide their feelings.

But secrets do not last long around me. My work is about putting all the secrets and past abuses on the table and taking away any power they have over you. When we talk about this issue and they acknowledge their feelings, I just unconditionally love them, do not judge them, and do not make an issue about it. I tell them, "Okay, now another person knows your secret. So what? Let us move on. Do whatever you want in the sex department with whomever you want to be with. I hope you are very happy as long as you choose to be together." Spirit offers the term androgynous as an explanation for this situation. This implies that you are attracted to and love all people. This does not even need to translate into sex.

## Your Past Ends When You Allow It To

I refer clients to *The Four Agreements* book by Don Miguel Ruiz, because it teaches them to question all of their perceptions about themselves, as well as all those ideas, rules, and customs passed on to them by churches, parents, educational systems, schools, society and culture. They can make their own connection with God and evaluate themselves in this new light, coming to realize that they are an amazing person. God made you that way, own up to it!

As I have said throughout this book, it is hard when you finally take control of your life. It is hard mentally, emotionally and even physically. It will crush many of your ideas and beliefs that you have had your whole life. It is like you are being given a pair of glasses for the first time in your life. Ignorance, short-sightedness and lack will be gone in an instant. If you try too hard to be constantly balanced and perfect according to your old standards or those of others, it is even harder. Give it up! Life is about ebb and flow. A natural balance will resume at a higher spiritual level in your life shortly.

When people come for my assistance I feel like a triage nurse in an emergency room. They have several things we could work on but trying to do too much at once is overwhelming to them, so I try to address the top one or two issues. Then I plant seeds of restorative change knowing that they will grow when the client is ready for them. The seeds are hope, compassion, understanding, forgiveness and patience.

Healing can happen on many levels. When people try to do the right thing for their families, friends, business associates and customers, good things will happen. This is the Spirit of Good (the Spirit of God) that lives in each of us and is brought out best when we love ourselves, and then love our neighbors in small or large ways.

I can be the catalyst to healing, but I am also the witness to healing. These spiritual gifts come through me but do not originate here. Unfortunately, fear often triggers a need for healing. It motivates and imprisons many people in the world. Much of society is fear-based, whether it's fear of disease, or fear of not having enough life or disaster insurance. It makes some people (corporations, for example) huge fortunes. Elements of society based on love, understanding and compassion often help people tremendously, but by contrast, these activities are not as popular with some people because they have little monetary reward.

As we have outlined previously, mental or physical illness is the result of DNA, karma, worry, fear and anger. Even when we do encounter illness, we can learn from it and move past it. It is what your soul needs to make you a better, stronger person. I have seen this happen in my work many times.

Illness is about fear. The medical establishment is about fear. The pharmaceutical companies market fear. The Government promotes fear. Wall Street and insurance companies also operate on fear and profit from it.

Control and fear of loss changes people and destroys relationships.

## Exit Counseling - You Get Healed, But You Still Die

Exit counseling is done when a client is near or preparing for death; it prepares them, their family, and their friends for the journey. A woman was suffering from cancer and I was brought in to do exit counseling. She was in her early sixties and very beautiful. She had been poisoned by toxic chemicals. A local company had dumped the waste into the water supply. She had all the indignity and suffering of a cancer patient who had tried everything, and she was mad as hell at the inequity of it. The cancer was taking away her beauty, her hair, her ability to control her functions, and her dignity.

Her family had set up a hospital bed in her living room and hospice had been called in. She was a woman of strong words. When she came home from the hospital, she sat on the couch and her family could not get her into the bed. I had her hold my neck and transferred her to the bed. She said, "You nearly dropped me." I said, "No, you nearly let go." As I said, she was very angry to be dying. She had worked hard and raised a family she wanted to see prosper. She was mad.

It was a large Hispanic family and friends and neighbors came around to visit and pray. They brought tamales, tacos, rice, beans, shredded beef, barbacoa and menudo, a soup made out of cow's stomach, and many cakes and cookies. It was a feast, and it was a good-bye party for the person who was leaving. Slowly she slipped away and was asleep more and more each day. Day by day, she grew weaker. I could see her leave her body for the first time. She was still connected to her body by a silver cord. I told her it was okay and that she would be safe. Still, even while she was dying and beginning to separate from her body, she was mad that people were enjoying their time together.

In her anger, she went around the room (in spirit form) talking to people about events that had happened many years before. She had things to say and she was saying them. Some things were not so nice. This went on for two days. When she had told everyone what she needed them to hear, at least what their Spirit could hear, she was tired and pleased with herself. Then she and I talked about the cause of the death. She was worried about her money, her car, and her husband.

I told her they would all be fine; she did not need to worry about that anymore. Everything would be fine. She would be leaving behind on Earth all the pain, humiliation and indignities that the cancer had delivered into her life. Things were going to be amazing for her when she died.

The day before the woman died she and I both saw her deceased parents. We also saw the angel of death standing by her bed, and the tunnel with the light at the end of it. In her case, since she believed in Jesus Christ, He is who came through. I have seen different entities appear with people who have different beliefs. I explained to her how it all worked, that she would just slip away to the other side. She would be out of her body and not come back. She could stay around in spirit form for as long as she chose. She could see her memorial services and watch how people mourned her loss; see her burial and then she would pass into Heaven. She smiled. The next day, by the time I got there, the hospital bed was empty. She was healed emotionally and spiritually, relieved of her anger, fear and suffering, and it allowed her to peacefully cross over to the other side.

## Physical Healing: My first time nearly killed me!

The first time I ever did physical healing, I did not do it right. I used my own body's energy, and I was depleted and sick for two weeks afterwards. The healing was for a friend's mother who had had a stroke and was in a coma. This was a family that was very rigid and did not talk about things. My friend was the last of the family. His mother was expected to die at the time when I went to the hospital and prayed over her. I put her feet on my forehead, connected her energy to the Earth, and allowed the flow to go through me. She woke up. She was completely lucid and said everything she had never said to her son in his 52 years on Earth. Things like, "I love you!" and "Thanks for being a great son!" She died a week later, but those last days they had together were the best he ever remembered in his life. They both said what they wanted to say and it was magical.

After she died I went to his house to pay my condolences. I was walking up his sidewalk and I watched him lay out photos on the couch that he wanted to display at the funeral. I saw his mother dressed in her burial clothes, her best dress, with hair done up and makeup on. Her spirit was sitting in her favorite chair and smiling at him. She stayed there the entire visit. I did not tell him that, as I was not yet ready to talk to people about my spiritual gifts. But her recovery and her presence gave me great confirmation that I was on the right path. After that, I learned how to allow God's energy through me so I did not deplete my core energy.

## Breast Cancer

One client that had suffered greatly from a radical mastectomy which involved removal of the lymph nodes around the area, came for a healing. She was four and a half years into recovery. The popular wisdom is that if you can survive five years, you are considered healed. In reality, some still get cancer after that.

The woman was so worried about the bad news that she imagined I would tell her that she could not relax enough to start the reading. I listened to her describe "her cancer" and I said, "If you think of it as 'the cancer' it would help. If you think of it as an invader, not a resident, mind over matter will seek to make it something that you used to have."

We had trouble starting the reading because she was scared and upset. Finally, I looked her straight in the eyes and said, "You are going to die, your parents are going to die, your children are going to die, your brothers and sisters are all going to die. That is the result of life. You die! But you are not going to die for at least another 36 years. This is what Spirit told me."

Sometimes I tell people that I am hearing from Spirit the age when they will die because it plants the seed of longevity in them and helps them to move on. There are a million variables, but sometimes it is helpful. I said, "You dying is not as important as what you are going to do with the next 36 years. Who are you going to help, who are you going to love, what joy will you find and what joy will you make for others?" Death is a common fear and it is amazing to me that so many people forget that death comes to us all. Knowing that death is in your future, and that things will be all right if you have some minimal understanding of the process, makes it something to not be feared.

Fear invites abuse, worry, anger, unemployment, eviction, foreclosure, despair and depression. Fear, worry and regret can bring an early death.

## Spiritual, Mental, Emotional and Physical Healing

One of the first times I did healing in a hospital setting was for a 74-year-old man. Part of his right foot had been cut out due to complications from untreated diabetes. When I saw him the wound had turned the foot almost black and gangrene had set in. He was depressed and wanted to die. The doctor wanted to cut the foot and leg off up to just below his knee. I laid my hands over the wound area as I talked and prayed, and let the healing energy come through me. I saw the angel of death in the room with him. He looked very close to death and was unresponsive as I did my prayers and hands-on healing. I said, "I'm going to pray for you tonight, and I'll see you tomorrow. I love you." He was too sick to even respond.

The next day when I came into the room, he was sitting up in the bed surrounded by family. The foot had gone from almost black to bright pink. His body and soul were reinvigorated from the prayers. He said, "Rich how are you today? I forgot to tell you yesterday that I love you! I'm sorry about that." His wife chimed in and said, "He's been saying that he loves everyone today." This was despite the fact that in the 40 years of their marriage he never said "I love you" or "I am sorry" to his wife for anything.

He was raised to believe that if he provided for and educated them; his family would know that he loved them. That is what his father had taught him. He said all that love talk was for women, not men. It was understood through their lives that they had that connection; he just had never verbalized it.

We were able to resolve many other issues that had been depleting him of his energy. On my last visit he was in very good spirits and was healing, until the doctor came and talked to him for two hours, in what he described later as a session of fear, about why they he needed to cut off the leg. The doctor used fear to advocate that surely the gangrene would reappear and spread, and that he should still cut off the leg below the knee. Although it appeared that it was not medically necessary at the time, they cut off the leg as a preventative. He adapted to an artificial leg and is now happy in his life. The last time I saw him he was positively glowing. Losing the leg was part of another of his karmic lessons. He and his wife are fine now. Some people have harder lessons to learn than others do.

## The Dead Healing the Living

In one reading with a young man, a Jewish Holocaust survivor came through in spirit; he had died the week before. Originally, he was scheduled to die in 1942. He was a child standing in a line of men who were awaiting a firing squad. The shots were fired and the men all fell to the ground. But a bullet did not hit him. One of the dying men collapsed on him and he was trapped under him. This saved his life. Then Jewish prisoners came to remove the bodies and found and freed the boy. He lived until the age of 79. In his comments to his grandson that day, he told him that "the lesson of life is to not worry about death. Death is going to happen no matter what you do. You have no choice in when or how. So why worry about it? "He said that "he found joy in a cup of coffee, a good meal, a beautiful woman and a fat baby." He said that when "you enjoy your life by staying busy and helping others, you will be happy. That is the best thing that you can do to help yourself." Then he asked his grandson to congratulate him on his death. The grandson, now in tears said, "Mazel Tov on your passing!" It was a joy-filled moment for all of us.

When we lose touch with who we are and why we are here, we lose touch with our souls and our spirits. That invites illness, disorder, and stress. If we try to stay in touch with what we need to live and enjoy our time in our bodies, wonderful things can happen. Even in sadness, joy can be found.

One man I'd counseled seven years' prior called me one day. He told me all that I had told him so long ago and that he had not followed any of my advice. My predictions about his life came true. He remembered that I had told him, "If you are with this woman, your life will be filled with pain and suffering." Their relationship and marriage was based on a negative past life connection, and the marriage deteriorated after the first year. She had a cocaine and alcohol problem that fueled her sex addiction. She refused to work, and constantly berated this man. She told him he was an unworthy piece of garbage. She started bringing her lovers home and humiliated him. One night he was asleep on the couch and his wife was in their bedroom with a lover. He remembered the words I had told him, *"Love Yourself First, Best and Always."* He opened his eyes and saw an angel sitting at the end of the couch. The angel said, "So are you loving yourself?" The next day he left. He lost everything he had and was $100,000 in debt, but he said it was worth it because he was free. He said, "Praise God! I am free!"

## Sexual Abuse Healing

Almost half the people I work with have experienced sexual abuse. I tell them that they are in control of their lives and show them how they can release themselves from this past if they forgive and turn the abuser over to God. When you are a grown up, you are in control, though some people act as if they are not. I show them that they are in control now, and to forgive themselves and others who have hurt them and get on with their lives. If you love yourself enough you can let go of the anger, shame, hurt and regret. You have the power. You do not need lengthy counseling bringing up old memories and suffering again. You just need love to clean up your life.

Your mind/ego seeks to help you avoid unpleasantness, strife and change, unless you will directly benefit from it, to protect yourself. But avoidance hurts you mentally and spiritually.

Remember, or allow the thought, that we are all born perfect, exactly as God created us. God does not make junk. All life is beautiful. As we learn to appreciate this, we learn to appreciate others and ourselves. We have a chance of seeing it in ourselves.

One man said that he never liked himself and his father always used to tell him, "Shit happens. Get over the events in your life." He felt empty and alone until he reconnected to the Universal energy.

Spiritual and emotional healing are the fastest forms of healing to take effect. Muscle and soft tissue healing comes next. Bone/skeleton healing takes more time, at least for me at the level of healing that I am able to offer right now. The very subject of pain is also a big deal. When you do not suffer pain your whole life will change. When you are debilitated to the point that the pain overtakes your life, it is time to change your life, and change your attitude about yourself. It is easier to change yourself than to suffer increasing pain and loss of function.

Small healings, such as when you stub your toe, are bleeding, or when your children have pain, are very easy when you align to the energy and push out the energy disruption. Headaches, backaches and menstrual pains are quick to leave as well. Longer term healing always involves more work. I teach people how to gather pain and cast it out into the ground and, with practice, it gets easier.

## Discovering Who You Really Are

The "real you" is quietly functioning inside you all the time. This may not be the person that your mate, friends, or employer sees. Often that is a persona, a mask, you created to help you function in the world. When you seek to combine all of your "selves" into one "you," then this will allow you to be who you really are so you can pursue what it is that you want in life. The role that you have for work is not who you really are; people in business create a persona all the time.

I found this out from personal experience being the IRS bad guy (in some people's opinions). Having a business persona keeps business from bleeding into your home or personal life. This can go two ways because if you want to be officious and abusive, the persona can allow you greater freedom to do so.

I can always see the good part of any person; I am sometimes the only one who can. Just because that goodness and love is in them, that does not mean it has to come out in this life. That is all part of the process. There is no timeline; there is only learning. Sometimes we learn the same lesson many times until we are ready to let it go.

## Past Life Healings

Many healings happen after we have done past life hypnosis. A man was suffering from sudden unexplained neck pain as his 42nd birthday approached. He regressed back to a life in London in 1746 where he was a barrister who had just turned 42. The carriage he had been riding in flipped over, throwing him out onto the cobblestones and breaking his neck. After the memory surfaced, the man never experienced neck pain again.

Another past life regression was shocking to my clients, a couple who were dating and having relationship problems. It was also shocking to me. The man said the problems were because they had a poor sex life since she always complained of pain in her shoulders, upper back and lower back, but the doctors were not able to find anything.

During the regression, the man described a prior life during Roman rule in England. The man was standing beside a tree weeping over his lost lover/fiancé. In the current life, the man's girlfriend was the female from that past life. She was troubled physically but there was no medical explanation.

I asked what had happened and he said that he loved her so much but he suspected her of cheating on him. That day he decided that she must die so he had her tied to four horses going in opposite directions (drawn and quartered) and his lover died a horrible death. After that he wept over her grave. It was later found to be untrue that his lover had been cheating on him, but that was one of his karmic lessons in that life. He could not trust and always acted too quickly, learning to rue the day he made many of his poor decisions.

When we did past life work with each of them, they both healed emotionally and physically. They did break up later, but simply because they had resolved why they had come together.

# CHAPTER 17

## *Looking Forward*

How many lives are you currently leading? As a partner, spouse, son, daughter, lover, friend, father, mother, employee, employer? There are so many personas we need to have in order to be functional in the world. Sometimes we even come to believe that those roles we play are really who we are. We feel we have to perform the roles that we have allowed others to place on us.

My life has been about building bridges between who I really am inside and who I had to be in my various personas to function in life. I am amazing and special, and have many spiritual gifts. I am also a person who sees the best, the greatest and highest good, in each person even when they do not see it themselves. I was taught to think that in my life I had to "just go along, to get along." I discovered it was not enough. I went to a place where I thought I could deal with anything God or man threw my way. I thought, "You don't need to get over it, you just need to get through it." That was not enough either.

Being patient and loving to yourself is hard when the complete Western culture is working against you. Americans are sold the lie that if they just work hard they can be rich. They can live lifestyles of the Rockefellers, Trumps and Kardashians. Television shows support this lie. We live in a place of abundance but have no money; we have "stuff" and great debt. We now need both mothers and fathers to work just to stay in the middle class. We have strangers raising our children. We work harder and for less than at any time in our history. We mistreat the elderly, veterans (12% of veterans are homeless), the mentally ill, and the poor. You don't get to any safe station in the future, you always have to keep paying. Paying and paying; there is no living off the fat that you accumulated in your younger years because the government, society, and big business have taken it. We have become like drugged sheep being led to our slaughter.

TV and the Internet constantly seek our attention to show us more stuff we do not have and make us think we need. Seeds of discontent and fear are planted, and you are hungry for more stuff. You need rest and relief from the punishment that your life has become. You need an end to the prescribed medications and self-medications that maintain and blind you to the dark energies around you.

You deserve to go back to the earth, back to a connection with something greater than yourself. You deserve peace, love, compassion and joy. Yes, this could include finding and hugging a tree.

We are constantly told of the rewards that await us down the road if we just keep working hard, and paying into the system. The end of the line is your death, with many people unable to even afford a decent funeral. The system does not care about us. It sucks! It will suck the life right out of you unless you reconnect energetically to a higher power.

Striving for more stuff, more status and more power works for most people for many years. The sheep herd is always moving forward. When you reach the end, you get to retire, or you get old or sick and you are cast away from the herd. You will feel overwhelmed and frustrated by how quickly you are out of the game. Whatever you had been working on in your life is suddenly taken away and, upon evaluation, you will find that your business, your career, your money and your assets all add up to a big fat zero – nothing. No matter how wealthy you are, life is fragile and, in the end, you still die. None of that will have added to the quality of your life at all. Perhaps you are at that place now.

It is hard to rediscover who you were born to be. It is harder still to stay strong enough to discover what you are supposed in your life now. Perhaps you have forgotten to care for and love yourself, and care for and love other people. Or perhaps you have loved too much. The system has trained you that way. It has given you crumbs while others have enjoyed the whole cookie. The systems of government, politics, church and business are all committed to enslaving you, using and abusing your natural talents. They insist that you need something from them that only they can offer, such as Social Security, a place in Heaven, or a secure pension, but they really want your soul. You need to stay strong and buck the system. When you stay strong, you will find people that share your interests and talents and will connect with you. Like-minded people will support and encourage you. People will unconditionally love you, will be caring and honest and want nothing more than to bask in the glow of your spirit. Perhaps this is why the Bible is so clear in speaking about Eternal Life. That is where to invest your time and money. What you do for yourself and others here on Earth is what will come back to you over and over again. It is funny how Eternal Life sure seems like they are describing a soul that is reincarnating.

When you recognize and value what is important to your soul, you grow. Do not wait around for other people to tell you what is good for you and what you want. We are moving away from the "Keeping up with the Joneses" mentality which leaves you broke and sitting in a house full of stuff, feeling empty and alone even though family and friends may surround you.

When you have tried to "Keep up with the Joneses", you learned that there is never enough money, time, or stuff. That great car you have, those clothes you need for social events and business, the big house – all cost so much that you have no time for anything else and you are spiritually exhausted from feeding the money monster.

Dream about something that makes you feel good, happy, relaxed, and excited. Think about the last time you did the things that made you feel that way. It is probably easier to remember the last time you drove the kids to school, went to work, made dinner, paid the bills, fixed the car, and all the things you have to do. So much of your life has been about supporting you so that you can have a life of joy, but the work hours, the commute time and the diminishing return in your paycheck and its purchasing power drains you. You have so little time to enjoy life. The purpose of our lives is to learn lessons, have fun and to be happy despite the trials we go through.

Many people have a two-week vacation where they spend lots of money having fun doing things that are different from their daily lives. Then they return to their "normal" lives filled with very little fun and lots of stress for the next 50 weeks. Is that all there is to life? You have a choice as to what you want your future life to be.

Positive thoughts, intentions and affirmations work when you realize that there is more to your life than you have right now. For instance, when you listen to yourself you will hear why you have not achieved what you want. Negative, self-sabotaging statements work very well to limit your life. If you say, "I wish I could lose this fat", then you are concentrating on the symptom, not the cause, of why you are fat. Your vibration is recognizing excess weight and empowering it, and causing you to leave the door open for more weight gain. Being realistic about your health, body type and genetics, and your self-assessment of how you look is essential. Keep your perceptions and judgment of yourself to a minimum. Keep it real! You may not look like some actor or model, but you can still be happy and healthy if you feel it inside your heart. You can restructure health and body statements to say, "I am healthy and strong so I can do what I want to do." Instead of saying or thinking, "I want the Universe to support me", you can say or think, "I know the Universe provides unlimited abundance for me." Then you are not coming from a place of need and want. See the difference?

If you cannot dream about tomorrow, you are blocking your life plan. You do not need to stay where you are. You have chosen to be there. Now ask that the lesson be successfully concluded. Before you disappear in the mud of the lesson, release it and move forward.

When people allow for more in their lives, and don't lose hope, they find that miracles happen every day - spiritual, mental, emotional and physical miracles. Sometimes you will attract things that you may want, but they turn out badly for you. However, even bad is good because you can learn a lesson from it and let it go! Bless the bad as well as the good. Sometimes good things are already present in your life, but you do not recognize or appreciate what you have standing before you since you have been trained to only see people and events in certain ways. It is all about creating new connections and recognizing them.

If you do not ask for what you want in your life, you are destined to receive more of the same – more of what you don't want. You will receive a lot more of the same experiences, jobs, relationships, and suffering you already have.

Positive affirmations that I like and are helpful in redirecting your energy and thoughts are:

I feel loved.

I like being of service to others.

I am good.

I am great.

I am complete.

I trust.

I believe.

I know.

All is well.

I am awesome.

Just leave these positive statements open. When your mind/ego stops trying to define, categorize, and control, everything gets better. You are allowing yourself to *Go with the Flow* more often and that feels good. My message is simple. If doing what you are doing makes you happy – do it more. If what you are doing makes you unhappy or feel bad, stop doing it. If you could only believe in and love yourself as much as God and the Universe do, you would have no problems, just glorious opportunities.

When you focus on what you don't have, you are focusing on the depressing and negative. When you are allowing God to help you in each moment, then every moment becomes precious. When you *Go with the Flow of Life,* you will be amazed at how fast things in your life will change. Sometimes your ego will take credit for good things that are happening in your life. Your mind will say that you are doing well because you are so smart or well educated or clever or a hundred other reasons. But that is a deception when you are in the flow; it is because you have surrendered part of yourself to the overall process of the Universe. You have joined the community of life and then are rewarded because of it.

Too many people complain of being frustrated and unhappy in their lives. I find that frustrating for me because I wish you to have the best, growth-filled experience that you can have here on Earth. I know you will have good and bad in your life, but as long as it is forward motion and you are in the joy and gratitude for the experience of the pleasure and the pain, you will be okay.

One thing I have learned from all the years of working with people in the IRS, and now doing readings, is that people are all very much alike. They have the same worries, fears, feelings and desires to find love, security, happiness and comfort. The only thing that makes each person different from any other person is how much they have loved and served others, and loved and served themselves.

Many clients ask me how to be happy. I say, "If you want to be happy then be happy. If something feels good, continue doing that. If something feels bad, stop doing that." Some clients ask how to stop being sad. I say, "Stop being sad." The same goes for everything else you do not want in your life. How do you stop being lonely, sick, worried, angry, and fearful? Just let go of it. Drop that crutch you have used in your life. Volunteer for something you care about. It will stop you from thinking too much about yourself and your own circumstances.

When you set your mind to something, it is like planting a seed. When you bless each moment of your life you will find that the good feels great and the bad does not last a moment longer than it takes to learn what the lesson was all about.

Even if you are unable to get around well or get out of the house, there is much that can be accomplished just sitting in your favorite chair. You can do telephone and computer work – paid or volunteer – to help organizations and charities that you care about. You can get involved in on-line study programs that enrich your knowledge. There are prayer groups and work that can be done in helping and supporting the growth of other human beings. Because once you set your mind to something (dream) then God will provide you with opportunities.

When you restrict the access that dark energy has in your life, from television news, newspapers and even phone calls of complaining or gossiping friends and family, you will find that you won't feel as bad as you have in the past. When you are passionate and love yourself, you are establishing a pattern that the Universe will reinforce.

You do not need to allow the abuse that the world uses to hold you down. Freedom and love will come in through your times of communication with the God energy, through meditation, contemplation, and adoration of something greater than you in your body. I believe that we all worship the same God energy, but each of us seeks to identify it by a name that is comfortable to us. That is okay. Who am I to tell you how to love and know God?

I have done readings and counseling with clients all around the world on Skype and a common thread is that each of them wants what everyone wants - food, clothing, home, heat or cooling, family, friends, jobs and security. Governments want territory, war and domination. Society sometimes trains us to keep waiting for the next big high in life. Then when it happens and is over, we have memories and pictures, but we return to our routines. When we recognize the beauty in the routine moments – the little nothing moments – in our lives, we start to appreciate that life is really all about small moments you will miss or savor later. The quality of each moment is all we have in the end. No one can ever take those memories away from you. We were given life to experience love, joy, happiness and abundance, and very few find these before they die and start all over in the next incarnation.

I have long been fascinated by the idea of things happening for the last time because you usually do not know it will be the last time. Think back to the last time that you kissed someone, talked to them, made love with them, or the last time you saw them. Let every last moment be bathed in peace and love, even if you are angry with them at that last moment.

Every time you greet another person, bless them and be thankful that they have crossed your path. Every time you leave a person, bless them and wish them peace. You may not agree with or understand or even support them, but you can still bless them and let God figure the rest out.

## What You Need to Start the Change

Desire and determination to want something different in your life will begin to move you toward the changes you seek. Be firm but fair with yourself. Making progress is better than seeking perfection. Life is all about the journey, and the destination for us all is death. Why rush to the end?

Read your self-help, motivating books and articles; seek out those people who will enlighten you and encourage you. Be the change that you wish to be that comes from dreaming the dream of what you desire. This allows your dream to become your reality. Then you do nothing. Having faith, hope and "knowing" will allow your dream to manifest.

Accept and allow change to start in your life. There will be new things and, potentially, there will be partings with old friends and family, but you will be progressing, not regressing, every day. Allow joy and fun into your life.

By serving yourself first, then you create the strength to serve others, if that is your path. Some lives are all about just serving yourself and that is okay. When you *Go with the Flow,* major changes will rapidly happen in your life.

When you imagine your life in the future, it will come. Your future will arise from how you deal with your past. The connections you make with the higher spiritual connection will allow you to resolve your physical and emotional pain. The mind over matter approach does eliminate pain and the causes of your illness and distress. It is similar to the placebo effect and it just works.

Dream the dream that you want your life to be; see it, feel it, smell it, touch it, and hear it. The more details you allow to be provided to you, the more you make ready the path.

Your mind reacts to a thought the same as if it is something already happening on a physical level. It cannot tell the difference. If you are thinking about taking a walk, allowing your body to respond accordingly will cause the body to start internal processes that will produce healthy, stress-relieving results.

**How to Sustain the Change**

The only way that I have found to make any change is to want it. Someone else cannot want it for you. You must want it and allow for it.

Praying, meditating, shutting up and listening will allow you to develop your intuition. The way you receive and interpret the messages will develop your discernment. You could do this all alone like a lone Buddhist meditating for years in a temple, or you could ask to be surrounded by and connected to people who have already done this and can support the change that you wish to see. Everything happens so much more quickly when you let it go, when you stop fighting the changes and the blessings the Universe holds in store for you.

Remember that you co-created your own destiny with God before you were born. Now you need to check back in to see if you got lost somewhere along the line. Getting lost makes you stronger, but it is also nice to be on your path occasionally.

When you place your order with the Universe, you will be broadcasting from your third dimensional body. You will be co-creating your own life, your own destiny… and God wants to give it to you. Your soul also wants the best for you, your highest and greatest purpose, all the time. This will include joy and pain, health and illness, loss and emptiness, and compassion. All these things work when we are open to them. The key is to fully experience whatever is going on in your life. Thank God for sending the experience and ask what you are supposed to learn, how that will benefit you and make you wiser and stronger. Then conclude those questions and move on. Bless it and move on, and that moment of faith will bring you healing in whatever form is appropriate for you.

If what you are doing in your life or religion works for you, stick with it. But if you are reading this book, maybe you suspect that there is something more to life. I want to give you the inside scoop and from my pain and confusion, you will benefit. You are more likely to sustain the change if you can just stick with it the first 30 days, just because you will feel different and will start to feel better.

## If You Do Not Change

You will have more of the same until it gets worse and you get sick, then sicker yet, and then you will die. When you insist on swimming against the current of the Universal flow of love, you get tired. When you do not *go with the flow* of love, time grows longer, and pain and boredom comes. It is in this way that you learn that we are all connected. Hurting someone else is, in fact, hurting you. The qualities of forgiveness and mercy are important.

When you face yourself, you face your own destruction or victory. Just choose! It is very difficult for some clients when I say that they are 50 percent responsible for everything happening in their lives. They are accustomed to blaming the world, their boss or the people around them. When you have tried over and over to do the "right thing," and gotten nowhere, you need to think about who told you what was the "right thing." When you are beyond anything you thought you would ever be capable of, then and only then are you ready to begin to change.

I once had a dream that there was a door I had never seen before because I was not ready to see it. My mind/ego had me so busy thinking and planning things, that I could not even see that the door existed. One day, when I was emotionally exhausted and depressed, suddenly the door was clearly visible. I opened the door and in the space of infinity was everything I had ever wanted or needed, and even more. It was all waiting there for me. I just needed to feel worthy to receive it. I was always worthy, but my mind/ego hid it from me. When I allowed it, my life changed.

I am an example of a normal person in a normal profession and still God found me right where I was - when I allowed it. Now, when I *go with the flow*, everything goes better. When I stand firm against the flow, my whole life is harder.

When you envision how your dream will look and feel, you plant the seed for it to become real. If we pray for something, we are empowering it, but, here is the tricky part: when you pray for something to occur you are also empowering the thing that you don't have. You give energy to the lack, the want or the need, of the thing. Be careful to *not* empower the very condition, the lack or the loneliness, that you are seeking to replace.

Dreaming, visualizing and imagining are the tools you need and I have found this is the hardest part. Sometimes I had to pretend that I was watching a movie of my life and I was one of the characters, and then my mind/ego could relax enough to see what was going to happen for my character.

I could see who was around me and who was no longer around me. I could actually feel the breeze on my face, smell my dinner cooking, and feel the love and compassion of those around me.

Watching my life movie all at once was overwhelming to me so I hit the pause button in my mind a lot. There is an outcome no matter if it appears positive or negative. When you allow the change that karmic lessons bring, they will come through and leave quickly.

Want does not bring you what you want. It prevents what you desire from happening. We are conditioned to want from our very limited perspective. The Universe wants to give you so much more than you could ever imagine. Want does not bring wealth, love, prosperity, joy and comfort. Enjoying, being happy and grateful for what has already been provided will send up the vibration that you are happy with your life. You do not need to dwell on what is missing in your life. Your dreams and desires will address that.

## Why "The Secret" Failed to Deliver

At times, the more you want something, the more you keep pushing it away. In my experience, people who have tried systems like "The Secret" get so excited and then are slapped with the cold, hard reality that they have failed. What they want does not come to them.

For some of my clients, watching their lives as though they were watching a movie or looking into a dollhouse allows the creative dream process to begin. Do not judge yourself for where you are right now. It is all good and you will, and have, learned from your experiences, which you will realize especially when you have turned the corner and try to look back. Appraise your life now and be real in your appraisal. Your mind/ego will jump to attention and tell you all the changes are not possible because you lack money, power, knowledge, education or opportunity. Learn about this negative part of yourself and you will soon learn how to stop listening to it too much.

When you find things do not come your way despite your wishes, you must ask the Universe why. Then you must turn off your mind/ego and listen to the response. Perhaps the choices are too limiting, perhaps you have more karmic issues to resolve in a situation or with a person or group of people, perhaps you are not seeing the big picture, or perhaps you haven't looked outside of the constraints you have placed on what it is you want. Perhaps it is not the right time or it may not ever be the right time for what you desire to occur in your present life.

Self-limiting thoughts, self-criticism and self-sabotage all cancel out the process and kill your dreams. Stop allowing anyone or anything, including you, to kill your dreams. You are too special and amazing for that. Soul will show you what you need. Access the power you already have.

We look to the experts in the field of business for examples. Henry Ford had two failed companies and was unable to find funding to start Ford Motor Company. But he had a dream and it happened. Once he was in the flow, the Universe cooperated with his desire and the lives of billions of people were changed.

Thomas Edison freely credited the power of quiet contemplation, meditation and envisioning what is available from the Universe. He talked about receiving visions of the various inventions that he created. This was followed by hard work where he set ideas down on paper and conducted experiments. Since this was his passion in life it was not a work of labor, but of joy.

Even though you may dream about what you desire in your future life, you must be open to receiving it, and sometimes some work on your part is required. Thomas Edison said "Great success can come from many failures." His life and works are proof of that. He also maintained a positive mental attitude in pursuing his works. He searched for years for the best material to be used as a filament for his electric light bulb. Many others would have given up long before. He said, "I have not failed. I have just found 10,000 ways that won't work."

It is not a question of you wanting something bad enough, but about you allowing it. Allowing requires no effort. Wanting and needing requires a lot of effort and, at first, even allowing takes a lot of effort, since we are taught to work hard and try to do everything ourselves. But after a while, you become used to allowing because you are in the flow.

When you pray from a position of gratitude, of comfort in whatever you have in your life, pain or positive, you are a generating station of gratitude, love and positive energy. Organized religion has taken away the power that so many of us have to be able to step away to see the big picture, which is our power of wonder and dreams.

Many people dream of winning the lottery and have no plans after that. There have been television shows and many stories about how winners' lives were ruined. Other people I have worked with who have money and privilege, live in gated communities and are locked away in mansions with valuable objects, expensive cars, and large brokerage accounts are so insulated from other people and life that they feel empty and alone. I know a 67-year-old woman who is a widow and so lonely and sad, despite the fact that she is a successful, wealthy concert pianist. She drives a BMW Z4 Roadster and has such a large house that she has a 1,600 square foot room just to house her Teddy Bear collection. She said that room brings her the happiest memories of all the various people who presented her with those Teddy Bears. It seems like such a waste that she just shut her life down years ago when her husband died.

When you allow yourself to see the dream as a movie, you will experience joy. Baby steps are required in the beginning as you learn what will lead you into your joy, and your progress will depend on what you allow to grow and develop in your life.

If you say, "I want *XXX* to happen in my life because I need/want it", then you do not get that outcome. The Universe does not respond to your words but to your vibrational frequency or the intention behind your words. When you are able to see things more from a vibrational energy level, much more of life will make sense to you.

The Universe loves grateful and thankful people and will give you more to be grateful for when you *let go and let God work in your life and go with the flow.*

You become like God when you forgive others. From a practical standpoint, if you are still angry and unforgiving with someone, they are still in control of your mind because you maintain a connection of anger and unforgiveness that keeps both of you trapped.

*I am only one, but still I am one. I cannot do everything, but I can do something and because I cannot do everything, I will not refuse to do the something that I can do. -Edward Everett Hale*

**The Enemy is Real**

One of the factors that disrupts the model of projecting out to the Universe what you want is that there are energies of chaos, deception and manipulation that seek to confuse, challenge and destroy you on your path. Call it The Enemy, Satan, Lucifer, Beelzebub, Mastema, the Devil, the darkness - whatever. The energy is one that comes up frequently in my work and it seeks to subdue and force you into a miserable submission to the world and its treasures. When you realize the rewards that you gain at a spirit/soul level, you will be surprised how different that vibration is from this dark energy that I describe here.

There are demons that you create for yourself which consist of all those negative feelings, thoughts and ideas you have and are found on "The List." You may notice some people in your life who allow demons to come through them - actual demon forces. You will hear them say some bizarre things from time to time and wonder where that came from. Now you know. Sometimes demons will come directly into your life – usually when you allow them access through prolonged depression, or drug and alcohol abuse. The more effort you make toward soul growth, the more darkness you will attract. The more you are in the light, the more the dark will seek to suppress you.

By your growth you are actually drawing energy away from the dark forces. Your growth converts darkness into light. The idea that any of this is bad is very confusing. You cannot read the stories in the Bible that talk about God and not for a moment believe that God could crush this darkness in a second. It is all part of the plan, the plan to help you in your soul growth. Remember, the Universe is exactly balanced on a grander scale than you could ever imagine, and you will have times when you are moving from one to another.

In Hebrew folklore there is an angel named Mastema who carries out punishments for God. He tempts humans and tests their faith. He asked God to have demons as his subordinates. He is the angel of disaster and chaos, the father of all evil, and a flatterer of God. His names in Hebrew means "hatred", "hostility", "enmity", or "persecution". His function is to serve God. Mastema is the tester of humans with God's permission. According to Wikipedia, this is from the ancient Jewish work used by early Christians but was suppressed in the 4th century and is known as the Book of Jubilees.

What attracts this negative attention to you is you allowing your spiritual growth. Also, what is called "generational sin" brings this type of attention and is also known as "The Sins of the Father", as discussed in the Bible. You may be a good person but in your genetic line there may have been people up to seven generations back who are attracting negative attention to you today. See the Appendix for the "Family Healing Prayer" to help dissolve the generational dark energies.

Negative thoughts, habits, and behaviors, and associating with people who allow these things to occur, will bring you down and hurt you. Spirit tells me that any connection with tarot cards, Ouija boards, black magic, Satanists or those who champion the dark will hurt you. Any connection or association with dark or negative energy such as organizations that promote distrust, hate, or ideas that you are better than any one of your brothers will bring you down. Sometimes living in a society or country that is doing harm to others will also affect you (situational karma.) Even associating or being part of religions that do not promote love, compassion and understanding of all people no matter their race, creed, sex, sexual orientation or nationality will make you part of the collective negative consciousness.

Sometimes negative ideas can be introduced through literature, movies, or actions you witness. The negative culture in you starts when you feel angry, worried or fearful. As it is allowed to grow it will attract negative past life connections and you will encounter a whole range of emotional experiences, abuses and problems. All the negative thoughts that you have created for yourself, including unworthiness, as well as allowing the negative thoughts that others project onto you, can harm you.

At the same time, you cannot live a life that hurts yourself or other people and expect a good result in this or future lives.

You cannot be afraid or passive. Life is ever-changing, and this is important to know. When you live in the *energy of the flow* then nothing will be able to knock you off course.

It is usually difficult for a good-hearted, well-meaning person to understand why others would be so self-destructive to themselves and want to hurt others, or control or manipulate them. It is by deception that these energies will try to get into your life and then attack you. This all goes away when you *Pray, Meditate, and Shut Up and Listen.* When you establish direct connections with the God energy, you will be in a good place to use your inborn discernment (gut feelings) to figure out what is truth and what are lies. You will feel in your solar plexus who around you is good and who is bad.

Know that you are not alone in seeking to release yourself from the power of these dark energies. People who really try my patience are those who both moan about their circumstances, then say things like, "Better the devil we know than the devil we don't know" or, "At least I know what to expect from him/her" or perhaps "It may not be pleasant but he/she cannot hurt me more than he/she already has so that is why I stay." Others say, "If that so-and-so was not on my back I could succeed" or, "If I had not married this person my life would be a dream." And there are other similar sayings that bring negative energy.

## So What Do You Do Now?

You have many choices. You can do nothing and continue to complain about your life and blame others for your troubles, or you can evaluate what I have written, the methods, processes and thoughts I offer, and you can decide that today will be the first day of the rest of your life. When you do these simple things consistently, your life will change.

# CHAPTER 18

## *How to Allow Change to Happen*

I advocate that my clients allow change by recognizing they have two parts: their front part, the future, and their back part, which contains the past. These are opposites in the same body and are like the old you and the new you. In the past you may have had worry, fear and anger, but you do not want them in the future, so you must first release those feelings in the present moment. Some people try to plan the future from the ashes of the past; they color their future with fear then wonder why they don't change.

I was very scared growing up. There was much upheaval and chaos around me. I thought the best way to avoid the fear was to think and plan, and try to control people, situations and events in my life. That is what the old Richard would do, but this is very time consuming and makes for a very fragile balance.

The old Richard crashed after illness, stress from work and worry caused his world to crash. I could not continue being who I was not. I could not be the Revenue Officer who caused the most hurt to his customers, or the man who gave away all his gifts to people who did not appreciate them.

I used to go along with what life dealt me, thinking about all those years that I had no real control. I learned early that you "go along to get along." I rarely complained about my life; I just existed, and sometimes suffered through it. I thought that nothing I could do would make any difference. But when I did have control over circumstances, I went into hyper-control mode. In time I learned that that used up too much of my energy.

Then from the depths the new Richard emerged. The new Richard is guided by Spirit. The new Richard has moved forward rapidly in many directions at the same time, making huge soul growth simply because he allowed it and did not try to direct it. By allowing old Richard to chill out, growth and blessings flourish in the present moment.

When I have friends or clients who are going through events in their lives, I am there for them. I listen to them and counsel them, and I care for them the first two times they tell me their troubles. They are free to choose whatever they want to do. Staying in their own misery and complaining is not one of the positive aspects of change. If they come with complaints a third time, I redirect them back to our earlier conversations.

Being empathic can be like an unhealed wound. It is important that I stay strong, encourage and support their changes, but if they refuse to take action and grow after all of my encouragement and education, it is important for my own self-preservation to distance myself from them until they are ready to make the change. Otherwise, their negative energies will begin to affect me. This is very hard to do at first.

Learning how to honor and respect my feelings changed everything. I did not feel good being around people who drained my energy. This has resulted in me letting go of people who do not have complementary energy to mine much more easily than in the past.

Celebrating my victories and those of the people around me is very important. Life is all about progress, not perfection. In the past I had allowed self-defeating behaviors to control my life, thinking I was doing the right thing because that is what society told me I was supposed to do. Like attracts like, so I attracted more self-defeating behaviors and people like me because that was the message I put out to the Universe. I learned that when I tried to change to make other people happy, it did not work. When I learned to change for myself because I was learning to love me, change came very quickly.

It is very easy to talk about making changes and it is very easy to put yourself in a position where you feel forced to make changes by circumstances and the actions of other people in your life. I want to encourage you to look deeper into what you really need and want from life. What is your mission? What makes you happy? What brings you joy? Missions usually affect a number of people you have no responsibility or obligation to. I want you to share some of the joy of becoming and embodying the change within yourself which will support change in others as well.

Envisioning change, and allowing yourself to stop fighting change, is the beginning of major growth. Many times we do not have the courage or incentive to make changes. It is easier to complain about our circumstances than it is to change them.

When your life brings you more pain than pleasure, when you feel trapped in the places you have decided to be, then you are ready for change. When you decide to leave your old emotions and your emotional baggage at the curb and check into a new hotel, or a new life, you are starting to take power over your own life. I am not advocating running away from the obligations of your job, your partner or relationships. In every situation you can achieve independence in your existing world when you take control of your day and the interactions you have with other people.

It is an issue with many because they have believed ideas that were not their own and were fed ideas that were foreign to their spirit. Many people have a secret room where they keep all the old memories of past pain, abuse, and neglect. (see Elevator Exercise). When you learn that your soul has already learned and recorded everything you needed to know from all those emotional interactions and painful life lessons you have experienced, it makes it easier to turn it over to God.

Everything happens for a reason and everything is a blessing. Life is about receiving and releasing. It is all a blessing. When you realize this, you begin to see that there are no random occurrences in your life. Things were planned for a reason. This allows you to release the feelings of powerlessness and hopelessness that have erupted in your life. It is only when we lose hope, faith and trust that we start to lose ourselves in our body and our lives. When you visualize your future, it will be created for you.

The use of visualization is a powerful tool. To see, to imagine what your life can be like in the future without leaving the obligations or circumstances you are in, is very exciting. It allows for amazing changes to begin happening now. Releasing old beliefs enables you to see what your true capabilities are and allows you to see a brighter tomorrow in everything. First, we need to believe we can allow change to happen.

## Hope-Believe-Visualize the Change That You Seek

Visualization is important because you release yourself and have access to a higher source energy; you also allow yourself a glimpse of what the energy is trying to show you. Visualization involves allowing, dreaming, imagining, and study. Often many people are limited in their dreams, wants and desires. Their lives can be so much greater than they could ever envision if they would only *allow* themselves to imagine. Everything that comes will be for the good of your soul.

Many clients want nothing but good things in their lives. When you pair this with a long list of incarnations, using the idea of reincarnation, some clients will have lives of wealth, love and contentment. Others will have lives of poverty, hunger and pain. Many clients have settled for mediocrity in their present and past lives, because that is as much as they can handle.

The easiest way to visualize is to think how you felt when you looked into a dollhouse or watched a movie. Imagine that you were the person who lived in the dollhouse or starred in the movie. It can be very simple or very elaborate. You did not know what you could or could not do, so everything was possible. You not only dreamed, you also believed, and good things happened to you. You get the idea. Imagine what your dollhouse looks like and what happens there, down to the smallest details. This is like writing your own script for the movie of your life. It must all be created in your mind first, before you can put it together in the right way, the way that pleases you. Or you can use the idea of watching a movie and imagining that you are the star of the movie. You make all the choices – where you will be, what you will do and what your life will contain.

You have already done this as co-creator of your own destiny, before you were born. It was just you, God, and some spiritual advisors who helped your soul plan all the details, lessons, and situations you would require in the coming life so that you could have maximum soul growth.

God has a plan for your life and so does the devil; be wise enough to know which one to embrace.

Now you can begin to see how this works. If you apply it to things in your own life, you will notice what makes you feel good, whole, satisfied or complete and it is setting off a vibrational energy within you. You are doing or pursuing something that makes you feel good. You are sending a signal off to the Universe that you would like more of the same feeling back – please!

You often need help from a person or thing outside of your sphere to initiate and sustain the change that you seek. Every thought, feeling, desire and emotion you feel is also sending out a vibration. That is why every thought is a prayer. Every word is a prayer as well. You may be consciously seeking change for something you hope, but the intention (the prayer behind the prayer) is what will be honored. If you are sending off the quiet vibration that you are not worthy of what it is you are praying for, then you are canceling your own prayer.

What you say with your words, you create with your words. You manifest your own reality. Every thought, word, feeling and emotion is being picked up and recorded by the Universe and the Universe is seeking to match what you are sending out. Like attracts like.

*"When you forget how to live, you begin to die quietly inside.*

*If you live long enough you will have regrets.*
*The ones that nag at you most are the ones where you knew you had a choice.*
*The ones where you knew you could have stopped yourself and you did not.*
*The ones where you and everything good inside of you looked into the mirror and said,* **Don't do this; don't do this**. *And you ended up doing it anyway.*

*So you did something stupid or harmful to yourself or others and suffered some abuse or indignity.*

*I got it!*

*Now get over yourself! We all make mistakes. That is how we learn.*
*Try to forgive and forget; turn your troubles over to God. Then move on!*

*God has a lot of fresh challenges for you in your life. Resolve the past.*

*It is time to move on!*

*If I could give you anything back, I would give you yourself back. "*
*- Received from Spirit*

I was thinking about Plotinus, a Roman philosopher, who said:
    "That we can forget who we are and descend into the world, the

real world, the world we can touch and see, we allow ourselves to get bound up with sensuality and overpowered by lust."

We make contracts and allow lower energies to tempt and seduce us. We are greatly pleased that we seem victorious in those moments.

We can get negative power from our ability to dazzle and delight, capture, confuse, and control others for sex, money, power, position and influence. But this is not an energy that makes you, or the person it is directed towards, happy. Even when God calls our attention back to the light, we may experience healing and a rise in our frequency (our vibration), but it is slightly painful because the old ways were more fun and familiar. Many fall back to their old ways, sometimes repeatedly, but people still have that quiet desire to have something more in their lives. We all eventually return to the light.

One day you will feel an instant calm, knowing that nothing more is expected of you in life and nothing else is required. You are done. Good or bad, the record of your life will speak for itself. Joy and peace may quickly follow. The people you leave behind will be affected, but you cannot control that. Hopefully, they will have had great moments with you that they can remember for the rest of their lives. For most of us, though, that day is not today. You still have time to set your vibrational frequency to dream mode and see the abundance and blessings awaiting you in this life.

The most amazing part of our lives is that we are never the same person we were five minutes ago. Heraclitus, a Greek philosopher, has several great quotes that fit this situation. I like this one:

"You can never step twice into the same river.
Everything flows; nothing stands still.
Nothing endures but change."

We are often very resistant to change, but it is all a fallacy as change is happening all around us, all the time. It is not about living in the dollhouse, for one day it will crumble, it is about living in the world but not being of the world. Remembering your soul connection allows you to do that. Some call this a soul agreement, or soul contract, that you make with God. When you experience déjà vu you are simply remembering watching the movie of your life played out like it is on a big screen. It gives you a tingle of recognition that you are indeed in the right place doing what you had agreed and planned to do.

Staying in touch with the present, who you are now and not who you were when you were a child, a student, or first married, will enable you to access the stream of consciousness that is *the flow,* and very swift changes will happen in your life. I like to imagine this is a decision you make that allows you to dream and create your future reality. You fake it, imagine it, until you make it!

Martin Luther King, Jr. said, "I have a dream!" To keep your dream alive, find victory where you are right now. Have small victories that will encourage you to dream about and pursue what you desire in your life. The powers of the world want to keep you exactly where you are. God wants to you get where you want to be. Finding a victory where you are will empower you and allow your heart to continue seeking change. Every day is a victory.

It takes great courage and fortitude to make the decision to allow change in your life. Once you make the decision, you have nothing to do. You *just be and allow.* Being and allowing is very hard for people in Western culture who have been taught that hard work will bring you what you dream, but that is untrue and not necessary. The hardest work you have is finding time to meditate or pray. Allow God to come into your world. You do not need to come into God's world. You never left it. The essence of God is within you, it is a merely remembering who you are and why you are here.

In my days as an IRS instructor, I told my students to work smarter, not harder and stressed that "good was good enough." There is also another old saying, "close enough for government work." This meant you work your cases to a certain point and then arrive at a conclusion. The person can either pay or not pay. They can pay right now or not right now. They can pay in an installment agreement or not. I had a limited number of choices and options of what I could do for or against these people. After 33 years listening to pleadings of poverty and hardship, I am more reality based. I learned that you really can't get blood out of a stone.

When people with great wealth and possessions parade in front of us, they do so as an example to you that if you just work hard (for them), you too can one day achieve what they have. This is poison to your mind and has affected the way people see the value of their labors. Being smart, educated, beautiful or lucky does not guarantee that you will achieve your dreams. Look around; you can prove that yourself. Being lucky or allowing for more than you have now can work, and so can matching your vibration to the vibration of the person, possession or situation you want.

When you realize that we are all connected and dependent on each other, you learn to respect and love your neighbors. The whole world is a web of connections. Heraclitus said, "It is wise to listen, not to me but to the Word, and to confess that all things are one." When you determine what your mission is and why you are here, you will learn that your greatest joy can come from being in the right place at the right time. Supporting the growth of others, in fact, supports you personally as well. Knowing that your soul has your best interests at heart all the time allows you to feel connected to something greater than yourself again, perhaps for the first time in your current body.

For many people who have spiritual gifts, life can be drudgery because they are feeling confused and different, trying to survive in two worlds. A Spanish mystic, St. John of God, called it his "dark night of the soul." It is not depression as commonly defined. It is a time when you turn your back on God, usually due to some triggering event. Your baby died, you have cancer, you lost your job, your spouse left you, your country lost a war, or all of this. Some major thing happened that caused you to question where God was in that situation. You turn away from God. Your mind/ego thinks that it can feed and sustain you; it does work for a while, but it always fails in the end.

Sometimes clients try to address the voices in their head, their depression or other afflictions. You need to know that when you address them, you must speak louder than the voices of depression, louder than your illness. You need to command them away from you, now and forever, and you can only do this when you have access to higher spiritual energies.

When you look at all the times you needed God and you do not see God in your life, you may question to the point of non-belief. This causes you to harbor melancholy and parts of your spirit begin to atrophy. You die a little more each day when you are in the world all by yourself. You are like a person who wakes up confused and cannot find your glasses in an unfamiliar hotel. You have a very limited vision because you have no glasses. You question God and those who profess to believe in God. You taunt and test, or secretly turn these doubts on yourself. When you are in the worst of it, you feel you have been abandoned and are lost and alone. You live in anger, worry, fear and emptiness. Then, as if by some miracle, one day the doorbell rings and the UPS person delivers a package containing a new pair of very powerful glasses. You did not ask for this to happen, but the lonely, desperate signal of your heart was heard and this miraculous gift arrives.

Spiritual gifts are not given equally to all people at the same time. Each receives what he/she can handle in the moment. It would be too much to have them all at the same time since you do not yet remember what an amazing soul you are.

Slowly you come to realize you did not see the whole picture when you turned away from God. The important thing you learn is that God never turned away from you. God cannot turn away from his own – from his own creation. You do get tough love from God sometimes and, believe me, things do not always go your way, but bless everything that happens to you. There is a lesson in all of it.

For many people this "dark night" phase lasts for many years. When you allow it to be over there is great spiritual rejoicing. The example

Spirit gives me as I write this is when the shepherd in the Bible worries more about the one lost sheep rather than the other 99 that are safely in the fold. God does not worry about the people who are in church or making other spiritual connections. God is looking for those who are lost and on their own voyage of self-discovery. The lost sheep.

I have always liked that Jesus is shown as the shepherd who is gently guiding the direction of the herd. But each sheep is still in control of itself and its connections to the rest of the herd. This is how it is in our human lives as well. We are always in control of what we say and do, and our choices.

Then when you reawaken you are glowing with knowledge about both a life with God and a life without God. One of my favorite quotes from F. Scott Fitzgerald is, "In a real dark night of the soul, it is always three o'clock in the morning." Remember I said in an earlier chapter that 3 am is the Devil's hour? It all fits together.

Many people focus on being safe and secure before they think they are ready to make a change. This is not necessary. In fact, it will hinder the start of the change. You will be safe and secure during the time of the change, but first you have to start the change. There is nothing that prevents you from doing what you need to do and no reality that can stop you once you allow yourself to dream, except for you. The Hindu God Ganesha is credited with removing obstacles in a person's life. I have found from my own life that I was always the biggest obstacle.

It was not the family I was born to, or the places I lived, or the education that I received, or the jobs and relationships I had. It was *me*. My fear, anxiety, and worry controlled my life. I can see that now in retrospect. At the time, I was just going along to get along. Now, I can appreciate that I have no desire to go back and change anything, good or bad, because all of my life made me who I am today. I don't need a do-over. I need to let the dust of the past settle, look forward to this day, and not worry about tomorrow either.

Sometimes making the change, or making the decision to allow change, can be scary. Change, even the thought of change, can bring on physical and emotional pain. We get so excited to change. When we board the airplane to our future, we freak out. So, we get off the plane. We do this several times and feel foolish. Maybe half of us are really on the plane when it takes off. Not that those who are embracing the change are not still filled with angst, fear and worry, but they are allowing the future to come, even under their own very limited terms.

What I have seen in working with thousands of people is that many create lives where they are in a box without a top. They live their whole lives in the box. They cannot see anything or know anything that is not approved to be in their box. Even within the box, they may dig holes that will allow them to sink deeper and deeper into their own miseries and pain. Sometimes they can jump up and see that there is more available outside of the top of the box. They can get a glimpse of what else is out there in the world.

One of my editors, Christy White, had this view, "I think that most people believe they are just living their lives, but they can't help but organize and categorize everything that comes into their awareness. The end result is that they live in boxes, sometimes very pretty boxes. Sometimes the boxes are open topped, but sometimes they have side-to-side boundaries. Our skin is a boundary! Many people live in a series of boxes…some with closed tops (belief structures) as an example, and some with open top boxes (open to receiving, knowing they are worthy of receiving). Still, it's a box. The Universe may show you a hole underneath the box that people dig for themselves. It is emptiness, unworthiness, depression and hopelessness because they have no connection to their higher-selves (soul) and the Universe. No matter what they throw into that hole, though, it still remains empty because it a downward sucking black hole. The only filling that is effective is through love, hope, belief in something greater and upward connection."

Sometimes people dream about what they saw when they caught a glimpse outside their box, and sometimes they do not understand what they saw but are drawn to life outside of their prison-like box.

For some clients, I just cut a hole in the side of their box and they can see that the world has more to offer them than they realized.

When I talk about dreaming of a future life that they want, or visualizing or co-creating lives that they wish, sometimes they can dream and have that connection to the bigger picture. That is all it takes to begin the major changes that will happen in their lives. That spark, that recognition is like a seed being planted. It will grow if they feed it with their hopes, dreams, plans, aspirations and the ability to allow what they want to manifest in their lives.

Spirit tells me this has nothing to do with the good or bad of the dream; it is not judging the dream as being worthy or unworthy. It is just seeking to provide what you want in your life, in your karmic plan. When you are desperately seeking love, you will bring others into your life that are equally desperate for love. And who wants to be attracted to that energy? When you broadcast energy of connection, wellness, and completeness, then you will attract people who have that energy as well. It is a much better place to be.

The second part is not just dreaming about this in your mind/ego, but also accessing the energy of your soul and its intentions for you. The vibrational energy you radiate from spirit/soul is what actually creates the energy that you will link up with. That is why simply consciously wishing for something does not work. Many self-help books and programs have failed to share this part and people are left feeling that they are doing something wrong when their desires do not materialize.

Negative thinking, poor self-esteem and low self-confidence are bad habits. When you really listen to what you say and how you say it, you will at first be shocked. When you hear yourself saying negative things, immediately say, "I cancel that last thought or statement."

When you learn to have faith in yourself, your choices and decisions, you will find that the Universe will deliver exactly what you want in your life for maximum soul growth. God has a plan for your life. It is The Plan, not your limited version of the plan.

*Therefore, I tell you, whatever you ask for in prayer,*
*believe that you have already received it,*
*and it will be yours. - Mark 11:24*

Today we call that visualizing, or even dreaming. It works. I imagine standing in front of my own grave, looking at my tombstone to see what is written there. I imagine seeing what would be written if I were to die today. Try this exercise and then ask yourself: "Is that what I want? Is that the summary of my life that I want people to remember me by?" If you are not satisfied with what your tombstone might say, what would you envision and why? What do you want your tombstone to say about your life? Would it be about what you accomplished in life? Or would it be about what you wished you had done? What are you doing with your life now? What ideas, theories or worries are holding you back? When you succeed in releasing from the old you, who will you be instead? Seeing the new changes that you allow in your life becomes a no-brainer. It is so easy compared to being dead and helpless, without the power to change anything. When you have no fear about the outcome, you are allowing yourself to access who you really are.

When you release the power that other people have over you, the power that you grant them, you can begin to come out of your closet of fear, anger and worry. You begin to grow. You learn that it does not matter if other people think you are odd, crazy, psychic, or psychotic. You gain control over your life and reduce your anxiety about making the change. This allows the possibility of whatever it is you desire in your life to move forward confidently and joyfully. When you allow for it, it will come. It is important to release the old negative fears that are holding you back. It is also important to realize, as Einstein said, "to raise the energy you must raise your vibration to match the energy, behavior, or situation that you want in the future." Therefore, you have to imagine seeing what is not there, then it can come to you. It is very confusing when you first try to do this, but it really works. See the dream you wish was your life with your body, mind, spirit and soul.

Many clients allow fear, worry, and hopelessness to prevent them from making the big leap of faith to the place where they want to be in their lives. Many people have stopped even dreaming of anything different from the same drudgery of their day-to-day existence.

*He who does not expect will not find out the unexpected,*
*for it is trackless and unexplored. - Heraclitus*

This leap of faith, this use of imagination is like how it is when you are in Disneyland or Disney World. At first it is a fantasy, the streets are so clean and the buildings are so freshly painted, people are so cheerful and friendly, and you and everyone else is so happy. It is unlike our normal world and all like a dream. Then you touch a pillar and you see the horse pulling a trolley, and you learn that it is all real. It is a created reality from the mind of the Disney staff that becomes your reality because that is what you know during your visit.

What I'm saying is, you can create your own reality in much the same way, by envisioning what you want and then allowing circumstances to come together to make it happen. The problem with this concept is that many people want to go into control mode and retreat to a place where they control the access other people have into their lives. They lock themselves away from normal human interactions. This is the idea behind going into your gated community and wondering why the world is not chasing after you. You have found everything you want in this little self-created world, or prison, that is your life.

I have, over the course of many years as a tax collector, been to many million-dollar-plus houses and many dilapidated houses. The thing that is interesting to me is that I always feel the sense of community more strongly when the people are living poor. In richer communities, residents rarely even know their neighbors' names and stories.

The idea is not to build a wall around yourself. You need to be interacting with people, and not just with the sales clerk at the mall or other stores. You should have a part of your home that is your sanctuary, where you can reflect and rest, but then you need to get into life. Go out, meet and touch people emotionally, mentally or physically. Be a person who makes a difference in the lives of other people and it will greatly enrich your life. When you have opportunities to share and provide the gifts you have with others, major change happens in your life. You will be blessed many times.

In my readings, I am usually shown many possible parallel outcomes of events that will happen in a person's life. This can be rewarding as well as scary for the client. Sometimes we use fear as a positive motivator and a reason to allow change, maybe by saying I expect that you will be alive and functional for another 40 years based on information I'm getting you being to envision having that longer life. Do you plan to be miserable and unhappy and stay with your partner, or stay in the situation that you are in for the next 40 years? Or do you want to make changes so that you will learn to love yourself?

Learning that the pain, misery, worry and fear you allow into your life will make you sick is a blessing. Pain, disease, and illness always have a message! Remember that you are not your pain or disease or illness; all are essential for your growth. You can process through them and survive using the violet flame procedure.

When the pain of staying in your current situation is greater than the pain of change, you will change. You will stop a lifetime of self-medicating, re-creating situations and relationships that no longer serve you. You will release yourself from the jail you have created. It is very difficult for many people to move past this point because we are all so cognizant of our failings, shortcomings and "sins". It is easy for us to persecute ourselves daily, to bring ourselves before the judge, which is us and society, to condemn ourselves, and to sentence ourselves to a less than perfect setting and environment.

It is all about choices we make and choices we do not make. Mix in karmic payback of karmic concerns, and we are on a path of learning that never stops… hopefully…during our life.

You can also apply what you have learned when you provide service to others, but without judgment or demand or trying to force a certain outcome for some purpose. Again, this is a vibration you are sending out. The Universe will seek to provide you with more of it if is in the best interests of your soul growth. This is why it is so important to figure out what brings you joy, what turns you on in spirit, mind, heart and body. There is no judgment about what you are doing, just the quiet, ever-present notion that you need to be in motion in all these areas constantly to provide you with what you need in your Soul Plan.

To talk about vibrational energy does not make sense to most people; it sure did not make sense to me for a long time. You identify it as you begin to feel it. When you are with your family and having a good feeling, they and you are on the same vibrational frequency. When you are with a group of like-minded people, such as at school, work, church or a civic group, and you all share the same concerns, knowledge, ideas or goals, you all are putting out a similar vibrational energy. When you pray or meditate with other people who are concerned with the welfare of another, or are praying for the greatest and highest good to result for a person or a situation, you are matching vibrational energies.

Even base needs have a vibrational frequency. When you make love, versus having sex, with a partner who is totally connecting with you spiritually, mentally, emotionally and physically, then you are on the same vibrational level. When you are at school waiting in line for your lunch and you are hungry, so is everyone else in line. Each person is hungry at their own level, so it is a collective vibrational frequency of people who all want to eat. Some have a light appetite and some are very hungry, but all join in that place at that time for the one common goal – to eat. This also happens when you are at an event and you are in a line to use the bathroom. Those are all vibrations.

Vibrations can be higher, such as when you feel what you describe as love with something or someone else. You may love your dog, your partner, your children, your parents and your work, but each with a different vibrational energy. All share the common bond of love, defined here as a strong positive affection or shared feeling. Lower chakra energy centers generally emit lower vibrations. Your body requires food, shelter, clothing, sex, procreation. The higher up on the chakra system, the higher the vibration. When you get to the heart chakra, you are generating energy of both giving and receiving. This is a much higher energy, and vibrational energies continue to rise until you get to your crown chakra, which is above mental energy, then you rise into spiritual energy. Just because you are in spirit does not mean that your energy is high, good, and pure; that is reserved for your soul level.

Vibrations can also be mean, ugly and hateful and will produce killing, abusing, hurting or destroying people or societies that you oppose. These may be actions that you need to take to learn karmic lessons. You may either be taking these actions, the killer, or the one being killed, the victim.

Doing the right thing is not always going to bring you an immediate reward, it may never do so in this life; whereas, doing what could be judged as harmful to others or interpreted as wrong can bring you a great and immediate reward. Remember, rewards are simply results and may look attractive at first, but if they come from tainted deeds, you will incur karmic debt to repay in this life or another.

This is like the American idea that working harder will make you rich. I mean really, work harder? What kind of propaganda is that given to the masses? At Auschwitz, and other concentration camps, there was a sign that said "Arbeit macht frei" (Work makes you free). It was a manipulation of truth. It may have given some form of hope to some. None of us can live without hope for very long. The sign set a vibration of hard work, satisfying results and eventual freedom if the worker did their best work. It was a lie and a manipulation, but good people bought into it.

I have a tall stack of naturally magnetic stones on my desk. They all stick together when their energies are aligned, but if I take half of the magnets and turn them around, each half repels the other. Turning them around creates negative energy to the positive energy. When I lay the negative stack down on the desk, the positive stack will put out a force that will cause the magnets to swirl around on the tabletop until the energy becomes correctly aligned again as a positive energy. We can say "like attracts like" but it actually goes both ways. All the positives align and all the negatives align, but separately. Another curious thing is when I put the magnet stack next to any steel, it will be attracted to that, but when I put the stack next to a plant or a piece of brass, nothing happens. All other material is in a neutral state and the magnet stack is neither attracted nor repulsed.

Like attracts like, but like also attracts the opposite as we have heard opposites attract. Spirit tells me that this occurs because there is a force in one person or the other who wants to silently change, or to compel the other person to change their vibration to one more like what they prefer. Much like the magnets show us as they can magnetize a piece of steel, such as a nail.

Sometimes you will be in the stack and part of you will be out of the stack; different fields and energies draw you away. That is why when you are in a neutral field, such as being single, living alone or being in nature, you can feel rested and ready to receive from a higher source of energy. In that "happy place" you are neither negative nor positive. You can just "Be". Be happy, be relaxed, be industrious, be rested, and be replenished. When we apply this to people, we find that when you are in harmony with like-minded people, you feel a vibration that makes you feel good. It makes no difference whether what you are doing is good or bad, it will feel good if you are all doing the same thing because you will not be judged by those around you.

When you desire something, you are setting off the vibrations of desire in your physical body, vibrations of want, need, and lack. Given the idea that "like attracts like" which is proven in physics, you will attract what you want. However, most people are putting off negative vibrations so often and so consistently that they cancel out the intention of their prayers. This is expected because the mind/ego does not like unexplained objects or thoughts.

Some people say they want to change. They read self-help books and make attempts to change, but they usually return to the initial behavior they were trying to repel in the first place. When they find out such change will involve real change, like leaving a marriage or a bad job, they stop. Spirit shows me the example of a person shaving their head, even using a hair remover to remove all traces of their hair, and then declaring him or herself bald. They are only temporarily bald because the hair will grow back. The hair is rooted in their head, and is healthy and seeks to grow again. The root of their behavior is what holds people back from major change in life, besides the aura of worry, fear and anger – the idea that you can make changes from your mental state without regard to your behaviors are deeply rooted within you.

If you have a weight problem, too much or too little, this has a root in you. It may be related to not having had enough food when you were growing up, or having too much. This can come from this life or past lives. If you had starved in a prior life, it is natural for you to want to not only eat, but to eat and store for later. Understand? This can be from the way your mother treated food when you were growing up. Perhaps she told you that if you eat food you will get fat and then men will not be attracted to you, you will never marry or be happy, etc. It is combined with society's input with models, advertising and television telling you what their idea of a perfect woman's body should look like. Reject that. Seek a healthy body.

When you practice *Loving Yourself First, Best and Always* you are sending out a vibration of love to and from yourself. Other people will notice it and be attracted to it. It is not a vibration of vanity, selfishness or narcissistic love, but of pure love of yourself that grows every hour and every day.

When you are with people who have a neutral energy then they will neither attract nor repel you. When you trust the neutral energy, you can embrace whatever it represents. It can be a vibration you like, love, and can grow from. Like attracts like can get boring and repelling your opposite wears you out physically, mentally and emotionally. Being neutral and available to be used as a positive or negative charge opens up a host of new opportunities; joy, pain, relief, suffering, and especially lessons learned. Either way these are good things. Learning always elevates your vibration.

You can use magnets to reground yourself and release the charge that you have one way or another, and a completely new world of possibilities comes available to you. You can also use a gold, silver or copper bracelet that will ground you. When you surrender the old charge to God and release all the energy that went to sustaining that charge, you will be ready for new things in your life. When you release the root cause of the charge – the need to love or hate, or construct or destroy – then you are ready for a new world to begin.

Attracting people is fun and attracting people that you repel can be a fun challenge, at least for a while. But it gets old quickly. Like attracts like and opposites attract, but only if they allow changes like the magnet swirling around to join the force of the other magnets. This happens. Does it change the root energy of the magnet? No. Each magnet has a positive and a negative charge.

Self-help does not work for everyone because, while you might want to make changes in your life situation, you can only effect change for a short period since you have not gone back and attempted to change your basic wiring. You must remove the thorn that has pierced you and caused a huge knot of scar tissue. Some people spend their whole lives protecting the things in their core that hurt them and they feel bad, eventually getting sick. They never feel good enough about themselves in the present to completely release the past.

You must look at your motivation for making the change, because if it is not strong enough, the base vibration will not allow the change to occur. By neutralizing the charge, you can nullify its effects on your life.

Many people perpetuate and protect their sicknesses to protect themselves from growth in life. They subdue their natural impulses and intentions to other forces and they get sick, suffer, and eventually die because of it.

Many people have asked me, "Does God use sickness to make good people better? " or "Do we get sick because we don't have faith in God?" or "If God is a loving God, why am I sick?" Healing comes in different ways to different people at different times. Illness is just something new to learn, grow from and then release. It does not make you a good or bad person, just a wiser one. Illness is hard for mind/ego to deal with because it represents lack of control. The Apostle Paul had what was described as a "thorn in the flesh" - the actual infirmity was never described. But he struggled his whole life with it. Three times he called out to God for healing and did not receive it because he had not learned the lesson from the thorn yet. In the end he was forced to rely completely on God for his strength. We would all prefer that it would be another way, to avoid the pain, but God uses our weaknesses for our growth, and to build bridges of compassion and empathy to others.

When people are reconnected to source energy through prayer, meditation, and shutting up and listening, they are able to see past this self-limiting and damaging vision of themselves.

I have been using scientific terms regarding the positive and negative charges we are talking about, but, to be clear, this does not mean positive as in good or negative as in bad.

When you understand that all the actions you judge as being good and all the actions you judge as being bad are exactly what are needed in your life, you will grow. When you bless everything in your life and welcome it with a smile, instead of complaining and bitching to God all the time, you will experience things that will enrich and enlighten you, your fellow man and the human condition. There is no wrong or right. It is all a game where the soccer ball is in play, but without a need to score any points. If you don't learn something in this life, you will learn it in another life.

Remember how I talked about how our souls are like rough diamonds that have 1000 unpolished facets and each thought, event and emotion we feel in life, combined with every action we take or do not take, all results in one or more facets of the diamond being polished? That makes every life an exciting opportunity for growth.

You learn how it feels to be sick and die as a child, or to be old, or greedy, or in love. Each action benefits you on the spirit/soul level. Nothing happens without a reason. People are very stubborn and headstrong, but that does not mean that they will not learn the lessons. It just means that the lesson will be delayed. As I mentioned before, our diamond gets shinier and brighter, and reflects more light with every life. People begin to notice this light and, when you have learned all you needed in the many lives you have, all 1000 facets are highly polished. Even God notices that you are the brightest diamond of the day.

Other souls come and admire you. You bask in the love they share with you. Then you have the choice to either stay like that for eternity or melt back into the Source Energy, which is God, and you are bathed again in that love for all eternity. Some of us keep choosing to come back to a body on Earth because we are full of love and compassion for other living beings. That is what sparks love in our hearts. That is what we as souls love to do, to be - in motion. It is not all work and no play. The closer you are to what you enjoy doing, work will seem like play.

The concept of karma and reincarnation as practiced in the Far East is not what Spirit is sharing with me. It is not a hopeless, oppressive task that we come back repeatedly into mire and misery for eternity. If it were that way, it would not be an idea coming from the Creator God energy. Man makes toil and oppression, not God.

When we are born, we forget most of what we knew. We pass through the veil to Earth and forget who we really are. We learn to think as the body we find ourselves in is trained and programmed to think in our country, culture, society, government, heritage, and from how our parents think. Our soul does not sleep, ever. It is there to provide you with directions, memories and coaching as needed. Your body and spirit are always drawn back to your soul.

It is difficult to explain this to people who have been trained to reject reincarnation publicly by organized religion. For me the cool thing is that I have spoken to thousands of people who quietly, or even secretly, know and embrace the ideas of karma and reincarnation, but they are afraid to share or discuss them with others. There are so many instances where even the religious communities I have worked with are perplexed as to where their visions, thoughts, ideas and ecstasies come from due to their feelings of unworthiness. Many of them believe secretly in reincarnation as well. I am not telling you that you have to believe in these things, I merely wish you to entertain the idea of karma and reincarnation and let the evidence present itself before your mind/ego.

This inquiry will lead you to remember who you really are and how you are connected to Earth and every form of life on Earth. God becomes incarnate in every person and object on Earth because we all came from that connection to the Creator energy.

Even as I write the words in this book, I am connected to a transmission from God with a message of love, compassion, understanding, acceptance and love to share with you. The words I choose to express this are written on the page, but the feelings and emotions, the intention of my words, comes through these pages from my soul to your soul bringing you the opportunity for acceptance, understanding and healing no matter who you are or where you are in your life. My intention is to call you back to a place of neutrality and offer you unlimited options in your future. As I write, and as you read, I am sending an energy charge that seeks to reach your soul and spirit, and calm your heart as you begin the process of clearing and neutralizing old feelings which are not healthy or in your best interests. I want you to be able to clear your conscious, subconscious, and unconscious mind of all that is burdening you and leading you to feel unwell, unhappy, unloved, empty and alone. These words will get you to a neutral state so you can then evaluate and make choices for the future. Just because you are reading these words you are picking up the frequency that I am transmitting, and it is touching your heart if you are open to change and allowing and accepting the love vibration I am sending.

This concept may be new to you so you may need to reread this chapter again in a month. You will start to feel the love as well, but my transmission of unconditional love is without cost to you. You owe me nothing. I seek nothing from you. My wish is that you simply "pay it forward." Give what I am giving to you to another person; this is how it works. If you make a change within yourself, you also allow change in those around you and that can be your gift to them.

# CHAPTER 19

## *Final Thoughts*

I have brought you ideas and processes for achieving a higher spiritual connection, through prayer, meditation and contemplation. I have advocated that you should *Just Be and Allow Joy into Your Life.* I know this is stressful, but know that if you allow this spiritual reconnection you will benefit, you will heal, and you will grow.

When you seek to know more about any subject, like-minded people will enter your life to help you and support your journey, and you will also be drawn to other people to help you on your path. Each seeker of love, trust and beauty will find what they need in the energy of the Creator of the Universe. You may know this energy by many names, but you will benefit no matter what you call it. At the same time, opposing energies will be coming across your path as well. That is good and will give you a whole blend of ideas and choices to make. The key to all this is not to be afraid, but to seek support if you feel you need it for your growth. You can find spiritual connection in a church or temple as well as just walking barefoot on the grass. There is no right way to reconnect.

Spirit always tells me that humility is so important. If I am humble, I will not let my head swell up because of my spiritual gifts. If I focus on serving others and loving myself, I will stay in balance.

The key is using your discernment, your gut feeling, to know what is true and what is a deception. Both will come to you many times in your life.

In fact, Jesus made this very clear in *Matthew 7:15-20* and *Luke 6:43-45* when he instructed us that one way to discern who is being motivated by God is to look at the fruits their works produce. In *Matthew 22:36-40*, Jesus is asked what it takes to gain eternal life. Jesus said:

> *Keep my commandments.*
> *You should love God with all your heart,*
> *with all your soul and with your entire mind.*
> *This is the greatest first commandment.*
> *The second is that you shall love your neighbor as you love yourself.*
> *Everything depends on these two commandments.*

When you refrain from harming or doing evil to your neighbor, you are loving them and loving yourself. When you recognize we are all connected as people, no matter our sex, race, creed, color or nationality, we are on the path to true brotherhood. When we see that hurting others in the end is hurting ourselves, then we learn that it is bad.

Do not seek gurus, priests or ministers to define the work, to tell you what God wants you to do in your life. Seek those who put off a vibration of unconditional love, compassion and understanding, then connect with them. Seek people who will greet you as a brother or sister, as an equal, not someone who looks down on you. Read, study, think and feel.

When you are living the life you dreamed and you are in service to yourself and others, you may be tempted to accept people's praise of your works or your gifts. Remember that those works and gifts are coming through you; they are not yours. You are merely a conduit of the energy of love.

When you seek everything, you gain nothing. When you seek

nothing, everything will stand before you for the taking.

When you let the light shine through you it will both attract people to you and repel people from you. A Chinese saying is, "Do good, receive good. Do bad, receive bad." That is a good start for the rest of your life.

Love God, *Love Yourself First, Best and Always* and Love your Fellow Man and Woman.

Seek advisers like me and thousands of others. Read and evaluate articles and books. Attend seminars, webinars and courses that will enlighten you.

Reject anyone who wants you to listen only to his or her advice, or his or her method, or only worship their God.

Reject anyone who is making you pay uncomfortable amounts to share the knowledge, wisdom and experience that they have.

If you strive to incorporate these ideas into your life, you will find the love, purpose, and mission of your life. You will find God and God will find you – often, both in the same place.

You will find people to love and care about, and they will find you, but not until you stop looking and waiting for them.

Just do it! Start your new life today!

I send my prayers, love and blessings to you. I wish you peace in your future. Your future is determined by you.

## Disconnecting Cords Procedure

One of the greatest gifts and blessings you can do for yourself and for another person is to disconnect spiritual, emotion, mental, physical and ethereal cords with them. This allows you to see them as they really are in the present life. It resolves old karmic connections and debt, and has been known to change people's lives and relationships for the better. Disconnecting means forgiving them, praying for them and turning them over to God with love. You can also disconnect with your old self, your old emotions (self-defeating habits, anger, worry, fear, depression and anxiety) and people who have used or abused you.

Over the next three days you will see the person you are blessing in the Disconnection with new vision that will allow you to see who they truly are in this life. You will release old feelings, allowing for a fresh start in the relationship, if you choose.

Begin by asking God to bless and protect all involved in this process.

Then say: "Please come here in Spirit, _____" and read your list of names. You can call them out in spirit since spirit is not attached to their body.

The person or persons you are blessing will gather in spirit on your right side. On your left side is the Golden Doorway to Heaven.

Then say: "I'm doing this with the Love and Light of God.

As I set you free, you must set me free.

No two spirits should hold each other as we have.

Now it's time to let go.

I undo all that I have created in you.

I owe you nothing and you owe me nothing. All is forgiven."

Then tell the person you love them and bless them, and anything else you want to tell them.

Then say: "I dissolve all cords, contracts, commitments, agreements, vows, spells, curses and all other karmic connections with love. All connections between me and _____ (read your list) are null and void.

Remove any resistance and help us to let go.

You are no longer allowed in my energy on any level of my being unless you come with the Love and Light of God."

"Anything you do in any way to harm me or those around me will reflect back to you, and you and that which stands behind you will absorb all karma.

Whether it be by your actions or the actions of others created by you, you and that which stands behind you will absorb all karma."

Then say: "I let you go, and now undo all that I have created in you. I set you free."

Then say: "God - I give you ____ (read the list) — He/She/They are no longer my responsibility.

Take them where they need to go, to heal and grow.

I will not hold you anymore.

I set you free.

Go into the Light!"

When you feel this has happened, say: "Amen" or "So Be It" three times.

Then envision a giant bubble around you that protects you from any reconnection. Stay in the bubble for seven days. Do not discuss past or emotional issues with the person you are dissolving from. This will let you decide if you want them in your future.

The cord cutting gives you an opportunity to speak to the person safely and truthfully, without fear, while they are in Spirit form. You can say what you need to say, release what you need to release, express your love for them, and then turn them over to God. It is important to forgive the other person for whatever they have done against you. I used to tell people that they needed to forgive, not necessarily forget. However, that was short-sighted advice because while the forgiving part usually comes along, it creates another cord. We want to get rid of *all* those cords. This is important because once you release, it is not something that will come up in your memory and is simply part of your past.

The result is what I call baggage, such as old pains and abuse that you continue to carry around into every new situation in your life. When I talk about disconnecting from those old events and leaving all your baggage for God to store and deal with, you would be amazed how quickly you forget and grow.

## *Prayers*

### The Miracle Prayer

Divine Spirit-
I come before you just as I am.
I am sorry for my faults and shortcomings.
I regret all the times when I did not act out of love for myself and others.
Please forgive me and allow me to forgive myself.
I forgive all others for what they have done against me.
I renounce the darkness and evil that seeks my attention.
I surround all those around me who have used and abused me with love.
Heal me, change me, and strengthen me, in body, mind, soul and spirit.
All of you Angels and Spirit Guides please help me.
Amen.

## Family Healing Prayer

To the Creator of Heaven and Earth
I ask for you to bless me and my family and the family of man.
I have the DNA and blood of my ancestors in me, so together we
stand before you.
Without judging them or their actions, I seek peace that will resolve
old feelings of misunderstanding, bitterness and hatred.
I place my entire family and the family of man
in a bubble of pure, unconditional love.
This will help to heal past, present and future family members
from the effects of their actions, in what they had done or failed to do.
I ask for help and healing for my family's physical, mental and
emotional health.
Heal us from generational sin and the sins of our fathers
Heal us all, both living and dead.
Amen

## Prayer for the Healer

God, thank you for sharing with me your wonderful ministry of healing and deliverance. Thank you for the healing I have experienced
today. I realize that the sickness of evil is more than my humanity can
bear, so I ask that you please cleanse me of any sadness and negative
thinking or despair that I may have picked up during my intercession
for others.

If my ministry has tempted me to anger, impatience or lust, cleanse
me of those temptations and replace them with love, joy and peace. If
any evil spirits have attached themselves or oppressed me in any way, I
command them to depart from me now and send you straight to God,
for him to deal with as He wills.

Come Holy Spirit, renew me, fill me anew with your power, your life and your joy. Strengthen me where I feel weak and clothe me with your Light. God please send your Holy Angels to minister to me and protect me from all forms of sickness, harm and accidents. I thank you God. Amen.

## *Meditation*

Winter Robinsons' meditation called *Talley's Lullaby* is a guided imagery Meditation that is offered free and can be downloaded from youtube.com or Vimeo.com/37491591

## *Affirmations*

Love God-Do Good Works!
Trust God and Do Good!
I Love You God; I Love You Unconditionally!
Do Good to People Who Need Help!
All is Well!
I Can Do It; I Can Do Anything!
I Love You! (Say this while looking in a mirror at yourself)

## *Blessing for Holy Water and Holy Oil*

I bless this water and oil with all the goodness, love and power
available to me from God - the Light of the Universe.
I infuse it with love, compassion, understanding and peace.
Amen.

I leave my Holy Water in the sun and moon for 30 days and look at it every day saying the above words. Any oil can be blessed but I like the Frankincense/Myrrh combination in a cream form from Rodco-Ltd. com. It is called anointing oil. They also have the Christian blessing for Holy Water or oil at (**www.rodco-ltd.com**) The Bible gives you the spiritual authority to bless oil and water and anything else.

You can also bless the water by writing positive intentions on the water container. Write the words, peace, love, hope, trust, healing, and happiness on the water and it will be blessed with those intentions. Google the work of Dr. Masuru Emoto and his work with water and thoughts.

**Spiritual Gifts** – *I Corinthian's 12:4-11: "To each is given the manifestation of the Spirit for the common good. To one is given through the Spirit the utterance of wisdom, and to another the utterance of knowledge according to the same spirit, to another faith by the same Spirit, to another the gifts of healing by the one Spirit, to another the working of miracles, to another prophecy, to another the discernment of spirits, to another kinds of tongues, to another the interpretation of tongues. All of these are activated by one and the same Spirit, who allots to each one individually just as the Spirit chooses."*

I have received all of these spiritual gifts and it has made my life interesting and amazing.

I am advocating that the readers of this book cultivate their own direct connection with God.

It only takes one spark to reignite communication with Spirit. Like striking a match in a dark room, in the instant you strike the match the entire room is exposed to light. After that, you cannot abide in the darkness any longer. It will simply no longer feel good.

I love this quote from Buddha:

"Believe nothing, no matter where you read it or who has said it, not even if I have said it to you, unless it agrees with your own reason and your own common sense." I like this because it points out that we each must learn to discern the messages that come to us. Maybe I do not present it in the right way. Or you are not ready for my message. If it does not resonate in your soul, reject it. God will send it to you again through another messenger.

Learn to be good to yourself or no one will be good to you.

*Pray, Meditate, and Shut Up and Listen.* Establish your own direct connection to God.

Use your discernment and intuition to evaluate people or situations in your life. Remove anything that is not worthy of your time and energy.

Be open to the Flow of Love of the Universe! You will attract people that are like you, or your opposite, and they will cause you to grow rapidly.

Keep looking up!

## Books

**Energy Centers and Chakra Healing**
*Feelings – Buried Alive Never Die...* by Karol K. Truman
*Anatomy of the Spirit – The Seven Stages of Power and Healing* by Caroline Myss
*The Symbolic Message of Illness* by Calin V. Pop, M.D.

## Psychic Protection
*How to Protect Yourself from Psychic Attack*, by David Goddard
*Practical Psychic Self Defense Handbook – A Survival Guide* by Robert Bruce
*What the Bible Says about Getting Free of Demons* – http://www.tcata.com/wdtbs/freeofdemons

## Reincarnation and Karma
*Reincarnation for the Christian* - Quincy Howe Jr.
*Reincarnation- The Missing Link in Christianity* – Elizabeth Clare Prophet

## Emotional and Spiritual Growth
*The Four Agreements* by Don Miguel Ruiz

## Personality Disorders that Can Affect Relationships
This is a summary. Many books have been written on each subject. I will define these generally and then provide articles or books that I recommend. You should also Google/Bing search.

It can be very useful for self-diagnosis of yourself and others using tools on the internet. I recommend that in acute situations you consult a therapist or psychologist or other mental health care professional for help.

### Traits of Adult Children of Alcoholics
Behaviors control emotions and behaviors
Fear losing control
Seek approval from others
Over sensitive
Unable to have fun or relax
Harsh self-criticism and low self esteem
Difficulties with intimacy
Passive-aggressive

Seeks chaos and drama

Want relationships with people that they think that they can rescue

Fear abandonment and will do anything to save a relationship.

Are stressed out

Attract mental and physical illness

Emotionally unavailable because they did not have those connections with their parents

Trust issues

**Traits of Borderline Personality Disorder**

Moodiness, instability, chaotic and unstable interpersonal relationships. Anger, inappropriate mood swings, manipulation and deceit. See Wikipedia for a good description.

Search the internet for a free Borderline Personality Test.

**Traits of Dissociative Identity Disorder**

One client stated that it was like her husband had more than one personality. Like it depended on which side of the bed he got up on. This can be found in people who have substance abuse issues and suffer from PTSD.

Often resulting from childhood sexual or physical abuse in early life

See Wikipedia.

**Empaths**

Google these articles on the web.

-Empaths and Narcissists: Opposite Sides of the Coin of Dysfunction?

-Why the Narcissist Chooses Us

-30 Traits of an Empath (How to know if you are an Empath)

## Highly Sensitive People
See Huffpost Characteristics of Highly-Sensitive People 3-5-2012

## Traits of Histrionic Personality Disorder
Excessive emotions and attention-seeking. Inappropriate seductive behavior and excessive need for approval. See Google for more information.

## Traits of Narcissist Personality Disorder
Google these articles on the web.
-The Highly Sensitive Person and the Narcissist
-Narcissism is an unhealthy focus on self that affects others in unhealthy ways. Everything is about them.
-Relationship with a Narcissist...Why 90% Fail...Recovery Survival Disarming
-See – 3 Key Tells That You are in a Relationship with a Narcissist on web.
-The Dangers of a Relationship with a Narcissist by Dr. Neill Neill

## Traits of Passive-Aggressive Behavior
Passive-aggressive behavior is the indirect expression of hostility, such as through procrastination, stubbornness, sullen behavior, or deliberate or repeated failure to accomplish requested tasks for which one is (often explicitly) responsible. (Wikipedia)
One client said she had been subject to this for years, but did not know what it was called. See Wikipedia for general description. Once you learn more about it, you will probably have many memories of when it happened to you.

## Traits of a Psychopath
An unstable and aggressive person suffering from chronic mental disorder with abnormal or violent social behavior.
Search internet for Test for Psychopathy

Traits of Schizophrenia is a mental disorder characterized by abnormal social behavior and failure to understand what is real. Common symptoms include false beliefs, unclear or confused thinking, hearing voices, reduced social engagement and emotional expression, and a lack of motivation. People with schizophrenia often have additional mental health problems such as such as anxiety disorders, major depressive illness, or substance use disorder. (Source - Wikipedia)

**Traits of a Sociopath**
A person with a personality disorder manifesting itself in extreme antisocial attitudes and behavior and a lack of conscience.
Search internet for test for Sociopath.

**Twin Souls**
See web article - Phases of a Twin Flame Relationship